The Bolsheviks in Siberia, 1917–1918

The Bolsheviks in Siberia, 1917-1918

Russell E. Snow

RUTHERFORD ● MADISON ● TEANECK
FAIRLEIGH DICKINSON UNIVERSITY PRESS
LONDON: ASSOCIATED UNIVERSITY PRESSES

©1977 by Associated University Presses, Inc.

Associated University Presses, Inc.
Cranbury, New Jersey 08512

Associated University Presses
Magdalen House
136-148 Tooley Street
London SE1 2TT, England

Library of Congress Cataloging in Publication Data

Snow, Russell E   1938-
    The Bolsheviks in Siberia, 1917-1918.

    Bibliography: p.
    Includes index.
    1. Siberia—History—Revolution, 1917-1921.
2. Communism—Siberia—History. I. Title.
DK265.8.S5S6   957'.08'4   75-5247
ISBN 0-8386-1643-3

To my wife, Linda Elisabeth
and our children

Contents

Acknowledgments

I would like to express my appreciation to Professors George Jackson and John Marcus of Hofstra University dear friends and colleagues, who suffered with me and remained steadfast in their encouragement of me throughout the long and sometimes difficult process of writing this book. I would also like to thank my professors at S.U.N.Y., Stony Brook, for their help and guidance, especially Alan K. Wildman and Werner T. Angress, from whom I learned much, and David F. Trask, for his good and wise counsel.

I must also express my appreciation for the works of Soviet historians on the revolution and civil war. Were it not for their labors, this attempt to provide an account in English would not have been possible.

Introduction

The victory of Bolshevism in Russia during 1917 is a subject much discussed, but as yet poorly understood. With a few important exceptions, Western scholars of the Russian Revolution and the subsequent civil war treat Bolshevism as something alien to Russia, something forced upon a desperate people by Lenin and his followers.[1] As Robert V. Daniels put it in summing up the consensus of a symposium held at Harvard University to commemorate the revolution's fiftieth anniversary, "the Bolshevik Revolution and the Soviet path of development were neither necessary nor desirable, but constituted a historical anomaly produced by Lenin's imposing his will-to-power on a country so disorganized and divided that it could not resist him."[2]

Soviet scholars argue the opposite; the Bolshevik revolution *was* historically necessary. Only Lenin and his followers reflected and articulated the deep strivings of the workers, soldiers, and poorer peasants for socialism.

11

The triumphant march of Soviet power was planned, coordinated, and guided by Lenin and the Central Committee, which directed the activities of the local party organizations. Within these organizations were the true Bolshevik followers of Lenin and the pseudo-Bolsheviks who followed the views of Kamenev, Zinoviev, or Trotsky. The pseudo-Bolsheviks, of course, provide a convenient scapegoat to explain such embarrassing phenomena as local party organizations deviating from what has been defined as *the Leninist line* in the revolution or the failure of the Bolsheviks to win over the railroad workers from the Menshevik-internationalists.[3]

Whether or not one believes in such things as Marxian laws governing social processes or the dubious proposition that there are historical anomalies, at least in a secular sense, it must be admitted that the views of some Western and Soviet historians on the role of the Bolsheviks in the Russian revolution are premature, highly prejudicial, and based upon a paucity of evidence. They both seem to have been engaged in a strange contest to endow Lenin with superhuman attributes: in one case demonic, in the other godlike. The chief casualty in the conflict appears to be historical truth. In fairness to both the pro- and anti-Lenin schools, however, it must be pointed out that both suffer from handicaps not of their own choosing. Western scholars have been severely hampered in their work by not having access to archival materials; Soviet historians labor under ideological imperatives dictated from above that take precedence over the truth.

Granted, Lenin eventually did exert his will over Russia through the instrumentality of party control of the soviets, but how did he control the party and how did it in turn control the soviets? What were the relations between the local party organizations to Lenin, the Central

Committee, and to each other? What were the factions within the local groups? To answer these and other crucial questions concerning the victory of Bolshevism in Russia, one must investigate the character and structure of the party in 1917. One must analyze the role of the local Bolsheviks in all phases of the revolution from February 1917 to the transfers of power to the soviets during the winter of 1917–1918.

Naturally, such a task for the vast and variegated Russia empire must be undertaken on a regional basis. Until recently, Western scholars have been exclusively concerned with the revolution in Petrograd. At last, a study of the Bolsheviks in Baku has been published in English, which begins to shed light on their role in the localities.[4] Hopefully, this study of the Bolsheviks in Siberia from February 1917 to March 1918 will further illuminate the key role played by local party groups in the victory of Bolshevism during 1917.

Although Siberia became a major theater of civil war in 1918–1919, its importance to the victory of the Bolshevik victory in European Russia during the winter of 1917–1918 has not been recognized in the Western literature on the revolution and civil war. In terms of population and industrial development it was one of the most backward regions of the empire, but its geopolitical and agricultural significance to the Bolsheviks, their opponents, and the Allies predestined it to become a major theater of civil war. The contending forces were well aware that millions of poods* of grain were stored in the warehouses of Western Siberia. Its normal access to markets were choked off by the huge quantity of war supplies that strained the capacity of the Trans-Siberian railroad. With the breakdown of the market mechanism in Central Russia and the Germans in control of much

*1 pood = 36.11 pounds

of the Ukraine, Western Siberia was one of the most productive and convenient grain producing areas in Russia.

As early as June 1917, Lenin was concerned about the Siberian grain, which he knew could feed the workers and soldiers who supported the Bolsheviks in the capital. He was particularly worried that when the Bolsheviks took power in Petrograd, which for him was only a matter of time, they might suffer the fate of the Paris Commune, starved into submission by opponents who controlled the food-producing countryside. The Socialist Revolutionaries and Mensheviks, after all, also knew the history of revolutionary France. He told a leading Siberian Bolshevik that the Party's task in Siberia was to break the power of the Socialist Revolutionaries and Mensheviks in Novonikolaevsk and Irkutsk, lest they organize the rich and middle peasantry of Western Siberia and deny Petrograd and Moscow access to the region's foodstuffs.[5] Whether by accident or design, this is exactly what the moderate socialists tried and failed to do in November and December of 1917. Despite the efforts of the Socialist Revolutionaries to hamper them, the Bolsheviks shipped over seven million poods of grain from Omsk to Petrograd and Moscow between December 1917 and March 1918. Some Soviet historians attribute their staying power in the capital during this period to the Siberian grain.[6]

Soviet scholars, therefore, have long recognized the importance of the Bolshevik victory in Siberia in 1917 to their success in European Russia. As a result they have tried to come to grips with many of the questions raised above concerning the relations of local Bolsheviks to Lenin and the Central Committee. Despite its highly ideological character, conscious distortions, and tendency to omit all references to events that can not be interpreted in the "correct" manner, Soviet scholarship is far more valuable than Western studies in helping to shed light on the role of the local Bolsheviks in the revolution. Western historians have simply ignored what went on in the provinces.

During the 1920s, Soviet journals published a relatively large number of articles and memoirs concerning the role of the Bolsheviks in Siberia during 1917. Because so many political exiles were in Siberia at the time of the February revolution, a number of prominent Communists in the 1920s who played a role—E. Yaroslavskii, A. Shlikhter, E. A. Preobrazhenskii, I. N. Smirnov, and B. Z. Shumiatskii—wrote about their experiences. They raised questions, publicly, which subsequent Soviet historians have not been able to ignore. From 1957 on, Soviet scholars have published more source materials on Siberia than any other region in Russia.[7]

Two of the most important recent works dealing with the role of the Bolsheviks in the revolution in Siberia are by M. M. Shornikov[8] and V. P. Safronov.[9] These scholars are in fundamental disagreement on the relative strength and weakness of the Bolshevik party in Siberia. The gist of the matter concerns the reasons why they refused to split with the Mensheviks and recognize the party's Central Committee until the summer and early autumn of 1917.

Safronov claimed that the majority of Social Democrats in the united organizations during the spring and summer of 1917 were Bolsheviks. They, in fact, strongly influenced the character of the united organizations. Criticizing this view, Shornikov raises the critical issue for Soviet historiography.

If, by May 1917, the Mensheviks did not predominate in the united organizations, then obviously the Bolsheviks did. But one must ask what prevented the Social Democratic party in Siberia from recognizing the Bolshevik Central Committee, from joining the party? It must have been either one of two things: Either the Menshevik defensists and internationalists, supported by conciliators, dominated, or Bolsheviks predominated, who did not wish to be Bolsheviks, i.e., who did not want to go into the Bolshevik party.[10]

Part of the difficulty, he points out, is in the party label.

"A Bolshevik," he writes, "is a member of the Leninist party, who recognized its policies and tactics, who worked in one of its local organizations, who struggled to realize its decisions in life." In short, for Shornikov, a Bolshevik in 1917 had to be a Leninist. Safronov, therefore, erred because he considered anyone who called himself a Bolshevik to have been one. However unfounded this narrow construction of Bolshevism, it is necessary to the major thesis of Soviet historiography that Lenin and the Central Committee guided the party to victory in the country at large.[11]

Faced with the fact that a majority of those men in Siberia who called themselves Bolsheviks were successful politically, but were not Leninists, Shornikov has fallen back upon the device of magnifying out of all proportion the role of the Bolsheviks in Krasnoiarsk, where Leninists and Left-Bolsheviks were very prominent. The bulk of his monograph is devoted to proving that the victory of Bolshevism in Siberia was due in large part to the efforts of the Siberian Regional Bureau of the R.S.D.R.P.(b), created at Krasnoiarsk at the end of March. The fact that the majority of Bolsheviks in Western Siberia, and for much of the time in Central Siberia, ignored the policies of this bureau is explained away on the grounds they were not Leninists. Not explained, however, was the failure of the Central Committee to break off relations with or to censure the recalcitrants.

More importantly, Shornikov fails to explain how so
many Bolsheviks who were influential party leaders in
1917, but not Leninists by his definition, became leaders
of the independent Bolshevik organizations during the
autumn. Why was the leader of the Western Siberian
Bolsheviks, N. N. Yakovlev, who refused to recognize
the authority of the Siberian Regional Bureau, appointed as agent of the Central Committee? To parry
these questions, scholars such as Safronov and Shornikov
have woven into their monographs a built-in apologia.
They must argue that those who refuse to follow
Leninist policy during 1917 were mistaken, but add that
the mistakes were understandable given the conditions
in Siberia.

These scholars have argued that Siberia was poorly
industrialized, and hence, the proletarian base was too
narrow for the creation of a truly proletarian organization. This view D. M. Zol'nikov objected to on Marxist
grounds.[12] The fact that the Bolsheviks did come to
power in Siberian cities necessarily meant that the pre-
conditions for their victory existed from the
socioeconomic standpoint. Following Safronov, that the
majority of Social Democrats in Siberia were Bolsheviks,
he argues that there were many reasons why they did
not form independent party organizations.

> One reason was the theoretical weakness of the Bol-
> sheviks, another was the long period they had been in
> exile. One did not know, another did not understand,
> and a few—M. Frumkin, V. Sokolov, and others, con-
> sidered themselves Bolsheviks, but did not accept the
> theory of socialist revolution worked out by Lenin
> during the war years.[13]

These Bolsheviks, he asserts, misled the workers, and
only during the course of 1917 when the full signifi-

cance of Lenin's April theses became understood did independent party organizations begin to form.

Thus, in a fashion not unlike that of Western scholars, Soviet historians want to argue that the victory of Bolshevism in Siberia was necessarily linked to Lenin and Leninism. All agree that the failure of the Bolsheviks to split with the Menshevik-defensists retarded the development of the socialist revolution. All agree unquestioningly that the tactic was a mistake. But significantly, none have been able to produce evidence to sustain this point of view. Instead, they have been forced to distort their accounts of party history in Siberia to the point that they have greatly ignored such cities as Omsk and Irkutsk, and have yet to produce sufficient evidence revealing the party's response to the October seizure of power. The present work will illuminate some of these problems, and will present a characterization of the Bolsheviks in Siberia during 1917, which is somewhat closer to the truth than the one usually found in many Soviet works.

The Bolsheviks in Siberia, 1917–1918

1

Siberia on the Eve of Revolution

Soviet studies of the revolution and civil war in Siberia usually begin with an introductory chapter outlining the more significant features of Siberian life on the eve of revolution.[1] Although this discussion emphasizes the different aspects of prerevolutionary life more than is found in Soviet works, it is necessary for the same reason. One can not easily follow the complex process of revolution in Siberia without some knowledge of its political and economic structure in the immediate prerevolutionary period. Since the one, good, scholarly work in English on Siberia before the war is not adequate to that purpose, this chapter will provide a brief sketch of the region's geographic, economic, and social characteristics, as well as outline the old administrative structure.[2]

21

Geographically, Siberia includes all Russian territory east of the Urals, excluding the maritime provinces that are called *the Russian Far East*. In terms of revolutionary politics, the geographically significant region is a zone of about fifty miles on either side of the railroad, between Omsk and Chita. Most of the major cities and the best cultivatable lands were in this zone, with the exception of Tomsk gubernia and Akmolinsk oblast, a good part of each was fertile and productive.

The territory between Omsk and Krasnoiarsk, especially Akmolinsk and southern Tomsk, is the eastern extension of the black earth steppe, while to the north of the railroad unending forests of birch and fir reach all the way to the taiga. East of Krasnoiarsk the terrain becomes more rugged as one approaches the shores of Lake Baikal. On the eastern shore the land along the railroad is flat, grassy meadow and rolling hills, giving way to a more mountainous landscape as one reaches central Transbaikalia. The Yablonovy range, although not high in comparison with others, is quite rugged.

In 1917 the population of Siberia was about nine million. Almost eighty-five percent were peasant settlers of Russian and Ukrainian origin, a large percentage of whom lived in Western Siberia and had only recently arrived. Between 1897 and 1917, some five million settlers crossed the Urals to till the land, to work the mines, and to build the cities. During these years the population increased more than twice that of the U.S.S.R.[3] Although the bulk of the new immigrants went into the countryside, the urban population increased at a much faster rate than the rural. In Tomsk gubernia the urban increased 184 per cent, as compared to 102 for the rural. In Eniseisk the comparative rates were 160 to 64 per cent; Irkutsk, 107 to 14; and in Transbaikalia, 376 to 71.[4]

With respect to the revolution of 1917, the rapid growth of Siberian cities had the most profound consequences. Strung out along the railroad at intervals of several hundred miles, often at one of the great rivers, these commercial and administrative hubs increased their population two, three, and sometimes almost ten times in the two decades before the revolution. Such rapid change invariably entails serious social and political consequences. As the following table reveals, by European standards the major Siberian cities were small, but they were sufficiently large enough for them to dominate the surrounding countryside as centers of revolution.[5]

	1897	1917
Omsk	36,376	113,680
Tomsk	52,210	101,129
Barnaul	21,073	56,007
Novonikolaevsk	7,832	69,827
Krasnoiarsk	26,699	70,327
Irkutsk	51,200	90,413
Verkhneudinsk	7,000 (est.)	30,000 (est.)
Chita	30,000 (est.)	70,000 (est.)

Among the Siberian native population, only the Buriat-Mongols lived in and near the railroad zone, on either side of Lake Baikal. Numbering about 220,000, they had developed a significant national movement in 1917, which had been strongly influenced by two groups of Buriat intellectuals: the Russianizers and the Mongolophiles. The first group were often Socialist Revolutionaries, and in Transbaikalia they played an important role in the revolution of 1917. The second largest group of natives, the Yakuts, lived along the middle course Lena River in northern Irkutsk gubernia and did not play a revolutionary role in the railroad zone.[6]

With the opening of the Trans-Siberian railroad in the 1890s, Siberia was drawn more tightly into the mainstream of Russian national life. The railroad linked its resources and fertile expanses with the booming industrial economy and provided a cheap and efficient way to relieve rural overpopulation in European Russia. In the wake of the five million settlers who crossed the Urals followed an army of Tsarist officials, merchants, entrepreneurs, professionals, n'er-do-wells, foreign businessmen, and a large number of socialist exiles. The new arrivals found there an already heterogeneous population of old settlers, native peoples, Cossacks, former convicts, political exiles, religious dissenters, and various foreign nationals.

This great migration stimulated a dramatic increase in agricultural production, mining, related industries, commerce, and urban growth, and it also produced a host of social, national, and political antagonisms, which would fan the flames of revolution and civil war. Siberia was a frontier society in 1917, but without the democratic leveling experienced in the American West. It was a Russian hybrid, a curious mixture of authoritarian government, sharp national and class conflicts, and a strange, almost anarchic kind of freedom.

The most significant feature of Siberian life in the prerevolutionary years was the staggering growth and commercialization of agriculture. Between 1901 and 1910, Siberian grain exported to Russia and Europe increased from 6 to 56 million poods.[7] During the next few years it skyrocketed. In Tomsk gubernia alone, wheat production rose from 60 to 120 million poods.[8] By 1917, the total Siberian grain harvest is estimated to have reached 500 million poods, or about 17 percent of the entire Russian empire. Of this, only 80 million were shipped to European Russia.[9] The rest of the surplus grain was stored in Omsk and Novonikolaevsk, and it became a bone of contention between the Bolsheviks and their adversaries during the October revolution.

In addition to grain, Siberia exported relatively large quantities of butter, eggs, fish, meat, and agricultural by-products, such as tallow and leather. By 1910, 3.6 million poods of eggs and 4.3 million poods of butter were shipped to markets in Europe and Russia.[10] According to Treadgold, the 1907 butter export was the major resource for the empire, while the percentage of meat in the supply markets of Saint Petersburg and Moscow went from 12 percent in 1904 to 50 percent in 1911.[11]

A major reason for the high productivity of Siberian agriculture, along with the fertility of the soil and the energy of the peasants, was the widespread use of agricultural machinery, about half of which had been imported from the United States and Canada. Between 1900 and 1917, Siberian peasants purchased large numbers of reapers, threshers, harrows, plows, seeders, and mowers, which had been made especially for Siberian markets. The total value of the machinery sold between 1902 and 1912 was 118 million rubles.[12] A large share of this machinery was supplied by Massey-Ferguson and the International Harvester Company. According to one Soviet scholar, the International Harvester Company alone had 200 sales outlets in Siberia on the eve of the war.[13]

The 1917 agricultural census, despite its unreliability, reveals that Siberian agricultural progress was well on the road to modernization and mechanization by 1917. Between 60 to 80 percent of the peasant households in Altai, Tomsk, Eniseisk, and Irkutsk gubernias had improved machinery. Well over 90 percent had livestock, including milk cows. From 20 to 40 percent earned an income from handicrafts; the higher figures are for Eniseisk and Irkutsk gubernias, where conditions for agriculture were less favorable than they were in Western Siberia. These figures point to a healthy market economy in Siberia, based upon a prosperous and commercially minded class of peasants.[14]

Soviet scholars generally divide the peasantry into three classes for purposes of analysis: poor, middle, and rich. Their standard used to differentiate them is the number of horses owned and the amount of land under cultivation. Households cultivating 0–3 *dessiatines** of land and having 0–2 horses are considered poor; those cultivating 3–9 *dessiatines* and having 2–3 horses are middle; those above these levels are rich.[15] In 1912, not the most prosperous year for Siberia, only 9.5 percent of the households had no horses at all. More than half of the peasantry had more than ten *dessiatines* of land under cultivation and had four or more horses.[16] In 1917, only about 12 percent of the households in Tomsk gubernia had no working livestock and 10 percent cultivated no land. The figures are about the same for Altai and Eniseisk gubernias, and somewhat higher in Irkutsk.[17]

While they do not deny the generally high level of prosperity of the Siberian peasantry, Soviet historians point out that the commercialization of agriculture led to increased class differentiation in the villages. This, they argue, sharpened conflicts between kulaks and middle peasants on the one hand, and poor peasants and agricultural laborers on the other.[18] One scholar asserts that the development of a money economy increasingly pushed the poor and lower-middle ranks into the labor market. He points out that over 60 percent of the new settlers in Slavogorod uezd, Tomsk gubernia, and 23

*1 *dessiatine* = 2.7 acres

percent of the old settlers were poor in 1911.[19] And it is a fact that 37 percent of the peasants in Tomsk gubernia had no improved machinery in 1917, and that 10 to 12 percent had no livestock or cultivated no land. But whether or not there was a significant minority of poor peasants and a widening gap between rich and poor as a result of the development of capitalist relations in the village remains an open question, for the evidence presented is not convincing.

The World War, on the whole, tended to benefit the upper and upper-middle strata of peasants by accelarating the commercialization of agriculture and contributing to the growth of a money economy. And this, of course, may have hurt the more marginal producers. Until the Trans-Siberian railroad became overburdened with American military goods landed at Vladivostok, it expanded the market for Siberian grain and stimulated the growth of handicraft industries. More importantly, it resulted in the proliferation of numerous types of cooperatives, which greatly helped the peasants to respond to the wartime market. Many handicraft associations were formed specifically to meet the army's need for harness, boots, caps, coats, and other goods. They also produced for home consumption. One of the largest, the Union of Siberian Butter Artels, represented 563 artels and 502 artel shops in 1914. With offices in Omsk, Moscow, and London, it made handsome profits supplying the army with butter, cheese, hay, tallow, and meat. It was so successful that it expanded into other fields, establishing a cloth mill, a tannery, and a paper factory.[20]

On the eve of revolution, the cooperatives played an impressive role in Siberian economic life. In addition to the large producers' and credit cooperatives, which had many employees and which commanded impressive fi-

nancial resources, there were many consumers' cooperatives of various types. There were 90 workers' cooperatives, 114 all-citizen city cooperatives, and 6,757 village-
consumers' cooperatives with a combined membership of
over one million.[21]

The moving force behind the cooperative movement
were the Socialist Revolutionaries. They staffed the entire network of rural cooperatives and controlled the operations of the larger institutions. Their achievement
provided a way for the peasantry to respond to the
growing market economy, but at the same time to preserve many features of traditional peasant society. This
meant that the upper and upper-middle strata were able
to enjoy the best of both worlds: they were capable of
producing for a market economy without becoming too
dependent upon its rhythms.

The war, apart from the benefits it brought to the
more productive peasants, tended to sharpen existing
conflicts in rural Siberia and had a detrimental effect
upon the less successful minority. The natural hostility
of the poor toward the rich was compounded by the bit-
terness felt by many soldiers toward those at home, who
seemed to have gained from the war. By 1917, the
mobilization drained the villages of about fifty percent
of the adult male population.[22] By September, almost
500,000 peasants from Tomsk gubernia and 200,000
from Eastern Siberia had been called into the army, and
more than fifty percent of them had been sent to the
front.[23] Assuming that Siberian soldiers took casualties at
the same rate as the army as a whole, it is likely that
150,000 of them between the ages of eighteen and forty
were either killed or wounded.[24] For more marginal
households dependent upon the labor of fathers and
sons, the economic effects of mobilization alone caused
hardships. But the psychological consequences of

wrenching these men from the matrix of traditional society, even one in transition, and subjecting them to conditions at the front was devastating. Exposed to terrible
defeats, and to the logic of Bolshevik propaganda, the
survivors would return home politicized, embittered toward traditional authority, and they would return with
weapons.

As the war continued, the age of the peasant recruits
increased. The call-up of the forty-three-year olds may
well have been sufficient to change the mood of the garrisons. At the time of the revolution there were about
350,000 soldiers stationed in the larger cities, awaiting
shipment to the front. There were about 50,000 at
Omsk, 70,000 at Tomsk, 40,000 at Novonikolaevsk, and
25,000 each in Krasnoiarsk, Irkutsk, and Chita.[25] Called
to the colors at a time when the terrible conditions at the
front were becoming known at the rear, few of these
older men were keen about going off to war. They were
racked with fears about their wives and families, wartime
inflation, the government mobilization of horses, and the
scarcity of kerosene and other commodities. Life in the
villages, while not impossible, was becoming more difficult, especially for the poorer and more marginal middle peasants.

As capitalist relations continued to develop in the villages, many of the peasants who remained at home were
driven into the labor market. Between 1913 and 1917,
the number of workers in the mining industry increased
from 67,000 to 81,000, most of whom were peasants.[26]
By June 1916, seventy-two percent of the miners in the
twelve major coal mining districts were raw, unskilled
peasants.[27] Given the abysmal conditions in Siberian
mines, it is likely that they were motivated to work in
them by the need for a cash income. It is hard to image
a well-off or self-sufficient peasant tolerating the inflated

prices in company stores, the crude barracks, or the lack of adequate sanitation and medical facilities. In some mines, owners who were required by law to provide a doctor found it cheaper to pay an annual fine than to hire one.[28]

The same process, the need for money, drew the peasantry into the transportation industry, which increased from 90,000 to 123,000 during the war.[29] Many of these peasant-workers were part-timers and did not depend upon their jobs for the whole living, although this changed during the war. In 1914, between sixty-eight and eighty-eight percent of the workers on the Transbaikal railroad, for example, earned less than a subsistence level of income, which indicates strong ties to the land.[30] With the increasing volume of wartime traffic on the railroad, however, the income appears to have gone up and larger numbers of peasants worked full-time. The absence of any serious labor unrest among the railroad workers during the war is a strong indication that the Tsarist government raised their wages to keep pace with the inflation.

Together with the rapid growth and commercialization of agriculture, the infusion of poorer and middle peasants into the labor market, and the effects of the war, the most significant aspect of Siberian development, as has been seen, was the growth of cities. Given this extraordinary tempo and the character of Siberian society, an atmosphere of boom or bust seemed to pervade these Russian frontier cities. Two Americans traveling through Siberia in 1913 were struck by their similarity to American Western cities. Omsk reminded them of Chicago and they compared Irkutsk to San Francisco, calling it the "Golden Gomorrah of the East." In Tomsk, "a City of Orgies," they witnessed great extremes of wealth and poverty, a riotous nightlife, and they reported that murders and robberies were frequent occurrences. They were also impressed with the pace of commercial activities and the region's great economic potential.[31]

Four years earlier a British engineer, Henry G. Read, wrote a highly favorable account of the business opportunities in Siberia, particular for manufacturers. "Labor," he wrote, "is abundant and cheap . . . but the cost of living is higher than it should be, mainly because of the lack of local manufactories to compete with imported goods." He urged foreign businessmen to invest in Siberia, pointing out that "here, as elsewhere, it is only those who put experience, ability, and ceaseless energy into their undertakings in the country who will succeed, and for those who are prepared to do this there is no need to fear for the future."[32]

Despite its outwardly freewheeling appearance, however, the settlement and development of Siberia was very much an official enterprise of the Russian state. Most Siberian cities were originally built as forts by the Government in the sixteenth and seventeenth centuries to protect the fur traders who provided the government with huge revenues. During the eighteenth century, peasant-serfs, exiled Cossacks, and religious dissenters settled in and around the small outposts, which gradually developed into towns and cities. As the population began to increase, the government expanded the bureaucracy to insure its control of the recognizedly valuable region.[33]

By 1917, the Tsarist government in Siberia was a huge administrative complex, employing thousands of people.[34] A large number of them were socialist exiles, who were sentenced to remain in Siberia after they served their prison terms. According to the laws on

Siberian institutions published in 1892, Western and Central Siberia were divided into four *gubernias*, which were subdivided into *uezds*, and the uezds into *volosts*. During 1917, Tomsk gubernia was split into two; the other named Altai gubernia. It was only under the Provisional Government that *zemstvos* were introduced.

Tomsk gubernia had a governor and administration of its own and was not treated differently from the others. Eniseisk and Irkutsk gubernias and Transbaikal oblast' came under the jurisdiction of the Governor-General of Irkutsk, whose office was created in the eighteenth century. In 1903 he was designated a Lieutenant of the Empire and was delegated many of the powers of the Tsar in Siberia and the Far East. He even had his own foreign office to assist him in the formulation of policy and relations toward China and Mongolia.

The administrative machinery was extensive, elaborate, and often overlapping in its functions. There were inumerable offices dealing with all aspects of economic and social life, as well as those of the treasury, state domains, land administration, courts, prisons, and innumerable inspectors. In addition to the gubernatorial, there were five other administrative complexes: the offices for peasant affairs, for town affairs, for military service, and, after 1909, the Resettlement Administration. The fifth was the Uezd and Village Administration, run by the police, and headed by a district inspector, who reported to the governor. The police, of course, were everywhere.

Along with its police duties, the corp of rural bureaucrats carried on a number of judicial and economic functions, including the collection of taxes, settling disputes about harvesting grain, quartering and provisioning of troops. The village administration came under the jurisdiction of *Krestianskie nachal'niki*, who were first introduced in Siberia at the end of the nineteenth century. Their purpose was the same as the *Zemskie nachal'niki* in European Russia. They were charged with the management of public administration in the villages and with improving living conditions. The old settlers, however, generally regarded the introduction of these officials as a new and unwelcome interference in their private affairs, especially since they had the power to intervene in disputes that the peasants had formerly settled in their own volost courts.

Given this army of officials and government employees, it is not surprising that in Irkutsk alone they numbered over 12,000. In the major cities it is estimated that from twenty-five to fifty percent of the working population worked in government institutions. Their large numbers, combined with those who worked in commercial institutions, small businessmen, professionals, teachers, and so forth, gave the Siberian cities a decidedly middle- and lower-middle-class atmosphere.[35]

Unfortunately, it is extremely difficult to re-create a satisfactory picture of middle-class life on the eve of the revolution. Indications are that it made up from sixty–seventy percent of the population. It is known that Siberian urban life was not markedly different from other Russian cities, if one allows for the wild frontier atmosphere. Electrification had begun; there was telephone and telegraph service, movie houses, theaters, restaurants, stock exchanges, and cultural societies. At Tomsk, there was a fine university, an engineering school, and a teachers' college.

The working classes in these cities made up approximately 30–40 percent of their populations. There were 20,000 workers in Omsk, 10,000 in Tomsk, 4,000 in

Barnaul, 6,000 in Novonikolaevsk, 10,000 in Krasnoiarsk, and 7,000 in Irkutsk. The largest numbers were in railroading, metals, woodworking, printing, building, water transportation, textiles, and distilling. In Omsk, for example, there were 5,000 railroad workers and 2,100 who worked in water transportation. In Barnaul and Novonikolaevsk, the fastest growing cities, there were about 2,000 builders in each city. Krasnoiarsk had 3,000 railroad workers, 1,000 woodworkers, and 1,000 builders. Chita also had 3,000 railroad workers.[36]

With the exception of a few railroad shops that employed more than 2,000 workers in Omsk and Krasnaoirsk, and a few factories that had 500 workers, the majority of Siberian workers, in small enterprises of 25–50 people, were craftsmen or laborers. Only about 23 percent of the labor force worked in manufacturing and processing.[37]

Although estimates vary considerably, and statistics from this period are unreliable, the total Siberian working class, discounting hired agricultural laborers, appears to be as follows: 123,000 in railroad and water transportation; 81,000 in mining and related industries; 70,000 in manufacturing; and 25,000 in construction. Of this total of 300,000, only 50,000 were concentrated in the six largest cities. The rest, more than 80 percent, were scattered throughout the territory.[38] Naturally, under these conditions only the larger concentrations of workers in the cities had any connection with revolutionary Social Democracy or had ever organized themselves into trade unions. They were hardly class-conscious proletarians.

In general, the war appears to have caused somewhat less hardship for the urban population of Siberia than in European Russia. Food and fuel were plentiful and relatively cheap. Manufactured goods were scarce, but many of the shortages were made up with peasant handicraft goods. By 1917, over 100,000 of the 200,000 peasant households engaged in full-time handicraft industries employed one or two hired laborers.[39] Perhaps the most serious problem for many Siberians was the astronomical increase in the price of tobacco and the severe shortage of sugar.

By 1916, however, the destructive effects of the inflation seem to have been felt somewhat more acutely in Siberia. One Soviet scholar claims that real income of Siberian workers had declined 30–50 percent during the war, as compared to 15 percent for workers in European Russia.[40] But part of this disparity might be explained by the infusion of unskilled peasants into the Siberian workforce, who were paid less because they did not depend completely upon wages for their living. In any event, the poorer and least skilled of the working classes felt the effects of inflation sooner and were the first to respond.

The first to strike for higher pay were the stevedores in Novonikolaevsk in June 1915. After several battles with police, who failed to break the strike, they won a high pay increase and returned to work. Krasnoiarsk experienced labor unrest in the winter and troops had to be called out to put down the disorders. In October 1916, the Governor-General in Irkutsk received the following report:

> The mood in the Krasnoiarsk shop district was extremely tense and conditions are worsening every day because of rising costs. The workers were coming to the conclusion that their pay increases were going into the pockets of the merchants and were not easing their difficult conditions.[41]

Soon, the unrest in Krasnoirsk, where many of the merchants were Jews, turned anti-Semitic and it developed into a pogrom.[42]

As the situation in Russia became more critical, the government became more repressive. In 1916, Kniazev, the relatively liberal Governor-General of Irkutsk, was replaced by the arch conservative, Pilts'. This change alienated virtually all of the intelligentsia, who had been cooperating with the government's war effort. Evidentally, he regarded all private initiatives in this direction as subversive, for he soon arrested men like V. Gurevich, a Socialist Revolutionary lawyer, who had been helping European refugees in Krasnoiarsk. Pilts' also rounded up and arrested many of the active socialist exiles and took the unprecedented step of drafting a number of them into the army in the autumn. Finally, in January 1917, he formed an armed detachment of well-to-do citizens in Irkutsk to assist the police in putting down revolutionary disturbances and public disorders.[43]

But the police repression, both in Siberia and in European Russia, was too little and too late. The war, as the great engine of accelerated social change in Russia, created new fields for revolutionary activity and further broke down those traditions that kept the autocracy viable. It was the war, more than any other factor, that reinvigorated Russian Social Democracy and transformed it into Russian Communism. Soviet historians claim that there was an upsurge in party life and revolutionary movement even before the war, and, indeed, there was, but it is difficult to imagine the victory of Bolshevism in Russia if there had been no war.

In 1914, Siberian Social Democracy lay dormant. There were no functioning committees in any of the cities and almost no connections with the party center. Occasionally, someone would manage to smuggle news to various party members. The resolutions of the 1912 party conference, for example, were written on the inside of cigarette papers.[44] In the larger cities, individual

Social Democrats managed to keep up contacts with the railroad workers and with the illegal unions in Omsk, Krasnoiarsk, and Chita, but their activities were severely limited and arrests were frequent. Many who were fortunate enough to live in and around Irkutsk, Tomsk, or Krasnoiarsk worked in city-consumer cooperatives, workers' libraries, and various kinds of professional societies. These jobs gave them opportunities to make contacts with working people, but they had to be extremely careful lest they be discovered and the government close the institutions. Others found work in the Tsarist bureaucracy as office workers, clerks, or technical assistants. Some, usually the most militant who had been arrested for revolutionary activity in Siberia, or had been sent directly from European Russia, found themselves in tiny settlements far to the north, where their greatest enemy was boredom and isolation.

Still, despite the overwhelming handicaps of exile existence, they somehow managed to carry on a limited party life and continued to concern themselves with intraparty politics. Even before the war, one of the biggest issues was party unity. Among the rank and file Bolsheviks and Mensheviks, the desire for party unity was stronger than the old organizational issue and the peasant question that had earlier kept them apart. Factional splintering had reached the point where differences between mainstream Bolsheviks and Mensheviks were often not as great as differences with their respective camps. Both groups, for example, regarded liquidationism and a hard-line policy toward party organization as threats to the Social Democratic movement. To combat this, a large number of Bolshevik-conciliators and Menshevik-internationalists increasingly began to draw together. In 1912, in its resolution on liquidationism and party unity, the All-Russian Bolshevik party conference passed a resolution calling for Social Democrats of all tendencies to work together in underground organizations.[45]

The outbreak of war greatly strengthened the tendency toward party unity by increasing the process of fragmentation. The new ideological issues raised by the war, the legacy of 1905, the effectiveness of the reaction, liquidationism, and the old organizational question created new factional relationships that cut across Bolshevik and Menshevik lines. There were defensists and internationalists, organizational hards and softs, liquidators, Bundists, ultraleftists, Leninists, conciliators, as well as the "personals," men like Sukhanov who considered themselves above factional disputes. All this resulted in a kaleidoscope of shifting alignments on different issues, which, under the impact of the war, gradually firmed into a broad, antiwar coalition of Bolsheviks and Mensheviks, committed to party unity and the international socialist revolution.

In contrast to Europe, the entire Social Democratic bloc in the Tsarist Duma voted against war credits. This identified both Bolsheviks and Mensheviks with the tiny minority of Social Democrats in Europe, which would become the Zimmerwald left. The problem confronting the internationalist Social Democrats was how to define their attitude toward the war in a way that would not benefit any of the warring factions. The ideological formulations known as *Siberian Zimmerwaldism*, worked out during the winter of 1914–1915, went a long way toward further party unity in Siberia.[46]

Ironically, the fortunes of war brought the leading Bolsheviks and Mensheviks still in Russia together in Siberia to work out the new ideological formulations. In November 1914, the five Bolshevik members of the Duma, along with Stalin and Kamenev, were arrested and sent to Siberia. Already in exile were Tsereteli, Dan,

Woitinsky, Rozhkov, and such Bolshevik stalwarts as Sverdlov, Yaroslavskii, and N. N. Yakovlev. Led by Tsereteli, the intellectual Social Democrats in Irkutsk had already begun to formulate the principles of Siberian Zimmerwaldism. In the early winter, they attempted to launch a journal to disseminate their views. Although only two issues came out before it was suppressed by the police, they did provoke a lively controversy among the exiles that was carried on by mail.[47]

In 1915, a Bolshevik exile sent a questionnaire to 141 exiles in the far north soliciting their views on the war, the fate of the Second International, Social Democratic participation in the military-industrial committees, and a number of other questions of contemporary concern. Of the 90 Social Democrats who answered, including 53 Bolsheviks, 9 Mensheviks, 9 Liquidators, 5 Bundists, 9 nonfractionalists, 3 Latvians, and 3 Lithuanians, the overwhelming majority were antiwar and against participation in the military-industrial committees. Naturally, the author fails to mention that the predominant views of the exiles were those of Tsereteli, Woitinsky, and Dan.[48]

According to Woitinsky, the chief purpose of Siberian Zimmerwaldism was to work out a position on the war that would avoid the extremes of social patriotism and defeatism, both of which, they argued, ignored the military and political realities of the times.[49] This view fit very nicely with the desire of Bolshevik-conciliators and Menshevik-internationalists to unify the party, although many Leninists and ultraleftists, as well as the defensists, were quite unhappy with it.

In summing up his attitude toward the war, Tsereteli wrote in his memoirs that

the ultimate aim must not be the victory of either coalition, but a durable peace based upon justice. Neither the blind support of the national government nor crippling opposition to the war effort would serve that purpose. By undermining the military policy of the Tsarist government, Russian socialists might become tools of German militarism. Similarly, the German socialists, by challenging the Kaiser, might ultimately lend support to the forces of absolutism in Russia. The solution should be a coordinated movement on both sides for a negotiated peace with victors and vanquished, without annexations and indemnities.[50]

This position, with some modifications, was held by a large number of Bolsheviks, not only in Siberia, but also in European Russia. Kamenev, Stalin, and Muranov successfully imposed it upon the party, for about a month, when they returned to Petrograd to take control of *Pravda* in mid-March.

Despite sharp arguments over various aspects and points in its articulation, most party members in Siberia were prepared to live with it. Most Bolsheviks shared the position that the bourgeois opposition to Tsarism was ripening into opposition both in the Duma and in the military-industrial committees, but that socialists should not participate in these committees to help the revolution along. A central principle of Zimmerwaldism was that socialists should not work to bring on the bourgeois revolution at the expense of delaying the international socialist revolution. Participation in the military-industrial committees might help the bourgeois-democratic revolution along, but it would put the working class under the thumb of the bourgeoisie. The yardstick to be used to determine all Social Democratic activity was whether or not they would be productive of socialist revolution under the changed conditions brought on by the World War.[51]

This was a principle not even Lenin could quarrel with, although he would relentlessly argue that it was constantly being misapplied. Many Bolsheviks in Siberia undoubtedly shared this view, but they were prepared to hammer out their differences with the Mensheviks in united organizations engaged in practical, revolutionary activities. Thus, with the exception of a few purists, the majority of Social Democrats in Siberia, including those who considered themselves staunch Leninists, were prepared to be in the same organization with all Social Democrats, who would then work in underground organizations and conduct revolutionary activity among the workers and poor peasants. And in two specific situations, they were prepared to work in the same revolutionary organizations with like-minded Socialist Revolutionaries. Instinctively, the socialists in Russia felt that world revolution was at hand, and that it would begin in their own country. At this critical time in history, when cataclysmic events were about to unfold, no one was going to be read out of the Social Democratic movement for what, at the time, seemed like less than fundamental ideological differences. Under the increasing conditions of police repression, concrete party work was a far more crucial sign of one's revolutionary zeal than one's attitude toward the war or the International.

Underground party life returned to Siberia primarily because the war made it easier for the Socialist exiles to move about. In Irkutsk, the center of Siberian Social Democracy, a clandestine organization of Bolsheviks and Mensheviks formed with fifteen members. By November, it had grown to over 150, with the Bolsheviks outnumbering the Mensheviks by about two to one. Toward the end of the following summer, the more militant and daring members of the organization had organized several cells among the workers. This group, which called itself *the Union of Siberian Workers*, was mainly Bolshevik, although it included Mensheviks and a number of Socialist Revolutionaries. The workers' cells had 15 tailors, 16 sausagemakers, 12 printers, 10 metalworkers, 11 bakers, 8 wool- and leathermakers, and 20 teachers.[52]

During the next two years, the Irkutsk Social Democrats tried to hold several gubernia conferences, but each time they were broken up by the Tsarist police. They did, however, manage to elect a united party committee in which the Bolsheviks predominated.[53]

In Krasnoiarsk, there was no united Social Democratic party organization until 1917, but Bolshevik-conciliators and Menshevik-internationalists were active in organizing the railroad workers. They also gathered around the workers' cooperative, *Samodeiatel'nost'* *(Self Help),* and two or three working-class reading rooms. During 1916 and early 1917, the Bolsheviks were engaged in a fierce controversy among themselves concerning the role of *Samodeiatel'nost'* in the revolutionary movement. The ultraleftists and Leninists wanted to use it as a base to carry on the revolutionary struggle. They criticized the Bolshevik-conciliators who controlled it for their gradualist, cautious approach and their Menshevik mentality. The conciliators replied that it would be sheer foolishness to do anything that would cause the government to suppress the organization, especially when many workers in the city depended upon it to make ends meets. The ultras were also critical of the conciliators' stubborn desire to work for party unity.[54]

In Novonikolaevsk, the Social Democratic movement was dominated by the defensists, and even the Bolsheviks, who were a distinct minority, seemed to share these views, at least to a limited degree. In contrast to other Siberian cities, the Novonikolaevsk Social Democrats did decide to participate in the military-industrial committee. According to G. E. Dronin, an old Bolshevik exile active in Novonikolaevsk since 1914, he and the other Bolsheviks tried unsuccessfully to block this move. As he grandiosely put it, "we, with part of the proletarian mass, boycotted elections of the workers' group to the military-industrial committee," but the only part of the so-called proletarian mass that did not send representatives to the committee were the stevedores. What he does not specifically say, and what can be clearly inferred from his memoir, is that some Bolsheviks did go into it.[55]

None of the memoirists, of course, writing in the early 1920s, wish to reveal the extent of their cooperation with the Mensheviks and the Socialist Revolutionaries. Few of them really did share Lenin's uncompromising attitude and certainly the long years of suffering and hardship in exiles built human relationships that were not so easily broken. The bonds of personal friendship and mutual interdependence forged in the exile days created an atmosphere of human warmth and cooperation, which transcended party labels, blurred ideological differences, and helped to shape the character of the February revolution. The fact that this atmosphere changed so drastically during the revolution and civil war frequently causes scholars to overlook and underestimate the powerful trend toward party unity in the immediate prerevolutionary period, not only in Siberia, but also in much of Russia.

This tendency to subordinate ideological differences to practical, revolutionary work was seen in the formation of the Military-Socialist Union. The idea for this organization grew out of discussions about what the exiles ought to do if they were drafted into the army. A few argued that the socialists ought to serve if the government would grant amnesty to all political prisoners and exiles. A small group of Latvians and ultraleftist Bolsheviks took the opposite view: it was the duty of all socialist to desert at the first opportunity, if mobilized. The majority, including Bolsheviks, Mensheviks, and Socialist Revolutionaries, felt that the best course of action was to go into the army and to agitate against the war and for the revolution. Among them were Leninists, who could see the distinction between out-and-out defeatism that might result in a German victory and antiwar, revolutionary activity.[56]

Here is reflected the value of Siberian Zimmerwaldism as a broad ideological umbrella under which the socialist could conduct concrete political activities. By rejecting the defeatism of the Latvians and the "social patriotism" of the amnesty seekers, the majority of exiles saw this as an opportunity to walk the extremely narrow line between responsible, revolutionary internationalism and out-and-out defeatism. From the scholar's standpoint the line appears nonexistent, but if one suspends knowledge of what happened for a moment and sees the world as the Zimmerwaldists saw it, it is not difficult to understand why such a course of action would seem plausible. Not only did it make sense in terms of concrete, political activity, it provided yet another means to unite the party.

The Military-Socialist Union was founded in October 1916, when exiles in Narym were finally mobilized and sent off to the huge garrison at Tomsk. But before they were shipped, they managed to elect an Executive Bureau of five, which included I. N. Smirnov, Yakovlev, V. Kosarev, and the Socialist Revolutionary Kudriavtsev.[57] A fifth place was left open for a representative of the Tomsk antiwar socialists. At the same time, the other members of the union were shipped to garrisons at Novonikolaevsk and Krasnoiarsk. In Novonikolaevsk, agitational and propaganda work in the barracks were carried on by F. I. Gor'ban and Adolph Klepper, both old Bolsheviks. In Krasnoiarsk, the Union was under the influence of B. Z. Shumiatskii, E. F. Dymov, and V. M. Klipov, who arrived at the garrison from Tomsk in December. Evidently, the leading activists in Krasnoiarsk were all Bolsheviks.[58]

Unfortunately, since the extant memoir literature is written by Bolsheviks, the impression given is one of Bolshevik predominance. This is probably true in the case of Tomsk and Krasnoiarsk, but the fact that the garrison was so strongly influenced by the Socialist Revolutionaries in 1917 indicates that Novonikolaevsk is an exception. In both Tomsk and Krasnoiarsk the Bolsheviks had very strong personalities in the garrisons and the troops supported them from the first days of the revolution.

The major work of the Military-Socialist Union was conducted in Tomsk. When the original Executive Bureau arrived from Narym, it found already in the army one A. A. Zvezdov, an old Bolshevik exile, whom they quickly elected to the Bureau. They failed to include a member of the Tomsk antiwar Social Democrats, as they had planned to do, because they were so closely watched that they had little opportunity to contact them. Consequently, it was safer for the exiles to concentrate their activities in their own barracks.

During the first few days of the exiles' arrival, the soldiers, who had been warned by their officers about these wicked men, shunned them as if they had the plague. They would have nothing to do with the seditious politicals. One day, however, an exile miner from the Donets basin began to tinker with his harmonica. A noncommissioned officer walked over to him and asked him to play something. The big miner obliged and within fifteen minutes a large circle of soldiers had gathered around him. He soon began to play a number of lively dances, and, caught up in the spirit of the occasion, the Bolshevik Zvezdov began to dance. At this the soldiers, who had avoided all contact with the evil politicals, began to murmer: "What kind of seditious people are these...? Do these serious socialists actually play and dance? Why! These are simply gay fellows!?" With this the ice had broken and many important links began to be forged.[59]

From that point on, the exiles in the Tomsk barracks had little difficulty in obtaining an audience for their antiwar views. As Kosarev points out, their task became somewhat easier as the grim realities of war on the eastern front filtered back to the barracks in Siberia. During the winter of 1916–1917, as life became boring and anxiety about being sent to the front increased, general dissatisfaction with military life was openly expressed, especially among the noncommissioned officers. These men soon made it easier to spread propaganda and to carry on agitational work with the rank and file. It was then possible, for the first time, for members of the Military-Socialist Union to make contact with the local revolutionaries in Tomsk.[60]

The connection established between local revolutionaries and the exiles was important both for the resources that the locals put at the disposal of the exiles and for the establishment of future relationships. Although the Bolshevik members of the Military-Socialist Union did not join the local underground Social Democratic group in Tomsk, they did work quite closely with them.[61] Particularly helpful was the Bolshevik I. L. Nakhanovich, who worked as a typesetter on the newspaper *Sibirskaia Zhizn'*. Nakhanovich, his wife, and two other Bolsheviks let their homes be used for clandestine meetings, they scrounged up typographical facilities and supplies for propaganda leaflets, and they did the printing.[62] With their help the Union managed to get out one antiwar leaflet that was distributed throughout the barracks, but before they could develop other forms of revolutionary activity, or, perhaps, get themselves arrested, events in Petrograd soon made open work among the soldiers possible.

Regardless of the rather insignificant fruits of their labor, it is clear that the Bolsheviks, especially, benefited from the Union's short-lived activity. They made contact with the peasant-soldiers and gained their respect and confidence. The votes of the soldiers would soon give the Bolsheviks a strong voice in Tomsk city politics. This was true not only in Tomsk, but in other cities as well. Throughout Siberia, in both the cities and the garrisons, Bolsheviks known and trusted both by the workingmen and the soldiers would be on the scene in February creating the various institutions that would make up the political infrastructure.

2

The Structure of the February Revolution

The so-called February revolution in Siberia began with the sudden and unexpected collapse of the Tsarist government during the first three or four days in March (O.S.).[1] Strictly speaking, there had been no revolution. Senior Tsarist officials simply stepped down from office when it became clear that the revolution had succeeded in the capital, and they turned power over to various kinds of revolutionary committees formed by the socialist exiles and local intelligentsia. Once that happened, Siberia exploded in political activity as people began to organize themselves into a myriad of groups, committees, unions, soviets, and political parties.

Although in March each group regarded its own activities as a necessary step toward democracy in Russia,

48

the collapse of Tsarism in Siberia unleashed centrifugal forces that would soon plunge the region into anarchy and civil war. In the cities, the working classes formed soviets and trade unions to safeguard their class interests in the coming struggle with the bourgeoisie. Peasant-soldiers organized to break the power of officers and to make sure they received a fair share of the land settlement. The peasants in the countryside were slower to respond, but they, too, formed soviets and various committees to protect themselves. In Transbaikalia, a strong Buriat-Mongol movement surfaced and immediately revealed that it, too, was riven by class conflicts and tensions.

At the same time, however, the revolution unleashed new political and social forces that would make possible the creation of a new socialist, soviet order in Siberia. Many of the political movements that developed in 1917 would die during the course of the civil war, but the Bolshevik party, the soviets, and the trade unions would not. They would be the key elements of the revolutionary infrastructure, which became the foundation for the urban-based Soviet government in the winter of 1917–1918. This government was made possible by the fusion of left-wing socialists into the Communist party and its subsequent domination of the soviets and trade unions.[2]

From the outset, the Bolsheviks in Siberia played vital and leading roles in creating and participating in the revolutionary infrastructure. As part of the coalition of antiwar socialists, they put aside their differences and did what they could to make the revolution work. This securely established their personal authority and popularity as revolutionary leaders, which, in turn, extended the influence of the Social Democratic party, far beyond its weight in members. When the party began to move left in response to news from Petrograd—for example, the issue of a coalition ministry, the Kerensky offensive, the July days, and the Kornilov affair—the soviets and trade unions in Siberia moved with it. So did many of the elective organs of self-government.[3]

In a situation where all moral authority was breaking down, where each particular group was jealously safeguarding its own interests in the name of revolutionary principles, the charismatic, revolutionary leader became the fountainhead of authority and a source of moral order. His vision of the revolutionary future, with its moral, political, and social implications, was either accepted or rejected as a world view. To his followers, he was not only leader, but also a teacher of the revolution. Consequently, he should not move too far ahead of them. If he was a revolutionary Social Democrat, he should guide the masses toward the socialist revolution, but only in and through their own concrete revolutionary experiences.

In Siberia, the Bolsheviks were generally astute enough to realize that if they remained aloof from those political movements that appealed most to Siberians, such as regional autonomy, no one would listen to them. But at the same time, the best of them were well aware that such political activity was only a means to an end, under conditions viewed as somewhat less than favorable for a socialist revolution. Hence, the task before the Bolsheviks and Menshevik-internationalists were different from those of their colleagues in the revolutionary capital. In Siberia the dominant theme throughout 1917 was to prevent the coalescence of counterrevolution. Siberia, with its rich stores of grain, must not become part of a Russian vendee. For this reason, most Social Democrats tried to conduct their revolutionary activities in a manner to avoid pushing the middle classes and wealthier peasants to the side of reaction and counterrevolution.

In treating the role of the Bolsheviks in the February revolution, several additional points must be kept in mind. Although there is ample evidence that they were aware of the situation in the capital, it is difficult to reconstruct how much they actually knew or how they interpreted it during the first few weeks. By April some Siberian cities were receiving *Pravda*,[4] and other newspapers were probably received as well. Toward the end of March, several emissaries from the Provisional Government were sent to the gubernia and regional capitals to explain its creation and to seek out prospective commissars from the local intelligentsia.[5] A few Social Democrats traveled back and forth to the capital on party business from the end of March on.[6] In mid-April, the Central Committee began to establish relations with the Bolsheviks in Krasnoiarsk by letter and telegram,[7] and most likely also with Omsk. Soviet sources give no information about the Socialist Revolutionaries and Kadets, but there is no reason to suppose they knew less about the situation in Petrograd than the Social Democrats.

Second, throughout 1917, the socialist leadership in Siberia believed that the Constituent Assembly would decide the final political and economic order in Russia. In March, the Social Democrats were quite concerned to increase their party's influence in anticipation of the elections, a concern that the Bolsheviks in Siberia continued to express until after the October revolution. The soviets were not seen as organs of government, but as institutions to safeguard the interests of the most democratic layers of the population against betrayal by the bourgeois Provisional Government and the threat of counterrevolution.

A third point is that the majority of Siberians supported the war in the spring. Though conditions of life were becoming difficult, especially for the salaried employees who had no ties to the land, they were a far cry from those in the larger cities of European Russia. There is no evidence of food and fuel shortages or that the prices of basic necessities had gone beyond the ability of lower and middle classes to pay. The formulations of Siberian Zimmerwaldism allowed Russian Social Democrats to respond to the prowar sentiment in Siberia, yet still maintain their revolutionary internationalism. One can assume that in the eyes of the population the careful ideological distinctions between Zimmerwald Social Democrats and Mensheviks of the Plekhanov type were meaningless. It was only during April, when the Siberian Social Democrats became aware of the rising tide of antiwar sentiment in Petrograd, that the internationalists sought to make the distinctions between themselves and the defensists clearer.

Another factor that affected the responses of Social Democrats to the February revolution was the strong sentiment toward regional autonomy throughout Siberia. It found its expression differently in Western, Eastern, and Central Siberia, but the result was the same. The Provisional Government failed to establish its authority over the local organs of self-government, most socialist leaders, and much of the population. It succeeded only in Novonikolaevsk and Irkutsk, because its socialist supporters controlled the entire revolutionary infrastructure, with the exception of the trade unions. But the local autonomous organs of government were generally popular, so, if the left-wing Social Democrats wanted to have any influence, they, like all other parties, had to work within these institutions.

Finally, one must keep in mind that the Social Democrats in the major cities of Siberia were aware of what each group or party organization was doing from the first days of the revolution. During March and April, the

Krasnoiarsk and Tomsk organization newspapers began to report on the activities of Social Democrats in other cities. More important, many of the leading Social Democrats knew each other quite well, from the days of exile in Narym or Turukhansk. Some, in Tomsk and Krasnoiarsk, had been linked together through the Military-Socialist Union. While Social Democratic activities during the spring do not appear to have been coordinated on an intercity basis until the last two weeks in April, this common awareness of the activities of other groups must have been an important factor in their behavior.

THE REVOLUTIONARY CITIZENS' COMMITTEES

Virtually all the citizens' committees that took power from the Tsarist government were created by socialist exiles and the local intelligentsia. In many of the cities they were formed at meetings of the Town Dumas, which were called in response to an official telegram from the Provisional Committee of the State Duma. In Tomsk, a special meeting of the Town Duma was called by Mayor Lomovitskii on March 2nd, which included several socialist exiles, among whom were the Social Democrats A. F. Ivanov[8] and A. Shotman.[9] Lomovitskii told of the creation of a Provisional Committee in the State Duma and that its president sent a circular telegram to the chairmen of gubernia zemstvos and mayors of gubernia and regional cities calling for the unanimous support of the Provisional Government. A number of Town Duma deputies made speeches expressing a fear of excesses and public disorder. These included B. M. Gan[10] and S. V. Alexandrowskii, who became part of a Committee of Public Order and Safety, which was organized at the meeting. This Committee initially included three other Social Democrats (Ivanov, Denisov,[11] and Shotman), one Socialist Revolutionary, and four nonparty members. Denisov represented the United Social Democrats, and Ivanov, the city's consumer cooperative.[12]

On March 3rd, Colonel Biron, commander of the Tomsk garrison, issued public orders to his troops announcing the recognition of the Provisional Government and the Tomsk Committee of Public Order and Safety.[13] During the next day, the Committee negotiated with Biron concerning the question of allowing soldiers to send representatives into the Committee, to which he agreed. He also agreed that a military parade would be held so the soldiers could pass in review of the Committee that same day, but only if the socialist exiles refrained from making propagandistic speeches before the troops.[14]

Between the 3rd and 4th, new delegates joined the Committee by the hour. When it had enlarged considerably, an Executive Bureau was formed that became the real civil power in the city; it included three Social Democrats, all of whom were Bolsheviks,[15] two Socialist Revolutionaries, and two nonparty members. According to Shotman, the Social Democrats exercised de facto control of the Executive Bureau, since the two nonparty delegates were Social Democratic sympathizers.[16]

From its inception, the Tomsk Committee of Public Safety took energetic revolutionary measures and quickly achieved prestige in the eyes of the civilian population and among the soldiers. It unhesitatingly took upon itself all the authority of local government, arresting the governor, the police chief, the officers of the gendarmes, and other ranking Tsarist officials.[17] It did not succeed, initially, in its efforts to take over the actual administrative apparatus of the gubernia, a factor that prompted it to undertake a revolution in local government, without regard to the wishes of the Provisional Government.[18]

It also took bold steps to establish its authority over the garrison. According to Shotman's account, despite Biron's public orders to the troops, opposition among the officers began to develop on March 4th. Many resented the inclusion of rank-and-file troops into the Tomsk Committee of Public Safety and they feared a complete breakdown of discipline in the barracks. The inclusion of Yakovlev into the Executive Bureau may have been interpreted unfavorably, since they were aware not only that he was an important Bolshevik exile, but also of his activities in the Military-Socialist Union. After several ugly incidents during the next two days, in which a member of the Executive Bureau had his horse shot from beneath him, the Executive Bureau decided to arrest Biron and the ranking officers of the garrison. Since it had no armed force at its disposal, except for a few Tomsk University students who functioned as a militia, it decided to resort to bluff. It arranged for the officers to come to the Bureau's headquarters on a pretext and placed them under arrest. To the members' surprise, the officers surrendered without resistance.[19]

The Novonikolaevsk Committee of Public Order and Safety was also created at a special Town Duma meeting on March 3rd, but under somewhat different circumstances. Upon receiving the circular telegram, Mayor Besedin made a flowery speech calling for a peaceful and dignified response to the event and adjourned the meeting. He may have been under the impression that the Town Duma would simply take over the Tsarist administration, but the Social Democrats and Socialist Revolutionaries, who had both been invited to the meeting registered a strong protest. They were aware that in

Tomsk a revolutionary committee had been formed and were determined to have one of their own. Under the energetic prodding of the influential Social Democrat, M. M. German-Kamenskii, the meeting reopened and lasted the entire night.[20]

Created that evening, the Committee of Public Order and Safety included representatives of the Social Democratic newspaper *Golos Sibiri*, the workers' group in the military-industrial committee, the Town Duma, the cooperatives, the Agricultural Society, and a few other organizations. The next day, the Committee increased its representation to include the two main socialist parties, workers, and employees from various commercial or industrial establishments. Approximately seventy-five percent of all the representatives were either Socialist Revolutionaries or Social Democrats. The executive committee included two Socialist Revolutionaries as President and Vice-President and one Social Democratic Vice-President (N. A. Rozhkov). Other Social Democratic members were German-Kamenskii, N. A. Gudkov, and V. P. Romanov.[21]

The Novonikolaevsk Committee was fairly slow in replacing Tsarist officials. On March 4th, it sent its representatives to the local police chief to inquire about his attitude toward the revolution. He said he would support the new government. They also went to General Reterner, who said that he would wait for orders but would make no move against the new government in the meantime. Later that day, the Committee must have learned of the parade in Tomsk and decided to have one of its own as a way to gain the support of the rank-and-file troops. At this the general balked. Zhernakov, the S. R. chairman of the committee, then confronted him with his own bluff. He said that if the general would not submit to the Committee on this matter he would be arrested. With that the general submitted and the parade was held without incident.[22]

Unfortunately, scholars have very little information concerning the role of the Social Democrats in creating the Omsk Provisional Coalitional Committee or the Barnaul Committee of Public Safety. The available Soviet primary and secondary sources, in fact, provide only glimpses of events in these cities during the spring of 1917. In Barnaul, the news was made public only on March 4th, at which time the Town Duma discussed forming a committee. It did not do so, however.[23] Interestingly, the Committee of Public Safety was formed by the Barnaul Soviet of Workers on March 8th, at its first meeting. Since the Soviet agreed that workers and Soldiers should send delegates to the Committee, one can assume that the Socialist Revolutionaries and Social Democrats created it themselves.[24] This is probably why Soviet historians provide no information about it; the idea of a soviet forming a "bourgeoisie committee" is too much even for Soviet casuistry! They also fail to provide any information about the Omsk Provisional Coalition Committee, since it included Kadets, Socialist Revolutionaries, and Social Democrats, as well as Soviet delegates.[25] Researchers do know that the Omsk Committee did take vigorous steps to arrest Tsarist officials.[26] Obviously, Soviet historians want to create the impression that the various committees that formed in Western Siberia were bourgeois organs, arising out of the old order, in which individual Bolsheviks mistakenly took part. But the situation in Omsk and Barnaul suggests that this was not the case.[27]

Confirmative evidence in this regard, assuming the plausibility of analogy, can be deduced from the role of the Social Democrats in creating the Krasnoiarsk, Irkutsk, and Verkhneudinsk committees, for which there are two valuable Socialist Revolutionary memoirs and an early Soviet source. Especially clear is the picture in Krasnoiarsk, which was the major center of Bolshevik strength in Siberia.

According to V. Gurevich, it was rumored among the exiles in Krasnoiarsk on March 1st that Governor Gololobov had received a telegram from Petrograd informing him of revolutionary events. The next morning, exile circles were informed by "trusted people," presumably friends who worked in the gubernia administration, that the rumors were true, and that the governor had gone to Irkutsk to consult with Pilts'. Immediately, they began to congregate in the offices of two cooperatives: *Samodeiatel'nost'*, a city-consumer cooperative run by the Social Democrats, and the much larger Eniseisk Gubernia Union of Consumer Societies, run mainly by the Socialist Revolutionaries.[28]

A few Socialist Revolutionaries, such as Gurevich, a lawyer who had only recently been released from four months of prison, went to the Union headquarters determined to act, but the majority of his colleagues on the board of administrators were just as determined to take a wait-and-see attitude. They were afraid that if Socialist Revolutionaries connected with the cooperatives acted in a revolutionary manner and it later turned out that the regime had weathered the storm in Petrograd, there would be severe retributions against the cooperative movement, the major source of Socialist Revolutionary strength in Siberia. This reveals that the exiles probably had only the sketchiest idea of the scope of events in the capital. Only the Socialist Revolutionary N. V. Fomin and the Social Democrat A. A. Baikalov[29] supported Gurevich's point of view, but to no avail.[30]

Consequently, Gurevich, Fomin, and Baikalov went over to the offices of *Samodeiatel'nost'*, where quite different attitudes prevailed. Summoned by telephone, about twenty left-wing Social Democrats gathered in the office to prepare a plan of action. Despite the fact that they had no concrete information, the meeting decided to prepare a revolutionary leaflet informing the population that a revolution had occurred and to create an inter-party committee of socialist exiles. They also agreed to call a meeting of representatives of "society" for six P.M. in the city's main theater. All representatives of the Town Duma, various public organizations, and political exiles were invited to attend.[31]

So as not to create the impression that the meeting was illegal, it was arranged that the mayor of the city would call the meeting. Many of the more conservative Duma deputies, however, would not even attend. Only such old narodnik deputies as V. M. Krutovksii took an active part, along with numerous Socialist Rev-olutionaries and Social Democrats. The major concern of the meeting was to play it safe. On the one hand, if a revolution had occurred in the capital and the Tsarist order were overthrown, it would be necessary to create an organ of civil authority to preserve order and to pre-vent bloodshed; on the other hand, every effort was made to avoid the appearance of a usurpation of author-ity in the case the news should prove unfounded. At the same time, a wary eye was cast toward the garrison, headed by General Kochengin, known to be a strict au-thoritarian and the loyal supporter of the Tsar.[32]

With all these reservations and trepidations, the meet-ing elected a Committee of Public Safety, designed to take over civil authority in the city. Elected to it were V. M. Krutovskii, chairman, A. G. Shlikhter,[33] Baikalov, and six Socialist Revolutionaries, including Gurevich and Fomin. The meeting then adjourned until the following day, when it was expected that representatives from other organizations and sections in the city would send delegates.[34] That night Baikalov composed the revolutionary proclamation he had been charged with writing during the morning meeting of socialists in the offices of *Samodeiatel'nost'*. It was published on the morning of March 3rd.[35]

> Citizen! The old order has fallen. All the important adherents of the old order are arrested. A new Provisional Government has been formed. The people, in close agreement with the army, are organizing. Committees of Public Safety are being formed. People are taking the government and their destiny into their own hands. It is necessary that the process of organizing should go more quickly. Only organization can save the people from becoming a sacrifice.
>
> Therefore our word to you, citizens of Krasnoiarsk, is to organize.
>
> Organize urgently into professional unions, to send your delegates into the soviets, to the Committee of Public Safety.
>
> Power must be taken from the hands of the adherents of the old order, immediately, and turned over to the true representatives of the people.
>
> Citizens, we call on you to be concerned peacefully and seriously with events, to become conscious of your strength and not to waste it on unorganized adventures. Citizens, difficult times face us. The old government has shattered all the threads of popular life. It is necessary to correct all this. It is necessary to introduce order into this chaos, an order which will rid us of all traces of the old.
>
> For the present, we must consider the government only temporary. The people must set about immediately organizing a government that actually rep-

resents the people. This government can only be organized by a Constituent Assembly, elected by all the people, at the front and in the rear, by a general, direct, equal, and secret vote.

This assembly of true and genuine popular representatives will work out the new order of government in Russia to serve the interests of democracy.

Citizens, our second word to you is to call for a struggle for a Constituent Assembly. Long live the revolution! Long live the Constituent Assembly!

Significantly, this leaflet was published as a proclamation of the Russian Social Democratic Workers' Party, even before a legal party organization had formed. This meant that the Social Democrats seized the initiative as the party that took bold and decisive steps to lead the revolution, and it was an initiative they never lost.

The claim that the old officials had already been arrested, however, was not true. It was put in, most likely, to give the population confidence. The arrests did not take place until March 4th. Late in the previous evening, a left-wing Socialist Revolutionary, Sergei Lazo, came to the headquarters of the meeting and offered the services of himself and his company of soldiers to the Committee of Public Safety. In the early morning hours, the Committee members each took a detachment of soldiers and occupied the gubernia administration, the postal-telegraph offices, and the telephone exchange. The arrests of high-ranking officials did not occur until late the next day, until after a delegation of the Committee went to General Kochengin to sound him out. From their meeting with the ranking officers of the garrison, they received the same response that Biron had given the committee in Tomsk. The army would not support the revolution until clarification arrived from Petrograd, but that it would not interfere, meanwhile, in the creation of a new civil government.[36]

In the other cities of Central Siberia a similar pattern of events occurred. In Eniseisk, for example, the Committee of Public Safety was created on March 3rd by Socialist Revolutionary and Social Democratic exiles. On that day, it arrested the Tsarist uezd police officer, the head of the gendarmes, the head of the postal-telegraph office, and abolished the local police entirely. Commisars were elected within the Committee to take over all administrative services and a militia of seventy-five was formed to maintain order in the city.[37] It is not, however, known who the Committee members were, but it can inferred that they were all left-wing socialists from the fact that they refused to recognize the authority of the Provisional Government.[38] The same reasoning can apply to Achinsk and Kansk, for which there is no available information concerning the creation of the Committees of Public Safety.

In Eastern Siberia, the pattern of events was somewhat different. On the eve of the February revolution, Irkutsk lay in the grip of a police repression. Governor-General Pilts' issued orders to the gendarmes "to spare neither mother nor brother" in maintaining order.[39] But by March 1st, his fruitless efforts were rapidly being undermined by the force of events. On that day, a group of prominent citizens who had heard privately of the events in Petrograd went to see Pilts', advising him to step down and to turn authority over to the Town Duma. He stalled for one day, obviously hoping that order might be restored in the capital, but by March 2nd news was received that a Provisional Government was being established and that the Tsar had abdicated. Presumably this was the circular telegram sent to all mayors of gubernia cities.[40]

During the evening of March 2nd, while most of the population in Irkutsk yet remained in ignorance that there had been a revolution in Petrograd, Pilts' called a meeting in his official residence of local intelligentsia, well known public figures and leading political exiles. Attending were representatives of the Town Duma, the stock exchanges, the cooperatives, and various other public organizations, including the Church. Also attending were Socialist Revolutionary and Social Democratic exiles, among whom were A. F. Gots and I. G. Tsereteli. At this meeting a bureaucrat tiptoed in, as if on cue, and formally announced the news that everyone, by now, suspected. Plans were then drawn to create a local organ of Provisional Government, the Irkutsk Committee of Public Organizations, although everyone agreed that this organ in the city must appear to have been created independently of the old regime.[41]

The key questions discussed at the meeting were how to create this new organ of government and what its character would be. The socialists who dominated the meeting were obviously thinking of the new organ of government in ideological terms. According to one source, profound differences occurred among the Social Democrats. A few Bolsheviks argued that it was necessary to organize a soviet immediately and to make it the sole authority in Irkutsk. The majority, Bolsheviks and Mensheviks, considered this idea "untimely," and they were supported by the Socialist Revolutionaries. Both Tsereteli and Gots were convinced that the revolution could not succeed without the cooperation of the bourgeoisie and the proletariat. The socialists and the workers could hardly expect sympathy from the middle classes for the idea of giving all power to the working classes. They reasoned that the idea of a soviet government in Irkutsk with a bourgeois government in Petrograd was ridiculous. Consequently, the idea of a Committee of Public Safety, representing the broad strata of middle and lower classes, was adopted, but the Social Democrats and Socialist Revolutionaries would hold the key positions.[42]

From the Social Democratic point of view, this was ideologically sound. The revolution was bourgeois, but the tasks of Russian Social Democracy were to insure that it proceeded along a path toward a socialist revolution. A premature seizure of power by the working classes could only result in throwing the middle classes into the arms of a counterrevolution. The only hope for socialism in Russia, because of the backward development of its productive forces, was a socialist revolution in the West. The main task was to ensure the further development of the Russian revolution by protecting it from without until such time as the inevitable revolution began to unfold in Germany. This view, shared by a broad spectrum of Social Democrats in Irkutsk, fit nicely with the Socialist Revolutionary organic conception of the revolution. The thing to do then was to join with representatives of the middle class and to prevent reaction from within and coercion from without.

The creation of the Committee of Public Organizations took place on March 3rd, amid the noisy street celebrations and meetings of the population who learned of the revolution that morning. The mood of Irkutsk was somewhat reflective of the mood in Petrograd. Workers and soldiers spontaneously began to fraternize and swore to serve the interests of the revolution.[43] During the day various delegations of workers, Duma deputies, from the stock exchange and public organizations, the cooperatives, the church and the political parties went into the Committee and an executive committee was elected. Headed by Tsereteli and W. S. Woitinsky, it included ten Socialist Revolutionaries, nine Kadets, and six Social Democrats. Later, it included representatives of the Irkutsk Soviet.[44]

During the next four days, the Irkutsk Executive Committee of Public Organizations firmly established itself as the head of both the gubernia administration and over the garrison. Unfortunately, the details concerning how it did this are not available in the existing memoir literature. Researchers do know that the Socialist Revolutionaries effectively organized the entire garrison within this period under the jurisdiction of the Executive Committee members—Gots, Krakovetskii, and Bruderer. They also know that the majority of middle-ranking officers in the garrison were Socialist Revolutionaries, who supported the Committee, which acted quickly to help them restore discipline that had temporarily been destroyed.[45]

In the civilian sphere, it is clear from Tsereteli's account that the Committee of Public Safety abolished the city police and replaced it with a city militia. It is plausible to assume that this Committee received rather widespread support and had no difficulty in taking control of the gubernia administration.[46] Evidently, a large number of exiles and former exiles worked in the gubernia administration. This was a rather large pool of administrative talent that could be drawn upon, in contrast to Krasnoiarsk and Tomsk, where the majority of exiles in the regions did not actually live in the city.[47] Thus, in Irkutsk, and this will become clearer in the next chapter, there was a much smoother integration of the new revolutionary authority with the old administrative order.

As far as can be determined, the situation in Transbaikalia was not markedly different than elsewhere in Siberia.[48] In Verkhneudinsk, as in Barnaul, the Committee of Public Organizations was created by the Verkh-

neudinsk Soviet and it was staffed, primarily, with Social Democrats. In fact, the Executive Committee of the
Committee of Public Organizations and the Executive
Committee of the Soviet met jointly, although it is clear
that the former was a creature of the latter. In Chita,
the pattern was similar to Irkutsk. Into the Committee
went Socialist Revolutionaries, Social Democrats, and
Kadets. In both cities the Tsarist regime was liquidated
quietly and efficiently by the Committees.[49]

By March 10th, the major cities of Siberia were entirely in the hands of the Committees of Public Safety or
Public Organizations,[50] but in every case the Executive
Committees, usually controlled or influenced by Social
Democrats were the real governing authorities. In every
case, even in Irkutsk, these Committees were conceived
of as local organs of self-government and were highly
resistive to the idea of any control over themselves by
the Provisional Government.[51] In the eyes of a significant strata of the urban population, these Committees
were legitimate and prestigious. Naturally, this prestige
and influence accrued to the Social Democrats who participated in them, and many of these were to become
leading Bolsheviks in Siberia.

THE SOVIETS

If the role of the Social Democrats in the revolutionary committees contributed to their influence in
Siberia, their role in the soviets was an even more important factor, since the soviets would become the organs of authority among the more militant and poorer
strata of Siberian society, especially the army, the working classes, and the poorer peasants.

The creation of the soviets in Siberia began almost

simultaneously with the creation of the revolutionary committees and very often the same Social Democrats took part in both.

In Tomsk, a Soldiers' Soviet was created on March 4th, by the Military-Socialist Union during the elections of military representatives to the Tomsk Committee of Public Order and Safety. By March, the Union had approximately 200 members scattered through the barracks of the 70,000 man garrison. Headed by the Bolsheviks Yakovlev, Smirnov, and Kosarev, the Union quickly took command of organizing the garrison, not only in creating the Tomsk Soviet of Soldiers', but also military committees.[52] The first meeting of the Soviet, which took place on March 5th, included 124 delegates and 68 candidates. The Executive Committee elected at the meeting included nine members, among them were I. N. Smirnov, S. Kudriavtsev, N. N. Yakovlev, and V. Kosarev—all Bolshevik members of the Military-Socialist Union. Yakovlev and Smirnov were sent as representatives to the Tomsk Committee of Public Order and Safety.[53]

From the available protocols of the first Soviet meetings, it is apparent that the mood of the garrison was initially patriotic, but soon began to accept the Bolshevik interpretation of the war. At its third meeting on March 9th, a number of speakers, including representatives of the Committee of Public Order and Safety, were loudly cheered as they called upon the soldiers to be prepared to defend their homeland with weapons in their hands,[54] but they would not fight an aggressive war. The primary concerns of the Soviet appear to have been establishing firm connections with the Committee, a restructuring of the garrison, and the removal of unpopular officers.[55] By the 15th a collegiate form of regimental and company committees had been created, which, under the jurisdiction of the Soviet's Executive Committee, had the right to confirm all military orders.[56] During this period, the Bolsheviks headed by Yakovlev, gained complete control of the Executive Bureau, and the first resolution of the Soviet on war, peace, and relations to the Provisional Government reflected their ideological influence.[57]

The Tomsk Soviet of Workers' Deputies was not created until March 29th, reflecting the fact that most of the energies of the Social Democrats and the Socialist Revolutionaries in the city were spent in the creation of the Committee of Public Order and Safety and in the Soldiers' Soviet. One reason for this lag was the relative insignificance of the working classes in the city. But in its first declarations calling for solidarity with the Tomsk Soldiers' Soviet and the socialist parties in their struggle against the bourgeoisie, the ideological consciousness of its Social Democratic and Socialist Revolutionary leaders is reflected. Unfortunately, the leaders and structure of the Workers' Soviet are not revealed in the available sources.[58]

In Novonikolaevsk, a Workers' and Soldiers' Soviet was formed on March 3rd. Of the 132 delegates to the Soviet, representing about 8,000 workers and 40,000 soldiers, not more than 30 were Social Democrats. The rest were either Socialist Revolutionaries or nonparty delegates. Nonetheless, two Social Democrats, German-Kamenskii and S. I. Kanatchikov, were elected as chairman and secretary. Among the other Social Democratic delegates were the Bolsheviks F. I. Gor'ban, G. E. Dronin, A. Klepper, V. R. Romanov, F. P. Serebrennikov, S. A. Schwartz, A. A. Cherepanov, and S. I. Yakushev. Altogether, the Executive Committee consisted of eleven delegates from the working classes, including the salaried employees, and four delegates from the military.[59]

In Omsk and Barnaul, the Soviets were created on March 3rd[60] and March 9th.[61] Both came under the influence of Social Democrats. In Barnaul the Socialist Revolutionaries were also influential, but in Omsk the Soviet of Workers' and Soldiers' Deputies was almost entirely in the hands of Social Democrats. The actual process of creating the Soviets in Omsk and Barnaul is not revealed in the available sources, nor is the role of the Social Democrats in the garrison. It is clear, however, that from the first, the Omsk Soviet took a firm, class position with respect to the Provisional Government.[62]

This was true of all of the urban soviets in Western Siberia, reflecting, no doubt, the ideological influence of its Zimmerwaldist Social Democratic leaders, and the fact that they followed the lead of the Petrograd Soviet.[63] The Provisional Government had to be supported because it was constituted to carry the country toward a Constituent Assembly and because a government was necessary to deal with the war. So long as the Provisional Government was moving toward its stated objectives, it deserved the support of the soviets. These were class institutions. Their purpose was to organize the forces of the most democratic layers of the population, the working classes, for a victory at the Constituent Assembly, and most importantly, to serve as a bulwark against counterrevolution. They were to prod, pressure, and push the bourgeois organs of government toward the realization of democracy in Russia, during which time the working classes could gain such concessions as the introduction of an eight-hour working day, improvement of working conditions, and in many cases, the use of lands by the peasantry.[64]

But the exact character of the relationship of the soviets and the committees varied widely from city to city, depending upon both conditions and upon the types of leadership. In Tomsk and Novonikolaevsk there was such a close interrelationship because the leading members of both institutions were the same men. In Tomsk left-wing tendencies prevailed in both institutions, while in Novonikolaevsk there was a definite tendency to support the Provisional Government. These differences reflected the ideological predispositions that characterized the Social Democrats as a group in either city.

The situation in Krasnoiarsk was quite different. Here the Social Democratic leadership of the Soviet was much further to the left than those Social Democrats who went into the United Bureau of the Committee of Public Safety. The Krasnoiarsk Soviet of Workers' and Soldiers' Deputies was organized on March 3rd and 4th. During the evening of March 2nd, members of the Krasnoiarsk Military-Socialist Union went to the barracks and created soldiers' committees in preparation for elections to a soviet. Headed by B. Z. Shumiatskii[65] and V. M. Klipov,[66] the Union had to spend many hours convincing the soldiers that a revolution in Petrograd had taken place. By morning, all the barracks in the city elected delegates except the Cossacks.[67] The next day, Ya. F. Dubrovinskii,[68] A. I. Okulov,[69] and A. G. Rogov[70] began to organize meetings in the railroad workshops. Shumiatskii, I. I. Belopol'skii,[71] and Frumkin[72] began to organize other workers in the city.

The next day, March 5th, the Krasnoiarsk Soviet held its first meeting and from the outset radical tendencies predominated even though a few moderate Social Democrats and Socialist Revolutionaries held influential posts in the Executive Committee for a few days.[73] According to Gurevich, the mood of the Soviet was a mixture of boisterous self-assertedness of the delegates and a desire for vengeance against all who were connected with the Tsarist regime. The delegates, in general, were hostile to the idea of a Committee of Public Safety. As newly elected delegates arrived at the Soviet during the next day, the mood grew even more ugly since many were fired up by the vitriolic speeches of such ultraleft-wing Social Democrats as Shumiatskii and Belopol'skii, who were organizing the elections in the barracks, the factories, and the railroad workshops. These speeches roundly denounced the "bourgeois committee and the compromising socialists who went into it." This hostility toward the Committee was unique to Krasnoiarsk, although later a United Bureau included delegates from the Soviet.

On March 6th, at the second meeting of the Soviet, speeches were heard pointing to the dangers of counter-revolution, about the intrigues of the bourgeoisie, and about the necessity of a peoples' court to deal ruthlessly with the servants of the Tsarist regime. Throughout the city, meetings were held that inflamed popular feeling against the Tsarist regime, and in one instance, the "crowd had to be restrained from resorting to lynch-law." Under these circumstances even the radical Social Democratic leaders of the soviet—Dubrovinskii, Okulov, and Shumiatskii—began to fear the consequences of anarchy and tried to calm the situation down.[74]

On March 7th, the Executive Committee of the Soviet,[75] headed by Dubrovinskii, convinced the Executive Committee of the Committee of Public Safety to arrest various Tsarist officials, and the situation began to stabilize. By then, the leaders of the Soviet recognized that some kind of arrangement had to be worked out between itself and the Committee of Public Safety, since they were obviously not prepared to take power in the city in the name of the Soviet. In fact, members of the Committee challenged them to do just that. Gurevich reports that the Executive Committee pointed out to the Soviet leaders that it could not function without the support of the Soviet, and if it was not prepared to take power, it had no choice but to support the United Bureau.

After a series of negotiations the Executive Committee of the Soviet decided it would send six representatives into the United Bureau. These delegates, however, would have no part in the actual functioning of the Bureau, "but would serve as critics and unmaskers of the compromisers, and would try to pressure it into the correct course of action." However, not one important member of the Soviet went into the delegation.[76]

In Eastern Siberia, the creation of the soviets was quite similar to the pattern in Western Siberia. In Irkutsk, Verkhneudinsk, and Chita, Social Democrats were elected to the highest posts in the Executive Committees of the Soviet, but the majority of the delegates were Socialist Revolutionaries or nonparty members.[77] All of these Soviets, however, regardless of the ideological tendencies among the Social Democrats, firmly supported the Committees. And in contrast to Krasnoiarsk, many of the more important leaders of the Committees also went into them.

Like in the cities of Western Siberia, the soviets in Eastern Siberia were conceived as class organs and safeguards against counterrevolution. Unlike Irkutsk, however, the Soviets in Verkhneudinsk and Chita were far more popular than the Committees of Public Organizations. In Verkhneudinsk, the Soviet, created on March 6th, was completely under the influence of V. M. Serov,[78] a former Bolshevik deputy to the Second State Duma. It was his conception of the relationship between the Committee of Public Organizations and the Soviet that was adopted on March 20th.

The Soviet of Workers' and Soldiers' Deputies, as the organization which represents the most democratic layers of the population, will be a kind of controlling apparatus over the attitudes of the Public Committee, and it follows that no single action of the committee should deviate from the announced principles of the new government and the democratic elements in the population. The Soviet not only wants to proliferate these principles, but strongly advocates compulsory adherence to them.[79]

Since all of the members of the Executive Committee of the Committee of Public Organization in Verkhneudinsk were Social Democrats (E. A. Petrov, I. A. Piatidesiatnikov, and M. I. Shister), this view, no doubt, reflected the realities of the situation. In Chita, the Soviet also dictated terms to the Committee of Public Organizations, and the same men were leaders in both.[80]

Unfortunately, scholars have only the scantiest information about the political complexion and makeup of the rank and file of Soviet members when the offices were created. One may guess that although the majority of the Soviet leaders were Social Democrats, the rank and file of the delegates, insofar as they had a party affiliation, were Socialist Revolutionaries. The exception was Krasnoiarsk, where the Social Democrats, mainly Bolsheviks, had 180 delegates out of approximately 250.[81]

The fact that so many Social Democrats achieved leading positions in the urban soviets had much to do with their influence among the political exiles and their personal prestige. N. N. Yakovlev, A. Shotman, and I. N. Smirnov were known and trusted by the Tomsk garrison for their activities in the Military-Socialist Union. In Novonikolaevsk, German-Kamenskii, Kanachikov, Dronin, and Romanov had been active in intellectual and working-class educational circles throughout the war. B.

Z. Shumiatskii had been active in Krasnoiarsk during the revolution of 1905, and was a member of the Military-Socialist Union. Rogov grew up in Krasnoiarsk and had been a leader of the railroad workers since 1901. Dubrovinskii, Okulov, and Rogov worked together in an illegal railroad union since 1913. In Irkutsk, Tsereteli and Woitinsky were widely respected, not only among the 2,000 exiles, but also among such groups as the postal-telegraph employees that Tsereteli organized. And In Verkhneudinsk, V. M. Serov and A. M. Buiko were known and respected throughout the territory. Serov, a former Social Democratic deputy to the Second State Duma, had lived in Verkhneudinsk since 1907.

It is important to realize that despite their initial weakness in terms of numbers, the Social Democrats in Siberia virtually controlled the urban soviets from the moment of their creation. That is because the executive committees of the soviets, to which they were elected, soon conducted the day to day business of the soviet. They formulated the resolutions, made proposals, and explained the character and course of the revolution to the rank and file. And most likely, as professional revolutionaries, they were the only ones who had the time and the resources to carry on sustained, initially unpaid, political activities. For this reason, the ideological tendency prevailing among the leading Social Democrats in any given soviet was generally reflected in its mood. In Omsk, Barnaul, Tomsk, Krasnoiarsk, and Verkhneudinsk, the soviets seem to have taken a fairly militant tack from the very beginning, since the majority of its leaders were Menshevik internationalists and Bolsheviks. In Novonikolaevsk, Irkutsk, and Chita, the Social Democratic leaders tended toward defensism and moderation. After October these were the last soviets to declare all power to the soviets.

THE TRADE UNIONS[82]

The trade unions in Siberia were organized almost exclusively by Social Democrats who were or became Bolsheviks during 1917. The strongest working-class unions were in the three major railroad centers—Omsk, Krasnoiarsk, and Chita—and in the mining regions of Tomsk gubernia. But in Novonikolaevsk and in Irkutsk all of the trades and crafts were organized into unions.

Prior to the February revolution, there were not more than sixteen unions in all of Siberia. By the autumn of 1917, there were over 200. Like the case of the committees of public safety and the soviets, knowledge of the actual process of creating trade unions during the first days of the February revolution is limited and distorted. Soviet scholars are simply unable or unwilling to provide much information about Social Democratic activities in general, because it might be too revealing of the influence of the Mensheviks, some of whom became Bolsheviks later. This is especially true of Omsk, where the strongest union, the railroad workers', was in the hands of Menshevik internationalists who opposed the Bolshevik seizure of power in October. On the other hand, it is clear that left-wing Social Democrats did create and control the unions during the spring, and that these were either the same men or were closely connected with those Social Democrats who went into the committees of public organizations and soviets.

In Novonikolaevsk, for example, Kanachikov, F. P. Serebrennikov, P. E. Dronin, and V. I. Romanov were among the leaders of unionization. Sometime during March, a Central Bureau of Trade Unions formed in the city, which included Dronin, I. Shamshurin, and P. Yakushev. The fact that no officers are listed by a leading Soviet account indicates that the Mensheviks may have been very influential in the Novonikolaevsk trade-union movement. And in fact, the Bolsheviks did not control this organ until the beginning of June.

In Krasnoiarsk and in Irkutsk, Bolsheviks seem to have created and controlled the trade-union movements entirely, with the exception of the Telegraph and Postal Employees' Union in Irkutsk. The Krasnoiarsk Central Bureau of Trade Unions, created in March, was headed by Belopol'skii, Shumiatskii, Dzhorov, and Frumkin. In Irkutsk, the president of the Central Bureau, also created early in March, was D. M. Trofimov. Its secretary was S. I. Lebedev, who was a member of the Committee of Public Organizations. The extent of Menshevik participation is not revealed, but it seems likely that they did play a role.

This process of trade unionization, which began somewhat slower in the mining areas continued throughout the spring and summer of 1917. As shall be seen in the next chapter, it became highly centralized in the mining districts, and virtually everywhere it was controlled by left-wing Social Democrats. In most large cities, the trade-union movement came under the jurisdiction of workers' commissions within the soviets. This guaranteed a tight bond between the union and the soviets, which provided the Bolsheviks with two bases of mass support during the winter of 1917–1918.

THE SOCIAL DEMOCRATIC PARTY[83]

Along with the various committees and soviets, political exiles formed legal party organizations during the first week in March. Following a pattern that had been established in the underground movement, Bolsheviks and Mensheviks joined together to form united committees. These party committees generally remained intact until about May. Unfortunately, scholars have very little concrete information about the actual formation of Social Democratic organizations in most of the cities. Soviet sources reveal nothing about Osmk, Chita, or Verkh neudinsk, and are just a little more complete with respect to Tomsk, Barnaul, Novonikolaevsk, and Irkutsk. Only for Krasnoiarsk is there enough materials for more than a mere sketch, but there is reason to believe that the situation of the party was not representative of Siberian cities.

In Tomsk, about twenty Social Democratic exiles and a few who lived in the city quietly formed their first legal committee on March 3rd. There is no evidence of any factional infighting concerning the character and direction of the organization. The rules for candidacy to the party committee reflected a rather broad though loose agreement on the principles of internationalism. All candidates were required to have a significant revolutionary past, to stand on the platform of Zimmerwald internationalism, and to share the view that the question of continuing the war could only be decided by the Constituent Assembly. The Committee included A. A. Naumov (chairman), A. Petrenko (secretary), V. M. Barkhatov, N. S. Vasiliev, M. M. Khismovich, A. A. Azletskii, and V. P. Denisov. Naumov, Petrenko, Vasiliev, and Azletskii were Bolsheviks, and Denisov was a Menshevik defensist. The factional affinities of the others are not revealed. This committee remained intact until the end of May.[84]

The formation of the United Social Democratic Committee in Novonikolaevsk took place on March 4th. Its members included: the Mensheviks A. K. Gastev, N. A. Gudkov, German-Kamenskii (chairman), and the Bolsheviks N. I. Teterin, S. I. Kanachikov, and P. E. Dronin. According to Teterin, the Novonikolaevsk organization, with the exception of a few members, stood on an internationalist point of view. This committee remained intact until mid-May.[85]

The exact date of the formation of the Barnaul United Social Democratic Committee is not given, but its membership, which did not change until June, included the Mensheviks V. I. Shemelev, V. I. Nikolaev, A. V. Spektorskii, E. P. Litvinenko, and N. V. Formoz and the Bolsheviks M. K. Tsaplin, I. I. Pankratov, A. V. Ustinov, and I. B. Prisiagin. At the time the Committee formed, however, the party did not have more than twenty members in the city. According to Nikolaev's account, there were ideological differences, but everyone agreed that their forces were so weak that they would be compelled to work together to organize the working classes. Consequently, they decided to ignore the question of war and peace, at least temporarily. Evidently, the Barnaul Social Democrats were either unaware of, or could not agree upon, the principles of Zimmerwald internationalism.[86]

In Krasnoiarsk, the situation was considerably more complicated. The first legal meeting of the party was held in the offices of *Samodeiatel'nost'*, late in the evening on March 2nd. Attending were Frumkin, Meshcheriakov, Shlikhter, Dubrovinskii, Okulov, Baikalov, and about ten others.[87] At this time, there were no more than fifty or sixty Social Democrats in the city who were known to each other. From Gurevich's and Frumkin's own accounts, it appears that both Frumkin and Meshcheriakov were seen as leaders of the Krasnoiarsk Social Democrats.[88] That is because both were former members of an underground committee that had become defunct by late 1916.

At the evening meeting, an organizational bureau was

formed that issued a call to all members of the party to take an active part in its new life.

> In view of the decisive wish of many members of the party to expand its activities and to have the organization play a leading role in the revolution, the former Krasnoiarsk Committee of the R.S.D.R.P. asks all members of the party, according to their abilities, to take part in this by paying personal dues and collecting money from those who sympathize with the tasks and aims of the working class.[89]

But in Krasnoiarsk, unlike Tomsk and Novonikolaevsk, there was no easy agreement among the Social Democrats as to the character and direction of the party.

It is important to note that the March 2nd meeting in the offices of *Samodeiatel'nost'* was not attended by the ultraleft Social Democrats who did not share the views of the majority. Whether men like Shumiatskii, Belopol'skii, Rogov, or Dzhorov were consciously not invited is difficult to establish, but one can well imagine that this may have been the case. It is clear that the ultraleftists in Krasnoiarsk considered themselves distinct and apart from the majority of Bolsheviks and Mensheviks in the city. During the war, they had bitterly attacked the administrators of the cooperative, Frumkin and Meshcheriakov, for not using the institution as a means of raising the political consciousness of the workers.[90] They were not, then, about to be drawn into a party organization with united defensists and compromisers.

In anticipation of a meeting to elect a party committee, called for March 5th, about twenty ultraleft Social Democrats met in the apartment of Dzhorov to discuss tactics and strategy. Unfortunately, the only account of this meeting is provided by Shumiatskii, who may have distorted his memoir to make it seem as if this group were following the principles of Leninism from the very beginning. Along with Shumiatskii and Dzhorov, the meeting was attended by Rogov, Belopol'skii, and Pekazh, and possibly, Bal'batov, Sokolov, Biriukov, and Gretsov.

According to Shumiatskii, a sharp battle developed at the meeting over whether or not this group, which called themselves *Bolshevik-Pravdists,* ought to go into a united party organization with Mensheviks. Some argued that it would be possible to join with Menshevik-internationalists, but not defensists. Others argued that there was no possibility of union at all. In the end, a compromise was worked out. The Bolshevik-Pravdists would remain within the party for one month in order to struggle for the adoption of their revolutionary line and so as not to confuse the workers.[91]

On March 5th, the first general meeting of the legal party organization, attended by almost 200 persons, elected the party committee. Unfortunately, none of the available sources list its membership, with the exception of Rogov.[92] There is good reason to believe it may have included Frumkin, Dubrovinskii, Teodorovich, and Okulov, all of whom played prominent roles in the life of the party from the beginning, and continued to do so throughout 1917. Soviet scholarship tends to attribute a decisive role in the creation of an independent Bolshevik party organization to the Krasnoiarsk-Pravdists, but this, as shall be seen, was simply not the case.[93] When the Pravdists first broke with the party at the end of May, they took with them only 106 of 2,500 members.[94]

The basis of party unity in Krasnoiarsk was the same as in Novonikolaevsk and in Tomsk: the principles of Siberian Zimmerwaldism. The majority of Bolsheviks and Mensheviks within the united organization considered themselves antiwar, internationalist Social Democrats. Their primary task was to organize the forces of the proletariat within the context of the present bourgeois-democratic revolution. The most efficient and effective way to do this was to maintain party unity, no matter what, especially since the defensist Social Democrats were a small minority. So long as the united party was internationalist in character, the defensist Social Democrats, some of whom were influential in Krasnoiarsk (for example,) could only increase the party's mass support.

This was apparently the situation throughout Western and Central Siberia. The majority of Social Democrats were Zimmerwald internationalists, Bolshevik and Menshevik, who controlled the united organizations from the moment of their creation. In all the major cities, there were probably influential Menshevik-defensists, whose inclusion within the united organization did not weaken its internationalist character, but yet brought it a measure of mass support. In the context of Siberia in March, there was simply no reason for any responsible Social Democratic leaders to follow the purist tactics of the Bolshevik-Pravdists in Krasnoiarsk. And in fact, not all the Bolshevik-Pravdists followed the line of Shumiatskii and Belopol'skii. According to Frumkin, a number of Pravdists decided to remain within the united organization after May 30th, on the grounds that the ultraleftists were not consistent with the policies of the Central Committee.[95]

In Eastern Siberia, where the evidence for the creation of Social Democratic organizations is almost nonexistent, one can imagine a similar bipartisan internationalist character of the party. Regardless of his ideological transformation in Petrograd, the leading Social Democrat in Irkutsk, I. Tsereteli, was a bona fide internationalist, as were the majority of Irkutsk Social Democrats. The 150–200 party members active in Irkutsk at the time of the February revolution can be divided into three main groups, each constituting about one third of the membership. There were the orthodox Bolsheviks, a number of whom were about as far to the left as the Krasnoiarsk Pravdists, the Bolshevik-conciliationists, and the Mensheviks. Despite profound differences on many other issues, it appears that the left and center were agreed on the principles of Zimmerwald internationalism, which constituted the common platform of the organization. According to Vel'man, the Bolshevik-conciliationists, the leader of whom was Ya. D. Yanson, played the most important role in the united organization. It was their determination to remain "united, no matter what," that held the united organization together until June, and, after a brief split, until the eve of the October revolution. A party committee of ten, including representatives of the three groups, was elected on March 6th, but the membership of the committee is not revealed in the sources.[96]

In Transbaikalia, researchers have virtually no information about the creation of the Social Democratic organizations in March. It can not be assured that they existed. According to V. Sokolov, the Social Democrats in Chita lived and worked in the underground as a "compact group." This group included Vagzhanov (Bolshevik, Second State Duma Deputy), E. A. Preobrazhenskii (Bolshevik), V. A. Anisimov (Menshevik, Second State Duma Deputy), V. N. Sokolov (Bolshevik), E. D. Sokolova (Bolshevik), S. F. Zavodskii (Menshevik), Martynich (Menshevik), and Kheladze (Menshevik), who were all exiles, and N. K. Senotrusov (Bolshevik), A. A. Voiloshnikov (Menshevik, Third State Duma Deputy), and a few young Mensheviks, who were not. These men probably went into a Social Democratic Committee in Chita.[97]

Researchers can infer from the available information on party conferences in Transbaikalia during July and September, that the majority of Social Democrats in both Verkhneudinsk and Chita were internationalists. Later, in December, they would form their own Social Democratic internationalist party that would stand for the positions taken by *Novaia Zhizn'* in Petrograd.

By March 10th, a day in which there were coordinated parades of revolution in all the major cities of Siberia, the revolutionary infrastructure was relatively complete, at least in the main cities. Within the infrastructure a large number of Social Democrats, who were or were to become Bolsheviks, were in key positions of power and authority. They retained their offices throughout 1917, and continued as officials of the new Soviet Government during the winter of 1917–1918.

It is important to note that none of the institutions created during the first week in March involved any guidance from the central revolutionary institutions in Petrograd. The Social Democrats, especially, acted completely on their own. During the party's formative period there was no contact with any of the central organs of the party. The spontaneous tendency toward unity reflected a powerful impulse within the Social Democratic movement generated by the impact of the war both in Russia and abroad.

The fact that Social Democrats throughout Russia either helped to create, participated in, or at least, supported the so-called bourgeois revolution showed that almost no one in Russia expected a socialist revolution in March. The tasks of the party—that is, furthering of the democratic aspects of the revolution, pushing for the realization of the minimum program, and preventing the bourgeoisie from joining forces with an inevitable counterrevolutionary trend, and organizing the working classes, in the light of general agreement on the principles of Zimmerwald internationalism—seemed to dictate the solidarity of all Social Democratic forces. And under Siberian conditions, it meant that Social Democrats either supported or went along with the powerful tendency toward local self-government, in cooperation with the regionalist bourgeoisie and socialist revolutionaries or suffer virtual isolation. It also meant that if the party wished to increase its mass support, it would have to adjust its rules to allow almost anyone who wanted to join.

Consequently, the Social Democratic party in Siberia was being infused with people who did not share the revolutionary heritage or the ideological commitments of the political exiles. Ideological purists and left-wing fanatics within the organizations were soon swamped.[98] It did not mean, however, that the professional revolutionary leadership of the party lost its influence. It simply meant that they would have to bend ideological considerations to the realities of the revolutionary mass politics under Siberian conditions. But before one can understand the development of the party itself, it will be useful to reflect on certain aspects of those conditions during the spring of 1917.

3

The Completion of the Edifice

Immediately following the creation of the revolutionary infrastructure early in March, the February revolution in Siberia developed into three distinct regional revolutions.[1] Until the revolution polarized, following the Kerensky offensive and the July days, the character of the regional revolutions had a more profound effect upon the behavior of the Bolsheviks than the course of events in Petrograd. In general, they subordinated ideological differences over the war and the character of the revolution to the practical tasks of reorganizing political life, preparing for the Constituent Assembly, and dealing with pressing economic and social issues.[2]

With much of the revolutionary infrastructure in the hands of the socialists, congenial power relations between the soviets and various revolutionary committees were quickly established. There is little doubt that if the Petrograd Soviet had declared itself the government of Russia in March 1917, the soviets in most Siberian cities were strong enough to follow suit. But the idea of Soviet government was alien to most socialists, with the exception of a small minority of Bolsheviks in Krasnoiarsk.

Despite the pronounced differences in the character of the revolutions in the three major regions of Siberia, there was one essential similarity. In each region—Western, Central, and Eastern Siberia—the revolutionary infrastructure began to resemble the bureaucratic, hierarchical government that it replaced. In all cases, the former gubernia or oblast' capitals set the pace for revolutionary developments. Organs of provisional government, soviets, political parties, and trade unions headquartered in these cities claimed authority throughout the gubernia or oblast'. Within the organs themselves, there was a trend toward the centralization of power in the executive committees.

One of the main reasons for this in Siberia, like in European Russia, was that the revolutionaries simply took over the Tsarist administrative machinery. They replaced upper-level Tsarist officials, but the rank-and-file employees remained at their jobs. This meant the administrative norms remained pretty much as they were.[3] Another reason was the tendency of the socialists throughout Russia to organize their parties, the soviets, and the trade unions in conferences and congresses in a hierarchical pyramid that reached its apex in Petrograd. During 1917 the two most highly organized and effective hierarchies became the Bolshevik party and the soviets.

During the spring and summer of 1917, the tendency toward hierarchy and bureaucracy in Siberia was somewhat masked by a spontaneous movement toward regional political autonomy. In Western Siberia, for example, the socialist leadership undertook a thoroughgoing restructuring of the gubernia administration in Tomsk by creating a hierarchy of popular assemblies. In Central Siberia, the soviets became the de facto authorities during the late spring.[4] In Transbaikalia, the socialist leadership conducted a thorough revolution on the land during April, without regard to the policies of the Provisional Government. Only in Irkutsk did the Executive Committee of Public Organizations become the leading governmental authority, primarily because the socialists there supported the Provisional Government.

Throughout most of Siberia, the Provisional Government had very little popular support during 1917. In the spring and summer, its natural supporters in Siberia, the middle classes, were politically inert. By midsummer and early autumn, when they did become politicized, they looked to the Kadets and the military. The lower classes, under the influence of radical socialists, were hostile to the Provisional Government from the beginning.

On the other hand, the Provisional Government had the power of the purse over much of Siberia. Overall, the national government spent more in Siberia than it collected in taxes and revenues. The financial dependence of many Siberian cities on Petrograd meant that the Provisional Government could not be ignored.

From the moment of its creation, the Provisional Government attempted to assert its political authority over Siberia. Although it was understood primarily as an interim regime to carry on the war and to convene a popularly elected Constituent Assembly, it was charged, as well, with carrying on all those governmental functions necessary to the well-being of the country. This, of course, enmeshed it deeply in such problems as the land, the nationalities question, finances, and local government.

In Siberia, where there had been no zemstvos, the issue of local self-government was particularly vexing.[5] The pressure from below stimulated a movement toward autonomy in self-government, but these institutions had to be created on the basis of laws and constitutional norms. In Petrograd, the Ministry of the Interior recognized that a reorganization of local government would be difficult and ought to be dealt with by a Constituent Assembly. It also realized, however, that the people in Siberia simply would not wait. Hence, it had no choice but to try to take over the movement.

The attempt and failure of the Provisional Government to establish its authority in Siberia in 1917 is one of the key factors in solidifying the popularity of the Social Democrats. In most of Siberia, they led the movement for local autonomy, and in Western Siberia, they played an important role in the creation of the popular assemblies. In Central Siberia, they controlled the soviets. While the Socialist Revolutionaries in both these regions generally resisted the attempt by the Provisional Government to undermine local autonomy, they generally supported its national policies. Alone, the majority of Social Democrats in Siberia consistently opposed the policies of the Provisional Government at all levels. As the war became increasingly unpopular in Siberia, Russian Social Democracy gained strength in the cities and became the focal point of opposition to the increasingly detested regime. This meant that during the spring and summer the ideological context in which revolutionary issues were discussed was primarily Social Democratic, which in Siberia had a distinctly Bolshevik cast.

THE PROVISIONAL GOVERNMENT

Beginning on March 5th, the Ministry of Interior of the new government began to issue a series of circulars on local government. The first proclamation "temporarily" removed all gubernia governors and vice-governors from the "execution of their function," which meant that it merely sanctioned what had already happened. More important, it promulgated the theory that old legislation on local government would remain in effect as long as it did not violate the spirit and principles of the revolution. In Siberia, this was construed by some to mean that the Town Dumas would take over the function of local government, but this was not acceptable in any of the larger cities.[6]

Having no real knowledge of conditions in Siberia, the Provisional Government decided to send several Siberian members of the State Duma and the State Council to sound out the situation. It is possible that members of the government feared a revival of Siberian regionalism in light of the fact that the Kadet-deputy Vostrotin had gone to Krasnoiarsk (in January) to sound out regionalist sentiment in case of revolution.[7] In any event, I. P. Laptev was sent to Omsk, E. L. Zubashev to Tomsk and Krasnoiarsk, P. I. Preobrazhenskii to Irkutsk, and Rusanov to Transbaikalia and the Far East. Before leaving for Siberia, Zubashev reports several meetings with Kerenskii, Tereshchenko, Guchkov, and L'vov. From the latter he received his commission:

Inform local society that a special commission of the government is urgently working on plans to convene a Constituent Assembly, not later than the autumn of this year, which will decide the state structure in Russia. Another commission will be working on laws for the creation of local government and for elections to local institutions. The law on local institutions will be published in the near future, and therefore, the Provisional Government advises retaining the old city administration, filling it, if necessary, with representatives of the various public and political organizations, as we have done with the Petrograd city administration.

Zubashev then pointed out to L'vov that in Siberia there was no zemstvo administration to take over the functions of government and wondered what would happen until the publication of the new laws. L'vov replied, more prophetically than he realized, "somehow they will exist."[8]

There is no doubt, however, that the Provisional Government meant to impose an interim order on the situation in the localities, which was to apply throughout the Empire. On March 14th, while Zubashev and the rest of the emissaries were on route, the government issued a new circular attempting to regulate relations between governmentally appointed or confirmed gubernia and uezd commissars and the local revolutionary committees:

> For purposes of coordination and of the systematic carrying out or forthcoming administrative tasks, the Provisional Government considers it necessary to unify the existing and newly arising committees into gubernia, uezd, and volost, and in the larger centers into municipal and village committees. The interests of all the groups of the population of the given localities should be represented in these committees. The gubernia committees should direct and unify the activity of the uezd, municipal, and other local committees. Coordinating their activities with the respective committees, the temporary gubernia commissars, who are entrusted with the duties of the governor, and uezd commissars are the persons locally delegated by and the local executive organs of the Provisional Government.[9]

With respect to Siberia, the above circular was almost worthless. It failed to take into account the popularity of the soviets and assumed that the local committees could be turned into local executive organs of the Provisional Government. The only exception was Irkutsk gubernia, but even in Eastern Siberia, the political reorganization was spontaneous and carried on without regard to circulars and guidelines from Petrograd.

EASTERN SIBERIA

Unfortunately, there is no evidence available pertaining to the arrival of P. I. Preobrazhenskii in Irkutsk or of Rusanov in Transbaikalia. Zubashev reached Tomsk at the end of March, so one can surmise that they reached their destinations early in April. During March and April, it appears as if the Executive Committee of Public Organizations in Irkutsk rather smoothly took over all areas of the Tsarist administration and claimed for itself the same kinds of powers and jurisdiction in Eastern Siberia that had been those of the Governor-Generalship. Despite the dearth of sources, it appears as if the Mensheviks and Socialist Revolutionaries who controlled the Committee, the Soviet, and the garrison had widespread popular support.

With its high number of governmental employees in the city and its low level of industrial development, the Irkutsk Soviet of Workers' Deputies was somewhat less influential than the soviets in Western and Central Siberia. Another perhaps more important reason for this was the fact that the soldiers and workers had not been joined together, like in Verkhneudinsk and Chita.

The Irkutsk Soviet was still regarded as important by the socialists, and the Executive Committee was forced to define its own powers and authority vis-a-vis the Soviet, since the Petrograd Soviet obviously had the support of the broad stratum of soldiers and workers. The socialist leadership in Irkutsk recognized that the Soviet was an organ that reflected class interests. Such items as working conditions, salaries, and labor disputes were seen as falling under its jurisdiction. And finally, the role of the soviets in the revolution was understood in terms of a rather widely held theory in Russia that the local organs of government were answerable to them for its actions.[10]

The Executive Committee naturally tried to subordinate the Irkutsk Soviet to its own authority, since a cantankerous and hostile Soviet might render the governing of the city impossible. An agreement was worked out on March 24th, which clearly assigned a passive role to the Soviet, but that expressed its theoretical supremacy in revolutionary matters:

> Recognizing that the basic tasks of the present are carrying through the revolution to its end and strengthening popular power and freedom, the Soviet of Workers' Deputies declares (1) it will continue to work for the strengthening of the forces of the proletariat, (2) that it relies on class organizations to support the local executive committee and the Provisional Government in their revolutionary steps, (3) it will be prepared to push the local executive committee and the Provisional Government to the left in those cases where it displays vacillation and undecisiveness, (4) that for realizing these aims it must strengthen its own representation in the Executive Committee of Public Organizations and recommends that all unions send their own representatives to that organ.[11]

As a result of this declaration, the Soviet increased its representation in the Executive Committee from one to six, three of whom were Bolsheviks. Following the

Soviet's advice, the professional unions' Central Bureau sent two delegates, both of whom were Bolsheviks. Interestingly, the Railroad Workers' Union, controlled by the Mensheviks, refused to send its own representatives into the Executive Committee, although they were invited to do so. Unfortunately, there is no evidence for their reason.

Meanwhile, the Irkutsk Executive Committee began to take measures to establish its authority as an organ of the Provisional Government for the whole of Eastern Siberia. As usual, there is precious little source material concerning these activities. It is known that in neighboring Verkhneudinsk the Executive Committee of Public Organizations announced on March 25th that it would take upon itself responsibility for organizing and uniting all of the activities of the local committees in Western Transbaikalia. It was doing so in conjunction with the Executive Committee of the Transbaikalia Regional Committee of Public Organizations and Safety. Both Transbaikal Committees were working in concert with the Irkutsk Committee.[12]

Just how the Irkutsk Committee went about organizing Irkutsk gubernia is impossible to establish from the available sources, but given the impetus toward broadly unified activity throughout Eastern Siberia, one can hypothesize that it was quite similar to the process in Transbaikalia, for which information does exist.

On March 20th, the Verkhneudinsk Soviet of Workers and Soldiers, which had actually formed the Committee of Public Organizations in the city, affirmed as follows its relationship to the bourgeois organ of government:

> The Soviet of Workers and Soldiers Deputies, as the organization which represents the most democratic layers of the population will be a kind of controlling apparatus over the attitudes of the Public Committee.

It follows, therefore, that no single action of the committee should deviate from the announced principles of the new government and the democratic elements of the population. The soviet not only seeks to proliferate these principles, but strongly advises compulsory adherence to them.[13]

In Chita, where the soviet actually took over the Committee of Public Organizations during the second week in March, there was no question that the bourgeois organ of government would not be responsive to it.

Thus, in Transbaikalia, as in Irkutsk, the reorganization of local government during the spring had the full backing of the soviets. On April 9th, the press in Verkhneudinsk announced that agreement had been reached with the Transbaikalia Regional Committee on a plan for the reorganization of local government in western Transbaikalia, and for the proper relations between uezd commissars and the oblast' commissar, as well as between the two Executive Committees. The Verkhneudinsk Committee of Public Organization was to unite the activities of the various rural and town committees of Pribaikalia along the same lines as would the Transbaikalia Regional Committee in eastern Transbaikalia. The Verkhneudinsk Committee would select its Uezd Commissars, whose activities would be guided by the Transbaikalia Regional Commissar in Chita. Similarly, the activities of the Verkhneudinsk Committee would be guided by the program and instructions of the Chita Committee. At the same time, two regional congresses of villages and towns were called, which would meet in April.[14]

By this time, Rusanov arrived in Transbaikalia. One can infer that he, like Zubashev, took part in the reorganization of local government. In theory, the arrangements announced in the Verkhneudinsk press reflects the ideas expressed in the government circular of March 14th, but in practice, the socialist leadership went far beyond anything envisioned by the government in Petrograd. This is why one suspects that their public support of the Provisional Government was pragmatic and was linked to financial considerations.

On April 15th, the First Transbaikalia Regional Congress of Village Deputies met in Chita to set up the machinery of local government, to discuss the land question, and to prepare for the forthcoming elections to the Constituent Assembly. As far as the majority of the delegates were concerned, the most important order of business was the land question. The head of the Transbaikalia Regional Committee, M. M. Bogdanov, a Buriat-Mongol Socialist Revolutionary, was elected chairman of the congress. He offered his party's land program as a basis for establishing an interim order on the land, which was adopted by a vote of 269 to 70. This resolution declared that land in Transbaikalia could no longer be bought and sold as a commodity. It called for the expropriation of landed estates and monastery and private monopoly lands, and it established that land was to be administered by popularly elected organs of self-government in concert with central government organs. This resolution was adopted verbatim by a congress, headed by the Bolshevik, V. M. Serov, that met in Pribaikalia about a week later. Both congresses set up machinery whereby local land committees would decide what size holdings would be confiscated and the quality as well as the amount of lands that were to be distributed according to the needs of those who worked the land. The Transbaikalia congress set up a Territorial Soviet of Village Deputies, which functioned as the highest rural authority, under the jurisdiction of the Executive Committee.[15] All this, of course, ignored and contradicted the official policies of the Provisional Government.

There is no evidence that a similar revolutionary order on the land was introduced in Irkutsk gubernia, but that may have been because it was unnecessary. Irkutsk was not an agriculturally productive gubernia. There is no evidence that the land question generated much popular pressure.

Paralleling the creation of a governmental hierarchy in Eastern Siberia during the spring was the organization of the soviet structure. In general, the Social Democrats, most of whom were or became Bolsheviks, led the movement. In Verkhneudinsk, for example, Social Democrats were elected to all the leading positions on the Executive Committee. V. M. Serov, a former Bolshevik deputy from the Second Duma, was elected chairman. Two other Bolsheviks, A. M. Buiko, an exiled worker from Saint Petersburg, and I. G. Maslov, chairman of the Berezovsk Garrison Committee, were elected as vice-chairmen. Two Mensheviks became its secretaries.[16]

In Chita, the composition of the Soviet's Executive Committee is carefully hidden in V. Sokolov's account of the February revolution. It is entirely possible that he or E. A. Preobrazhenskii, the left-Communist economist, headed the soviet. According to Vel'man, Preobrazhenskii, a conciliator, was the most influential Bolshevik in Eastern Siberia.[17] In Irkutsk the Bolsheviks played a role in the Soviet, but its Executive Committee was controlled by Mensheviks and Socialist Revolutionaries.

On April 7th, the First Congress of Eastern Siberian Soviets of Workers, Soldiers, and Peasants Deputies met in Irkutsk. Attending were 132 delegates with voting privileges and 37 with an advisory voice. Of the voting delegates, 49 were peasants' representatives, 51 were soldiers, and 32 were workers. According to Maksakov, the majority of delegates were right-Socialist Revolutionaries, but just as in the case of local soviets, the leading posts in the Congress's executive organ went to Social Democrats.[18] According to Vel'man, the Bolsheviks had only 18 delegates, but the executive organ, the Regional Bureau, consisted of 5 Bolsheviks, 3 Mensheviks, 2 Socialist Revolutionaries, and 2 nonparty members.[19]

From the scanty evidence available, it appears as if the congress passed resolutions identical to those adopted by the Irkutsk, Verkhneudinsk, and Chita soviets. It resolved to support the war to a victorious end, to work for the interests of the working classes, to support the Provisional Government in its revolutionary undertakings, and to follow the decisions of the All-Russian Congress of Soviets.[20] The leading Chita Bolshevik, E. A. Preobrazhenskii, expressing the sentiments of the Social Democrats in Eastern Siberia, declared:

> All know the merits of our revolutionary executive committee [in Irkutsk]. To us it is extremely important to establish that our [soviet] organization will act in concert with the committee, which must receive our moral support.[21]

Thus, the highest organ of the soviet structure had to support the highest organ of the governmental structure in Eastern Siberia.

The election of eight Social Democrats to the Soviet Regional Bureau reveals the extent of their prestige in Eastern Siberia. The fact that five were Bolsheviks, in an area where the Bolsheviks were their weakest, flatly contradicts M. M. Shornikov's assertion that the Bolsheviks were not influential in the united Social Democratic parties in Siberia. The Bolsheviks, one must infer, played a vital and active role in leading the revolution in Eastern Siberia in all its initial phases. They did so, primarily, because they were willing to cooperate with the other socialists in the practical tasks of organization.

During April and May, the issues of war, economic disintegration, labor unrest, and other manifestations of popular discontent did not polarize the revolution in Eastern Siberia. Consequently, there was little or no public opposition to the Provisional Government or to the war. By the end of April, Lenin's dramatic theses, with their antiwar declarations, became known throughout Siberia.[22] And he was an important enough figure for the Social Democrats to define their attitude toward his positions and for the Socialist Revolutionaries to launch a campaign of slander against him in their press.

In Verkhneudinsk, for example, a special session of the Soviet was called during the first week in May to discuss the problem. Buiko made a speech declaring that it was necessary to continue the war for as long as the aggressor occupied the Russian soil. He did not, however, refrain from defending Lenin's credentials as a true socialist leader. In fact, most Social Democrats, Mensheviks, and Bolsheviks rallied to Lenin's defense against the Socialist Revolutionaries' insinuations that he was a German agent. The Verkhneudinsk Soviet then passed a resolution that stated that while it did not agree with Lenin's position on the war, it certainly did not consider his activities criminal or dangerous.[23]

The prowar attitude of the Social Democrats in Eastern Siberia made sense because the population was extremely patriotic and because the full economic consequences of the war had not become felt. There is some evidence to indicate that the Eastern Siberian economy benefited from the war, at least until the late autumn of 1917. One indication is the absence of labor unrest in

Irkutsk, Verkhneudinsk, or Chita until April 1917, whereas strikes of workers in Western and Central Siberia over rising costs had broken out in 1915 and 1916. Another was the brisk trade between Transbaikalia and Manchuria. The tonnage of goods shipped from Manchuria to Transbaikalia increased from 1,117,050 poods in 1913 to 6,296,232 in 1917; this on the Chinese Eastern railroad alone.[24] The total imports of grain increased (in the same period) from 186,658 to 5,065,214 poods.[25] Foreign manufactured goods were shipped to Transbaikalia via the Manchurian border town of Manchouli, which connects with Chita by rail. By 1917, Manchouli had become the second largest exporting center in Manchuria, and the largest reexporter of foreign manufactured goods bound for Russia from her Western allies.[26] This trade, incidentally, was cut off only in December 1917 by the Chinese government, apparently under pressure from the Japanese.

WESTERN SIBERIA

The organization of local government in Western Siberia during March and April became deeply involved in the movement toward regional autonomy. Although a full-fledged regionalist movement did not get under way until midsummer, the influence of regionalism was very strong among the Socialist Revolutionaries, with whom the Social Democrats cooperated throughout 1917.[27] In contrast to Eastern Siberia, where the various revolutionary committees took over the gubernia and oblast' administrations with very little friction, the socialists in Tomsk gubernia met with resistance from the bureaucracy.

With the solid support of the Bolshevik-controlled

Tomsk Soldiers' Soviet, the Executive Committee of the Tomsk Committee of Public Safety, by the second week in March, decided to completely revolutionize local government and administration in the gubernia. Having gained control of the garrison with the assistance of the Military-Socialist Union, during which one of its members was murdered, the Executive Committee turned its efforts to the old Tsarist administration.[28]

First the Executive Committee created an administrative section that claimed to be the highest executive in the city and gubernia. This organ replaced the governorship. It included B. M. Gan (who was later named *Gubernia Commissar*) and N. Gotovskii, who were both nonparty members; V. I. Anuchin, M. B. Shatilov, and V. S. Sizikov, who were Socialist Revolutionaries; and N. N. Yakovlev and A. V. Danilov (Shotman), both Bolsheviks.[29]

At the same time (about the second week in March), the Committee organized an executive bureau, which actually took over all administrative offices. Its militia section was headed by the Bolshevik A. F. Ivanov. For the administration of the city and gubernia, it appointed a commissariat headed by P. V. Vologodskii, M. P. Markov, and Vosboinikov. (Vologodskii later became the Chairman of the Council of Ministers of the Provisional Government of Siberia during 1918.)[30]

Immediately, both the old Town Duma and the gubernia administration began to resist all attempts by the revolutionary administration to take over its offices. The Town Duma, knowing of the Provisional Government's desire that the old city administration continue to function pending a new election law, was reluctant to give up its authority. It sent letters to Petrograd complaining of the unlawful actions of the Committee of Public Order and Safety, and requested the immediate sending of a Commissar. Meanwhile, bureaucrats in the old gubernia administration refused to allow the new Commissariat any office space in its buildings. Later they reluctantly gave in.[31]

During this time, the Committee began to make plans for the creation of popularly elected organs of government in the villages, volosts, uezds, and cities, to be organized hierarchically, with the Tomsk Gubernia Popular Assembly as the highest power. The third week in March, with the support of the soviet, the Executive Committee announced its intention to organize elections to be held 'at the beginning of April.

It was in the midst of these elections that Zubashev arrived toward the end of March. He stopped first in Tatarsk, where he was informed about the plans of the Tomsk Committee of Public Order and Safety. In that city and the next, Kainsk, the Town Dumas had simply taken over the administration without any difficulty and the call to elections had been ignored. But in Novonikolaevsk, elections to the city assembly were taking place and delegates had already been sent to the Gubernia Assembly in Tomsk.

Upon his arrival in Tomsk, about March 30th, Zubashev had several meetings with local revolutionary leaders, informing them of events in Petrograd and the Provisional Government's plan to issue a general election law for reorganizing the Tomsk Duma. They informed him of what was already taking place. Evidently, he decided to appear before a large meeting of the garrison to sound out their support of the Provisional Government and to see whether or not it supported the local revolutionaries. Here he received somewhat of a shock as he describes in his own account.

Laying out for them the course of events in Petrograd and ending with the Provisional Government's intention of carrying through the war to a victorious end, I did not even hear the beginnings of anything sympathetic to the government's position. The meeting remained silent, which, although it was not clear to me then, was a protest. I then called attention to the fact that great portions of the Russian territory was occupied by our enemies and expressed doubt that the Russian armies would lay down its weapons while one foot of Russian land was in the hands of its enemies. After this, a young Social Democratic exile made a speech, which went something like this: The Russian people do not want to take part in an ,imperialist war, but neither do we want to give up our land. The Russian army will not lay down its weapons, so long as one enemy soldier occupies our land. We will not fight with peaceful peoples, but with imperialist invaders. Peace to the huts; war to the palaces.[32]

Because of the wild and stormy applause that greeted the speech of the unidentified Social Democrat, Zubashev wrongly interpreted this mood as a willingness to fight. One suspects that the phrase "peace to the huts; war to the palaces," triggered the cheering. He soon learned of his mistake. At the end of April, a contingent of 10,000 soldiers left Tomsk for the front. According to him, over 9,000 of them deserted before they reached the Urals.[33]

During his stay, Zubashev realized that there was little that he or anyone else in Petrograd could do to influence the situation in Tomsk. At one of the first meetings of the gubernia assembly held late in April, he advised the delegates that it was necessary for them to propose a candidate from their midst for the central government to confirm as Gubernia Commissar.

With this, N. N. Yakovlev, a moving spirit of the meetings, and now president of the Tomsk Soldiers' Soviet, made a speech. First of all, Yakovlev expressed amazement and dissatisfaction that the Provisional Government would send to Siberia a representative of the bourgeoisie and not a socialist, despite the fact that Zubashev was a well-known public figure in Tomsk. Then he declared: "We do not need a Provisional Government Commissar; we can run our own affairs and we ask Mr. Zubashev to leave Tomsk. He came here with a mandate from the former bourgeois government, and not the present one which has socialists in it." The noise of the applause reflected the agreement of the meeting with the declarations of Yakovlev.[34]

There is no evidence of the composition of the Tomsk Gubernia Assembly, but if it was similar to that of the Novonikolaevsk City Assembly, it was made up almost entirely of socialists, the majority of whom were Socialist Revolutionaries.[35] Throughout Western Siberia, especially in the larger cities—Omsk, Tomsk, Barnaul, and Novonikolaevsk—there was a clear distinction during the spring between socialists and the bourgeoisie. The latter had virtually no role in organizing the revolutionary infrastructure, but they were not without power and influence. This was to become clear during the late summer and autumn, when the Kadets began to gain strength.[36]

Fear of a bourgeois reaction in Tomsk was one of the key factors holding the socialists together and may account for the fact that the Socialist Revolutionary press in Tomsk did not slander Lenin. The bourgeois press did, however, and on April 27th, while expressing complete support of the Petrograd Soviet, the Tomsk Soldiers' Soviet passed a resolution of protest against "the lies of the counterrevolutionary bourgeoisie about Comrade Lenin."[37] Another reason was the influence of regionalist sentiment among the Socialist Revolutionaries and the hostility toward it by the Kadets. One can only surmise that the Bolsheviks and Menshevik-internationalists saw no threat in regionalism, since regional and local autonomy would naturally result from a European Socialist revolution.

Because of the absence of working-class activity in Tomsk, the garrison and the restructuring of local administration were the prime areas of activity. The Bolsheviks had to establish their influence there or not at all. One can only assume that they were actively involved in the movement toward regional autonomy since N. N. Yakovlev was, in fact, the most influential leader in Tomsk and a guiding spirit of the Tomsk Gubernia Popular Assembly.

At a meeting on May 10th, the Tomsk Gubernia Popular Assembly declared that:

> Siberia, because of its geographic distinctions from European Russia, and because of differences in ethnography and other local conditions, must receive the right of broad self-government. Although it must not sever its organic connection with the Russian Republic, Siberia must have its own All-Siberian Regional Duma, which will make laws concerning the internal life of Siberia; on questions of a general state order, Siberia must support All-Russian laws.[38]

During the next few weeks, plans were made for a Siberian Regional Congress to be held on August 2nd, but for unknown reasons it was not held until October 8th.

Despite the potential power and influence of the Tomsk Soldiers' Soviet, it played a rather secondary role in the political life of the Tomsk gubernia because the socialist leadership concentrated their main efforts in the Gubernia Assembly. The same was true in Novonikolaevsk and Barnaul. In fact, one can argue that these efforts retarded the development of soviets in the gubernia.

It is difficult for Soviet historians to deal with the fact

that the Menshevik controlled Omsk Soviet of Workers and Soldiers Deputies was the leading soviet in Western Siberia, and that Omsk was the focal point of soviet and trade-union activity during 1917. In contrast to Tomsk, where the socialists controlled all the organs of local self-government, the Coalition Committee in Omsk was bourgeois. Socialists took part in its formation, but the Soviet took a more standoffish position.

On March 12th the Omsk Executive Committee (of the Soviet) passed a resolution containing the following points: 1) it recognized the Soviet as the true representative of the working class; 2) it declared the Coalition Committee to be an organ of the bourgeois Provisional Government, and, hence, could not send its own representatives to it; and 3) it would send only an observer from the Soviet to the Coalition Committee for purposes of information.[39] The tone of this and subsequent Omsk Soviet declarations, (especially one protesting against an attempt by the officers in the garrison to split the soldiers from the workers), was quite militant. It also seemed to have had a great deal of power in the city, for, on the 18th of March, it declared the necessity of introducing the eight-hour working day in all Omsk enterprises.[40] When it ran into opposition, the Soviet, on April 4th, simply introduced it by fiat.[41]

Soviet scholars have studiously avoided producing any evidence of the Omsk Soviet's activities in the day-to-day economic life of the city, or its position toward the Provisional Government and the war. For those soviets controlled by the Bolsheviks, they have published key declarations; for those soviets controlled by Mensheviks and Socialist Revolutionaries, however, they have published only documents demonstrating their support of the government's policies. With respect to Omsk, one can conclude that the Soviet took a very militant stand toward the Provisional Government.

It is a fact that the Mensheviks and Socialist Revolutionaries in both Western and Eastern Siberia were much more active in organizing soviet congresses than the Bolsheviks were in Central Siberia. The First Western Siberian Congress of Peasants Soviets opened in Omsk on the 25th of March. Available evidence reveals only that it examined the questions of local self-government, the lands, the war, the Provisional Government, and other matters.[42] Unfortunately, there is no information at all about the Peasants' Congress in Omsk. Neither is there information about the First Congress of Western Siberian Soviets of Workers' and Soldiers' that met in Omsk on May 1st.[43] Scholars only know that the Bolsheviks did not get control of the soviets until the Third Congress, which met after the October revolution.

CENTRAL SIBERIA

The reorganization of local government in Central Siberia during the spring and early summer of 1917 resulted in a full-fledged soviet revolution. Although the soviets could not take power formally, because the Provisional Government controlled the flow of funds into Central Siberia, the Krasnoiarsk Soviet was the ruling authority in Eniseisk gubernia from the outset, and it was in the hands of the Social Democrats, most of whom were Bolsheviks and left-wing Mensheviks.

Despite bitter ideological conflicts among themselves, the Krasnoiarsk Social Democrats presented a rather militant front against the Socialist Revolutionaries. Why they refused to cooperate can only be surmised, but a good possibility is their power and numbers. Secondarily, it might have been their greater hostility to the Provisional Government, which the Socialist Revolutionaries supported.

In contrast to the relative calm that followed the February revolution in many Siberian cities, Krasnoiarsk experienced a rising tide of hostility and turmoil. The hostility of the rank-and-file soviet members toward the Executive Committee of Public Order and Safety, seen as early as March 4th, continued, and by March 12th, those moderate Socialist Revolutionaries and Mensheviks within the Soviet who had supported the Executive Committee lost their influence.

The Soviet formally cooperated with the Committee of Public Order and Safety and even sent its delegates to the United Bureau, which claimed to be the highest authority in the city. But such influential soviet leaders as Shumiatskii and Dubrovinskii were clearly hostile to it. Actually, the Bureau had no power in the city and the delegates to the Soviet knew it. When the Bureau failed to make a clean sweep of the Tsarist administration, many individual Soviet delegates, without authorization, began to make arrests.

The continuing popular unrest in the city during the first two weeks in March had a number of significant repercussions. First, it strengthened the hand of the militants and pushed the general Social Democratic leadership into a more radical posture. Compromise with those who supported the Bureau soon became almost impossible. Second, it created a fear of anarchy in the minds of the leaders of the Soviet's Executive Committee, which only strengthened their desire to take power. The initial response of Dubrovinskii was to lean on the United Bureau.

At a March 12th meeting of the Soviet's Executive Committee, Dubrovinskii pointed out that upon the signatures of the Executive Committee the United Bureau was obliged to conduct arrests and searches. He wanted the unauthorized arrests by individual deputies to stop, since they could only discredit the Soviet. But the issue

was more clearly put by the Bolshevik worker, Erkomashvili. He wanted to know how it would be possible
to suppress the actions of Soviet delegates. Also, he
wondered if it were desirable. They, after all, were the
only ones who were actually doing something to put a
stop to bootlegging and other such unwelcome activities.[44]

The issue that really determined whether the Soviet or
the United Bureau would have control over the use of
force in the city was the power of arrest, an issue decided by the Soviet without regard to the Bureau. It also
demonstrated that the Executive Committee meant to
have full control over Soviet members in this matter.

> The Executive Committee resolves that in extreme
> cases individual members of the Executive Committee
> had the right to detain private citizens, but that they
> must immediately inform the presidium within
> twenty-four hours. It would then decide whether to
> sanction the arrests. If the arrest took place during a
> sitting of the full Soviet, it would make the final deci-
> sion.[45]

The Krasnoiarsk Soviet did not wish to take power for
itself, formally, but it certainly saw itself as the leading
revolutionary organ in the city. And during the next
three weeks it continued to acquire new power and to
extend its jurisdiction over important spheres. It worked
out relations with the garrison, asserting its right to af-
firm or reject the commandant nominated by the officers; it became involved in the workers' control over industry, the creation of a city militia, and directed the
United Bureau to begin work on organizing elections to
a City Duma of free, equal, and direct voting. It also declared the introduction of an eight-hour working day.[46]

Meanwhile, the Soviet became increasingly hostile to
the Provisional Government and to the war. On March
21st, the Krasnoiarsk Soviet heard a speech by Ya. M.

Sverdlov denouncing the Provisional Government as a class organ of the imperialist bourgeoisie. As such, it was constitutionally incapable of ending the war, and all cooperation with it was a de facto support of the war. The leader of the Socialist Revolutionaries, E. E. Kolosov, answered him, speaking of the necessity to continue for as long as German aggression continued. Following the speeches, the Soviet passed an antiwar resolution by a vote of 136 to 91.[47]

The next day, the Soviet passed a resolution highly critical of the Provisional Government. It recognized that the government could not bring the war to an end or satisfy the revolutionary demands of the workers and peasants. Nonetheless, by a vote of 138 to 104, the Soviet resolved to support the Provisional Government "only insofar as its activities are in accord with the demands of the working class and revolutionary peasants." This resolution is not essentially dissimilar from the attitude expressed by the Omsk Soviet on March 12th toward the local organ of provisional government.[48]

Following the passage of the resolution on March 22nd, that denounced the Provisional Government, the soviet dealt with the disruptions of normal life in the city brought on by the collapse of Tsarist administration, revolutionary excesses, and increasing economic difficulties. One of the first areas of Soviet action was the sale and pricing of commodities. Citing the high cost of living for the working classes, and uncontrolled speculation, the Executive Committee of the Soviet appointed an accounting and price commission to take stock of all supplies in the shops and warehouses on April 4th. This was immediately seen by the Socialist Revolutionaries as a usurpation of the function of the Gubernia Supply Committee, which had been created by the local organ of the Provisional Government, the United Executive Bureau. In answering the objections of Kazantsev at the meeting of the Executive Committee of the Soviet, Okulov effectively argued that the Supply Committee was not a proletarian organization, but only a piece of the old structure. It was inactive and did not enjoy popular confidence. The Soviet, as a revolutionary organization, was impartial and was interested in establishing its authority with the population. The organization of supplies is a basic revolutionary affair. During April and May, the Soviet's Supply Commission conducted its surveys and gradually began to regulate the conditions of commodity sales by putting popular pressure on the shopkeepers and publishing information about hoarding, and so forth.[49]

Another area that the Soviet soon took under its control was the problem of drunkenness and bootlegging. Judging from the number of times the issue appeared on the agenda of Executive Committee meetings during April and May, the problem must have been rampant. So serious was it, undoubtedly because of the large quantities of grain used and the disorders drinking produced under the new conditions of freedom, that a special Bootlegging Commission was established to deal with it.[50]

By April 13th, new elections to the Executive Committee resulted in a majority of left-wing Social Democrats.[51] With the restraining influence of the Socialist Revolutionaries completely erased, the Soviet was fast becoming the only de facto government in Krasnoiarsk. The Executive Committee broke completely with the United Executive Bureau. On April 28th it recalled its delegates, pointing out that "further struggles of revolutionary democracy for the satisfactions of its basic demands absolutely requires a complete split with the agents of the Provisional Government, whose strengthening authority as a revolutionary institution can only be accomplished against the interests of the revolution."[52]

This rupture simply formalized what the representative of the Provisional Government in Eniseisk gubernia already knew. The Provisional Government had no mass support. And judging from the tone of the following telegram from Krutovskii, Gubernia Commissar to Prince L'vov, of April 22nd, there is little indication that he knew much else about the realities of the situation:

The Krasnoiarsk Soviet considers itself autonomous and refuses to recognize either the Provisional Government or the Petrograd Soviet. The question of granting credits to the Soviet has become aggravated. On this ground there is a possibility of serious conflict, since the actions of the Soviet make the population extremely nervous, causing them to withdraw funds from the banks, which has a disastrous effect on the land. Street women with illegimate children, supported by agitated soldiers, are demanding increased help. Credit is necessary to help amnestied criminals.[53]

It was the same elsewhere in the gubernia. Toward the end of April the Eniseisk Soviet of Workers' and Soldiers' Deputies, headed by the Bolshevik Pravdist, V.N. Yakovlev, sent a telegram to Petrograd that was commented on by Lenin and reprinted in the April 28th issue of *Pravda*:

The Soviet of Workers' and Soldiers' Deputies has taken cognizance of Minister L'vov's telegram to the appointed commissar of Eniseisk Gubernia, Krutovskii, sent to Eniseisk for guidance.

We protest against the intention to reintroduce bureaucracy. We declare, first, that we will not stand for being ruled by appointed officials. Second, there can be no return of officials who have been driven out by the peasants. Third, we recognize only such local bodies as have been set up in Eniseisk uezd by the people themselves. Fourth, appointed officials can rule here only over our dead bodies.[54]

In Kansk uezd the situation was even more decisive. On April 29th, Krutovskii sent a telegram to the Minister of Internal Affairs informing him that the Kansk Soviet of Peasants' Deputies had just declared itself to be the only executive organ in the uezd and announced that it was confiscating all privately held land.[55]

Krutovskii tried to deal with this direct challenge to the government's authority with the only weapon he had—money—but this proved to be ineffective. A massive fire in Eniseisk at the end of April provided the occasion. The Eniseisk Citizens' Committee of Public Organization, which was literally an organ of the Soviet, sent to Krasnoiarsk for relief funds. When these were not forthcoming, the Krasnoiarsk Soviet Executive Committee was contacted. At a meeting of the Executive Committee, Dubrovinskii remarked that he, personally, went to Krutovskii for help, but that he was dragging his feet because the Eniseisk Committee of Public Organizations would not recognize the authority of the Uezd Commissar. Dubrovinskii said that Petrograd had already wired 60,000 rubles for relief and that trains and supplies were available. Evidently, the Gubernia Commissar was forced to release the funds, since the matter was not again referred to in the minutes of the Krasnoiarsk Soviet.[56]

In any event, by this time fear of financial reprisals did not stop the Soviet in Krasnoiarsk from interfering even more deeply in the economic life of the city. During April and May there were increasing numbers of labor conflicts in the factories and disorders on the railroad and on the steamboat lines. A central factor was the unilateral declaration by the Soviet at the end of March of the introduction of an eight-hour working day. According to an article in *Sibirskaia Pravda*, 1 May 1917, the owners of the leather factory, Krasnoiarskii Kozhevnik, dismissed a number of workers, including a Soviet delegate, who began to leave work after eight hours. The workers apparently did not dare to do this until the second or third week in April, for it was not until April 25th that the Bolshevik-dominated leatherworkers' union and Central Bureau of Trade Unions decided to make an issue of it. On that day a commission of three delegates of the leatherworkers' union and two from the Central Bureau issued an ultimatum: either reinstate the workers on an eight-hour basis or face an immediate strike. The factory owners, who had originally claimed they were exempt from the eight-hour rule because they were engaged in defense work, capitulated after a short negotiation.[57]

A more serious conflict developed in the Abakan woodworking and milling factories. Following a strike, the management, according to the Bolshevik-dominated woodworking union, attempted a lockout. The situation was taken up on May 29th by the Executive Committee of the Soviet, which requisitioned the factories and turned them over to the control of the workers under the jurisdiction of the Workers' Commission of the Executive Committee. What this indicated, of course, was the fact that the Krasnoiarsk Soviet was simply taking over both the political and economic life of the city, and making good on their public pronouncements that embodied the fundamental principles of Bolshevism as expressed in Lenin's April theses.

By June 5th, the Executive Committee, whose actions invariably received the approval of the full Soviet, had evolved into a full-fledged organ of government, whose authority could not be effectively challenged. It divided itself into eight commissions: military, workers, supplies, finance, propaganda, provincial, transport, and bootlegging.[58] A similar evolution occurred in the other major cities of the gubernia, where the Bolsheviks had complete control of the executive committees.

During June, the atmosphere in these cities became more highly charged. as the garrisons learned of the plans to ship them to the front. The response of the soviets to this news provides a clear picture of the powerlessness of the Provisional Government. The fact that many units were not sent off was a result of Bolshevik influence and the reality that the rank-and-file soldiers simply did not want to go. This was quite clear from the resolution of the Kansk Soviet, which protested against the sending of any units to the front.[59] How many soldiers from Central Siberia actually got there is problematical. Judging from the desertion of nine-tenths of a 10,000 man contingent sent from Tomsk in April, one may guess that very few went.

Meanwhile, the tendency toward workers' control of industry initiated by the Soviet in May picked up steam due to the vigorous efforts of the Bolsheviks who controlled the labor unions. According to Shornikov, workers' control was established over all other enterprises in the city and over the railroad following the successful requisition of the Abakan factories. The motor force behind this was the creation of factory committees, which held a conference on June 28th and elected a Central Factory Committee, headed by Rogov, Dzhorov, and Belopol'skii.[60]

From the above, it is clear that the realities of political life in the three major regions of Siberia tended to differ from those in European Russia. The only significant exception appears to have been Krasnoiarsk. In Western Siberia, especially in Tomsk gubernia, the February revolution quickly manifested a desire for regional autonomy by a good part of the population. In Transbaikalia, a revolution in the countryside was undertaken without regard to the policies of the Provisional Government. In both of these areas, the Bolsheviks, Mensheviks, and Socialist Revolutionaries tended to cooperate on local issues. In Irkutsk, the Socialist Revolutionaries and Mensheviks simply assumed control of all institutions within the revolutionary infrastructure, with the Bolsheviks playing a definitely secondary role.

In the soviets, in the various committees, trade unions, and so forth, ideology and party politics were subordinated to the common task of creating a successful bourgeois-democratic revolution, but within the Russian Social Democratic party the larger issues of war and revolution loomed quite large. Thus far, little has been said of the development of the Social Democratic party during the spring. It was first necessary to examine some of the main features of revolutionary life, before the issues that undermined the honeymoon period in Petrograd began to make themselves felt in Siberia. Having done this, it is now possible to examine the party's development until the early summer, paying particular attention to the unwillingness of the Siberian Bolsheviks to break with the Mensheviks, even after the publication of the resolutions of the Bolshevik party's April conference held in Petrograd.

4

The Siberian Bolsheviks in the United Social Democratic Party Organization

The most important point to keep in mind about the Siberian Bolsheviks during the period when both factions of Social Democrats were united in Siberia is the fundamental assumption that party unity in the center was only a matter of time. This attitude prevailed not only in the provinces during March and April, but also in the highest echelons of the organization. There was, however, no consensus within the party on the ideological basis of formal unification, although many hoped that it would be on the basis of Zimmerwald internationalism.

In point of fact, there was no ideological basis for unification of Russian Social Democrats. The sentiment for unity and the actual unity achieved, most notably in Siberia, came as a result of subordinating differences to the practical tasks of creating and consolidating the revolutionary infrastructure. This, of course, is exactly what happened during the revolution of 1905.[1] Thus, under the new revolutionary conditions, when there "was not the slightest doubt that non-Bolshevik elements were pouring into our party," a meeting of the Petrograd Committee of March 18th declared that "it could not adhere to a strict formalism concerning the acceptance of members into the party."[2]

At the same meeting, an unidentified comrade from Siberia urged the Petrograd Committee to create the same kind of unity that existed in Siberia. He pointed out that "our forces are few, we should not divide them. Unity is possible on the basis upon which we already work."[3] In other words, it was not necessary to come to grips with the ideological divisions over the war and whether or not the revolution was socialist. The important task was to win control of the soviets, to strengthen Social Democratic influence among the workers and soldiers, and to create mass organizations.

This, apparently, was the prevailing viewpoint among the leading Bolsheviks in Petrograd until Lenin's return. On March 27th, for example, the Bureau of the Central Committee, then under the control of Kamenev, Stalin, and Nogin, convened an All-Russian conference of party workers to discuss the practical tasks of the party in the revolution. From the available protocols, it seems as if the issue of party unification was not discussed. Perhaps, since both Bolsheviks and Mensheviks attended, it was assumed that it had been accomplished and that formal unification could only come at a party congress. The fact that all of the major united party organizations in

Siberia—Omsk, Tomsk, Novonikolaevsk, Krasnoiarsk, and Irkutsk—sent delegates strongly indicates this possibility.[4] The day after the conference's close, a member of the Petrograd Committee remarked at an April 3rd meeting, "no one asks whether or not we have the symbols of the faith, the work of unification is being accomplished automatically. A few of the questions of unity have already been decided by our shortage of agitators and general lack of strength."[5]

Lenin's return to Petrograd late that evening, however, and the subsequent April crisis made mockery of that remark. Following a speech at the Finland station, to an audience of workers and soldiers who didn't seem to comprehend the purpose of his uncompromising stand toward the Provisional Government, he astounded a meeting of party stalwarts in Kshesinskaia's palace with a reading of his April theses. Some of the older Bolshevik leaders like Kamenev and Nogin were clearly dumbfounded by Lenin's call for a socialist revolution, but the younger party leaders went wild with enthusiasm. Clearly, from then on, if Lenin was to have any voice in the Central Committee, "symbols of the faith," that is, correct ideological formulations, were of paramount importance.

Immediately affected by Lenin's return were the terms upon which party unification would take place. In general, Lenin shared the viewpoint of the Petrograd Committee's declaration of March 28th:

> The Petersburg Committee considers it necessary and desirable to unite with the organization of Mensheviks (interdistrictites), who recognize the decisions of Zimmerwald and Kienthal, and who see the necessity and inevitability of a revolutionary struggle of the proletariat at the present time, not only for the political, but also for the economic party of the program

minimum of the R.S.D.R.P. For this purpose, it invites into its organizational commission representatives of the interdistrictite organization, the Polish Social Democrats, the Latvian Social Democrats, and Mensheviks who adhere to the above point of view.[6]

But Lenin went much further than this in his April theses. His form of Zimmerwald internationalism dictated no support for the Provisional Government. Tsereteli's brand, to him, was not true internationalism, but out-and-out defensism. This view, of course, was not shared by Kamenev, Stalin, Muranov, and Nogin, and they controlled the Central Committee.

On April 7th, Lenin published his April theses in *Pravda*. On the same page was an editorial by Kamenev, who pointed out that these were the personal views of Lenin and not those of the party. On April 8th, Zinoviev, who at this time followed Lenin's orientation, wrote an article condemning the party's leadership for falling under the "intoxification of Zimmerwaldism." He implied that the Central Committee was so bent on party unity, that it was willing to tolerate almost anyone in the organization. He also pointed out that Tsereteli's Zimmerwaldism was clearly an unacceptable basis for party unification. Again, Kamenev wrote an article in defense of his policies and made it clear that the decisions of the Central Committee would stand until the convening of a new party conference.[7]

Lenin, however, would not wait, and in defiance of his own rules, appealed to the leadership of the district committees of the capital for support. Meanwhile, Sverdlov returned from the Urals, where he stayed after leaving Krasnoiarsk, and Stalin swung around to Lenin's point of view. More important, his April theses corresponded much more closely to the mood of the workers and soldiers who were becoming suspicious and hostile to the Provisional Government and to its socialist supporters. By the convening of the Seventh All-Russian Party Conference on April 24th, Lenin had already gained control of the Central Committee, and the majority of the Bolshevik delegates shared his view on party unification as revealed in the conference's declaration.

Considering that:
1) the party of the Socialist Revolutionaries, the Social Democratic Mensheviks, and so forth, went over, in the majority of cases to "revolutionary defensism," that is, to support of the Provisional Government, which represents the interests of capital;
2) these parties' policies are conducted on the viewpoint and interests of the petit-bourgeoisie and corrupt the proletariat with the notion that it is possible to change the imperialist policies of the Government and creating encroachments of its freedom by means of compromises, "controls," going into the ministry, etc.;
3) this policy feeds and strengthens the relations of the trusting-unconscious masses to the capitalists; while such a relationship is the main obstacle to the further development to the revolution, which calls for a smashing of the forces of the landlords and the bourgeois counterrevolution; the conference declares
1) to recognize as impossible unification with parties and groups who follow that policy
2) to recognize a closeness and unity with those groups and tendencies who stand on the ground of internationalism—for a basic split with the petit-bourgeois policies of our socialists.[8]

Curiously lacking is any public declaration in *Pravda*, up to this point, on the manner and means by which unification could come about. There is no reference to the question of party organization, and the principles of democratic centralism in any issue of *Pravda* at this time, and this is crucial to an understanding of the development of the Bolshevik party in Siberia. Nor was it raised by Lenin in his article, "The question of uniting the internationalists," which appeared in the May 18th issue of *Pravda*. The Interdistrictites, he pointed out, were moving swiftly toward unity. Consequently, the Central Committee, which will be asked to set up an Organizing Commission to summon a party congress, will allow the Interdistrictite Committee to appoint two delegates. "If the Mensheviks, adherents of Martov, break with the 'defensists,' it would be desirable and essential to include their delegates on the above mentioned Committee." In other words, the major obstacle to the unification of the internationalists was not the old issue of party organization, but ideological attitudes toward the war and the course of revolution.[9]

Virtually all Soviet scholars of the revolution in Siberia claim that the failure of the Bolsheviks to split with the Mensheviks greatly retarded the party's growth in the region. They continually characterize this failure as a serious mistake, but from where the Bolsheviks stood in February 1917 it was, perhaps, the wisest possible course. Compared with the Socialist Revolutionaries in Siberia, the Social Democrats were exceedingly weak. In the largest railroad centers—Omsk, Krasnoiarsk, and Chita—Menshevik-internationalists were more influential. In view of the forthcoming Constituent Assembly, the continuing war, and a number of other issues that transcended the old battles within the movement, many Bolsheviks in Siberia sincerely believed party unity was not worth sacrificing since the Menshevik-defensists were not at all influential in the organizations.

From their standpoint, Lenin's April theses did not appear to contain the blueprint for immediate Bolshevik success in Siberia, although they quickly moved to this viewpoint as the revolution in Siberia became more radical. The Siberian Bolsheviks and many left-wing Mensheviks had failed to comprehend the manner in which rapidly changing conditions in the revolutionary center made necessary, changes in the ideological formulations of Siberian Zimmerwaldism to which they subscribed. Their very success in establishing themselves in key roles in the February revolution despite the strength of the Socialist Revolutionaries affected their attitude toward the legitimacy of the new power relations in Petrograd. Had they followed the course of revolutionary extremism advocated by such men as Shumiatskii and Belopol'skii, they would surely have isolated themselves from the masses and other revolutionary leaders, and would not have been able to achieve their positions of importance so early. Tomsk was a case in point. When the revolution in Siberia began to polarize, those Bolsheviks already established in the revolutionary infrastructure created during the first weeks in March became part of that coalition of Leninists, left-wing Bolsheviks, and left-wing Mensheviks that Daniels describes as "formally welded into a single party in which the majority of the leaders and the preponderant thinking were not specifically Leninist."[10]

The formation of united Social Democratic party organizations in the cities of Siberia took place immediately, but the rate of regional unification varied from one region to another, Eastern Siberia following a far more leisurely pace than either Central or Western Siberia. The first regional conference of Transbaikal Social Democrats and the first gubernia conference of Irkutsk Social Democrats was not held until mid-July. In contrast, the Social Democrats in Western Siberia attempted to organize their first regional conference in Novonikolaevsk on March 25th.[11] It was too small to call itself a conference and, consequently, the first official regional conference, which included delegates from Omsk to Krasnoiarsk, met on April 22nd.[12]

The dfficulties in dealing with the highly biased source materials are compounded when one tries to reconstruct the party's development between March and June in Siberia, for the simple reason that few of the Bolshevik memoirists wished to reveal the extent to which they cooperated with the Mensheviks. But as the following analysis will show, even the highly culled documents and biased memoirs can not hide the fact that the Bolsheviks predominated in most of the municipal party organizations and that very few of them were predisposed to recognize the authority of the Central Committee in Petrograd until after the July days.

Having reached ideological agreement on a reasonable antiwar resolution in the Zimmerwaldist formulations, the majority of Social Democrats in Siberia of both factions emerged from the underground in March determined "to preserve party unity before all else and no matter what." The bulwark of this coalition were the Menshevik-internationalists and the Bolshevik-conciliators, who had achieved a workable consensus on both the major and minor issues of the revolution. As the two available resolutions of the Krasnoiarsk April conference will show, agreement was reached by the Mensheviks taking a strong antiwar stance and by adopting the Bolshevik position on the agrarian question. The Bolsheviks gave in on the question of party organization and structure. During the late spring and early summer, the coalition held together, primarily because the Mensheviks moved further to the left on the war, while many of the Bolsheviks refused to budge on the organizational question, even under the prodding of the Siberian Pravdists. The first split in the united ranks, in fact, came when the extreme right wing of Menshevik defensists broke over the war issue, while the extreme left wing of the ultraleft and Leninist Bolsheviks broke on the issue of party structure.

The political complexion of the united Social Democratic Committees varied from city to city. In Omsk and in Krasnoiarsk it was quite radical, almost indistinguishable from the position of most Bolsheviks in Petrograd. In Irkutsk, on the other hand, it was far to the right, owing perhaps to the influence of a large number of right-wing Mensheviks and to the fact that a solid coalition of Mensheviks and Socialist Revolutionaries controlled all revolutionary institutions, except the small trade union movement, which was almost exclusively in the hands of the Bolsheviks.

EASTERN SIBERIA

In Irkutsk, the first legal party meeting of Social Democrats was held on March 5th. Attended by about 150 delegates, the party found itself split into several factions. According to the memoir of Vel'man, there were three main groups: Mensheviks, conciliators, and Bolsheviks. Based upon a careful reading of his account, in light of the party situation in other cities, this is a highly distorted representation. The characterization of *Bolshevik* in Vel'man's use means ultraleftist and Leninist Bolshevik. The conciliators included both Mensheviks and Bolsheviks, while the only term Menshevik refers to is *Menshevik defensists*. One can infer from this treatment of Tsereteli, that Vel'man has incorrectly lumped all Mensheviks together, overlooking the fact that many Mensheviks in Irkutsk were, in fact, internationalists.

On the war issue, for example, he attributes the passage of a resolution hostile to the war to the Bolsheviks, but this is clearly not the case. It was the united center of Mensheviks and Bolsheviks in Irkutsk who took a Zimmerwaldist stand on the war. The cooperation of the Menshevik-internationalist Tsereteli and the Bolshevik Woitinsky is symbolic of that agreement. So, too, are the agreements reached by the March 5th meeting on the creation of Organizational and Agitational-Propaganda Commissions and the resolution agreeing to support the Provisional Government "insofar as" it carried out the basic demands of the people.[13]

One can infer from Vel'man's account that agreements were not easily reached within the Irkutsk organization during March due to the extreme polarization. A number of Mensheviks were extremely prowar and there was a small but potent minority of radical Bolsheviks of the Shlyapnikov stripe, who were just as violently antiwar. Consequently, in various meetings a number of individuals, each claiming the mandate of the party Committee, came out with diametrically opposed views on the war. But the simple fact that the Irkutsk Bolsheviks did not attempt to split on the issue until June indicates its relative unimportance to the life of the party.

At the next party meetings held on March 11th and 13th, it became more and more obvious that the views of such left-wing Bolsheviks as Rosmirovich and Postyshev were not at all consonant with the general tone of the meetings. By this time, a number of new people had joined the organization and many exiles began to arrive in the city from the outlying areas. During the last half of March, Vel'man points to a distinct shift to the right against the views of the ultraleftists and Leninists. But he neglects to point out that the majority of Bolsheviks, themselves, must have been pulled to the right. He ar-

gues that by the end of April, the Mensheviks completely dominated the Irkutsk organization, but later in
the account he presents evidence to contradict this.

For example, the First Irkutsk Gubernia Conference
of the R.S.D.R.P. held in July was attended by twenty-
four delegates sent by the Irkutsk united party organization, fourteen of whom were listed as Bolsheviks. One of
the main purposes of the conference was to heal the rift
between the Menshevik right and the Bolshevik left, and
in this it was successful. The majority of Bolsheviks, led
by the Latvian Ya. D. Yanson, decided to hold fast to the
principle, "party unity, no matter what," and the ultraleftists and Leninists, such as Lebedev, Postyshev, and
Rozmirovich, decided to remain, also. The vote to remain united was 32 to 1, with 2 abstentions.[14]

In Transbaikalia, there is no evidence at all that the
Bolsheviks even contemplated leaving the united Social
Democratic organization before the end of September.
In fact, there is no evidence of any Social Democratic
party activities in the available source material prior to
April. In the small city of Nerchinsk, six Social Democrats led by the Bolshevik P. Okuntsov formed a small
group. By April it had grown to about fifty former
exiles and ten workers from the local leather factory.[15]
On Verkhneudinsk and Chita, the memoirists are reluctant to give any information at all. One reason for this,
perhaps, may be read out of the election results for the
Verkhneudinsk Citizens Committee, held on June 18th.
Here is found that the S.R.s and S.D.s ran a combined
list of candidates, which captured thirty-three of forty
seats.[16]

There is some evidence to indicate that the Bolsheviks
in Transbaikalia were more numerous and more powerful than the Mensheviks. The first regional conference
of the party was not held until July, and judging from

what was accomplished, the Social Democrats had just begun to organize their own party. The discussions centered around plans for organizing the party, and a small party cell was created to coordinate regional activities. A regional party Committee of five was elected, which was headed by V. M. Serov. According to Okuntsov's account, the Bolsheviks dominated the conference and the party Committee as well.[17]

Unfortunately, there is no direct evidence during the spring and summer of 1917 of an alliance of Bolshevik-conciliators and Menshevik-defensists similar to that which can be more clearly seen in Irkutsk, but the fact that the Transbaikalia organization of Social Democrats formally voted to become an independent organization of internationalists in the autumn suggests that a working alliance of left-wing Social Democrats had been achieved earlier.[18] This meant that if the Bolsheviks in Transbaikalia were preponderant, like their fellow fractionalists in Irkutsk, they were determined to maintain party unity no matter what.

It would seem that the only issue unsettled among the socialists in Transbaikalia was the war, and this issue did not break in upon them until September when the party, first in Chita, and soon after at the second regional conference, passed antiwar resolutions, at which time the Menshevik defensists left the united organization.[19] Thus, the following process of party development can be inferred in Transbaikalia between March and September. Initially, all socialists worked together to create the basic political infrastructure of the revolution; until July, Social Democrats worked very closely with the Socialist Revolutionaries. By the second week in July, party consciousness and conditions reached the point where the Social Democrats felt the need to create a regional party organization. All issues, except the war, that is, party organization and the agrarian question, had either been resolved or were not divisive. During the summer and autumn, under the impact of deteriorating local conditions and the news from European Russia, the war loomed ever larger. On this issue, a cleavage developed between Menshevik-internationalists and Bolsheviks on the one hand, and Menshevik-defensists and Socialist Revolutionaries on the other, culminating in the creation of an independent organization of left-wing Social Democrats, the majority of whom were Bolsheviks. Clearly, the desire for party unity above all else was the key factor in explaining this development.

CENTRAL SIBERIA

In Krasnoiarsk, the Social Democrats formed a united party organization on March 2nd, even before they took part in any other revolutionary activities in the city. The first legal meeting of the Krasnoiarsk Social Democrats took place late that evening in the office of *Samodeiatel'nost'*. With none of the hard core ultraleftists and Leninists present (they had, indeed, immediately begun revolutionary work among the workers and soldiers), a small group of Bolshevik-conciliators and Mensheviks laid plans to build a united organization. According to M. K. Frumkin who attended the meeting, an Organization Bureau was elected to get in touch with the fifty or sixty Social Democrats known to each other in the city.[20]

The reaction of the ultraleftists to the revolutionary caution expressed by their comrades was predictably hostile. Later that morning, a meeting of all influential socialist exiles gathered in the office of *Samodeiatel'nost'* to discuss the organization of a Soviet and the Committee of Public Safety. At this meeting the ultras were obviously in attendance, and one of them made a fiery speech calling for a revolutionary struggle with the bourgeoisie and the establishment of the dictatorship of the proletariat. He was, however, immediately attacked by another Bolshevik who spoke of the need of keeping one's feet firmly planted on the ground. For this speaker, the immediate tasks were the creation of a local organ of government, the preservation of law and order during the transition, and the organization of all democratic forces to guard against reaction. According to Gurevich, the debates became so vitriolic and acrimonious that a Menshevik standing next to him whispered somewhat prophetically that the revolution had just begun and already they were getting in each other's way.[21]

The ultraleftists, of course, were already alienated from the majority of Krasnoiarsk Social Democrats and these actions merely confirmed their hostility. The fact that a leading Bolshevik went into the Committee of Public Safety was unforgivable. This they regarded as the same kind of revolutionary timidity displayed by the administrators of *Samodeiatel'nost* during the war. Unlike Irkutsk, however, the revolutionary militancy of the ultraleftists in Krasnoiarsk could not be ignored since they were sufficiently numerous and influential among the workers and soldiers to make a genuine difference in the revolutionary temper of the city.

In the meantime, reacting against the timid attitude displayed at the March 2nd meeting of Social Democrats, a group of ultraleftists and Leninists met in the apartment of S. I. Dzhorov on the evening of March 4th. In discussing what their attitude should be toward the majority of Social Democrats, who would not accept Leninist principles of party organization, two points of view emerged. One group, the ultraleftists, argued for an immediate split with all other Social Democrats and for the formation of an independent Bolshevik party organization. The other pointed to the need for remaining within the united organization in order "to end the illusion of centrism, which was injected into the workers by the rich propagandistic literature and organizational forces of the united centrists." What this meant plainly is that they were clearly outnumbered and that a substantial percentage of the working class was influenced by Bolshevik-conciliationists and Menshevik-internationalists. Nonetheless, this meeting became so stormy and boisterous that it broke up twice during the night before anything was resolved. Finally, early in the morning of March 5th, an exhausted group of comrades managed a compromise. They decided to remain within the united party organization for one month in order to struggle for the adoption of their revolutionary line so as not to confuse the workers. Calling themselves Bolshevik Pravdists, these men actually created a Leninist form of organization within the united party, but they were without success until the summer of 1917.[22]

Once over the hurdle of their relationship to the rest of the Krasnoiarsk Social Democrats, they worked out the rules of conduct for members of the Pravdist group. Especially interesting are points four through seven of their organizational platform. According to Shumiatskii's account, all members were required to conduct revolutionary agitation and to spread propaganda among the workers and soldiers. They had to oppose all local institutions, including the local organ of the Provisional Government, which challenged the authority of the Soviet. They were required to attend all party and interparty meetings, to come out against revolutionary defensism, to speak out against any coalitions with the bourgeoisie, and to undermine support for the Provisional Government. Finally, all participants of the meeting were required to recognize unconditionally the Central Committee and to work to unify other Siberian Pravdists under its authority.[23]

On March 5th, following their own stormy meeting, the Pravdists attended a general meeting of the united party organization. In the elections to a temporary committee, the Pravdists put up Alexei Rogov; the rest of the committee were either Bolshevik-conciliators or Menshevik-internationalists. Shumiatskii contends that Rogov was sent to the committee purely for tactical reasons, but this does not seem to have been the case.[24] On March 10th, for example, a general meeting of Social Democrats declared their intention to negotiate with other Social Democratic committees for the purpose of convening a Siberian party conference of delegates from Omsk to Chita.[25] On the next day, organizational machinery in the form of a Temporary Commission was set up to try to organize the regional conference. Its members consisted of V. Leiman, S. Zhukovskii, and I. I. Belopol'skii, one of the most militant of the ultraleftists.[26] Thus the Bolshevik Pravdists were taking part in the life of the Committee. When this conference did convene late in April, it consisted primarily of Bolshevik-conciliators and Menshevik-internationalists.

It is true, however, that the Bolshevik Pravdists did conduct sharp polemics at party meetings throughout March, which zeroed in on an ominous problem within the united party organization. Although the majority of the Krasnoiarsk Social Democrats were antiwar and under the spell of Siberian Zimmerwaldism, there were a number of Menshevik-defensists in the organization. After passing several resolutions that embodied the formulation of Siberian Zimmerwaldism, including the notion that only the Constituent Assembly could resolve the war issue, the Pravdists launched their attack.[27] They claimed that a clear-cut failure to condemn the war and outline the party's position on all the major issues of the day played into the hands of the bourgeoisie. Social Democrats, after all, were supposed to be revolutionary Marxists, who could see that the Provisional Government was nothing more than a class organ, representing the interests of the bourgeoisie and the reactionary landlords, which continued the imperialist war for their own benefit. On this occasion, however, the majority of united centrists, who leaned toward the left-Bolshevik interpretation of the war, did not feel the need to press the issue, which would surely create problems for the organization. There were a number of Menshevik-defensists, such as A. G. Baikalov, whose close association with Bolsheviks like Frumkin, Shlikhter, and Meshcheriakov can not be underestimated. Moreover, although antiwar sentiment was growing in the city, the Pravdist arguments were, as yet, too radical for the masses. On March 15th, the Krasnoiarsk Committee called a mass meeting of citizens, which obtained popular approval for its Siberian Zimmerwald resolutions, passed on the 12th. And speaking for the resolutions were two Bolsheviks, Shlikhter and Okulov.[28]

The united centrists were taken by surprise, however, when Sverdlov was able to whip up hostility toward the war and the Provisional Government, upon his return from exile in the far north. Thus the united centrists were caught in an embarrassing position. The radicalism of the Krasnoiarsk Soviet forced them to state that they did, in fact, agree with the Bolshevik Pravdists on the war issue, and also on radical measures affecting the life of the city, but that they were determined to maintain party unity above all else.

Undaunted by the rebuffs within the united party organization, the Siberian Pravdists continued their struggle, and in this they were greatly buoyed up by the arrival of Sverdlov. He was an important member of the Central Committee, whose thinking was surprisingly in tune with Lenin's, considering his remote isolation. According to Shumiatskii, who is the only source for this, Sverdlov actually helped the Bolshevik Pravdists in Krasnoiarsk to develop a plan for organizing an independent Bolshevik party organization in Siberia. As he explained it, the Bolsheviks were to work for the transfer of power to the Soviet, or organize tight revolutionary formations among the workers, to expose the petit bourgeois consciousness of social patriots and united centrists, and, most important, to win support within the united organizations in order to force a split. Whether this split was between Bolsheviks and Menshevik-internationalists on the one hand, and Menshevik defensists-on the other is difficult to determine, but the silence of Soviet historians on this matter can be seen as an indication that the former may have been the case.[29] Finally, Sverdlov advised them to publish their own newspaper and to organize a Siberian Regional Bureau of the Central Committee, which would work for the Bolshevization of the party organization in Siberia.[30] Meanwhile, as has already been seen, the antiwar sentiment, which had been building up, finally burst forth in an antiwar and antigovernment resolution passed by the Krasnoiarsk Soviet.

Nonetheless, despite wide areas of agreement with the revolutionary conceptions of the Bolshevik Pravdists, the majority of Krasnoiarsk Bolsheviks and Menshevik-internationalists refused to yield to arguments calling for the adoption of Leninist principles of party organization. And this, it is clear, is the most important difference between a large number of Social Democrats and the small minority of Pravdists. Perhaps the most important reason for this was that except for this small minority, no one was thinking in terms of a Bolshevik party dictatorship. Almost everyone, including many on the Central Committee in Petrograd, were primarily concerned with the forthcoming elections to a Constituent Assembly.[31] In the spring, most of the Social Democrats in Krasnoiarsk thought Leninist principles of organization were unnecessarily divisive and in this they were in tune with the party in Petrograd. On March 26th, the Krasnoiarsk Committee passed a resolution approving the by-laws of the organization, the first of which said that members of the party are those who recognize its program, who pay their dues, and who adhere to party discipline. This, of course, was in direct conflict with the rules of party organization adopted by the Bolshevik Central Committee in March, where the recommendation of two members in a factory cell or barracks company were required.[32]

This form of party organization was intolerable to the Bolshevik Pravdists, but following the advice of Sverdlov, they continued to work within the united party. They did not, however, participate in the elections to a permanent Committee of the Krasnoiarsk R.S.D.R.P. Elected to that Committee were the left-wing Mensheviks, Dubrovinskii, G. C. Weinbaum, and the Bolsheviks, Shlikhter, Okulov, Meshcheriakov, Frumkin, Teodorovich, Staroverov, Savvteev, and Erkomashvili. Dubrovinskii's wife was also elected, but it is not clear whether whe was a Menshevik or a Bolshevik.[33] If the Committee was reflective of the balance of Bolshevik and Menshevik forces in the organization, it is clear that the Krasnoiarsk Social Democratic organization was overwhelmingly the former.

At this point, the conflict among the Krasnoiarsk Social Democrats raises some interesting questions about the policies of the Bolshevik Central Committee toward unification prior to the April crisis. On April 10th, the Central Committee in Petrograd discussed a telegram it had received from the Pravdists, asking the Committee to repudiate the united Committee of the Krasnoiarsk organization. The reply of the Central Committee was to request both groups to come to the forthcoming party conference with more detailed information.[34] Sverdlov, who knew about the situation in Krasnoiarsk, had returned to Petrograd, and the Central Committee secretary, Elena Stasova, probably had some idea of the kinds of factions in Krasnoiarsk, since she had been in exile in Achinsk, where Leninists and ultraleftists dominated the small Social Democratic organization. There is a good chance that she was aware of Sverdlov's action in Krasnoiarsk, for sometime between the 10th and the 14th, she sent a telegram confirming that the Central Committee recognized the authority of the newly formed Siberian Regional Bureau of the Central Committee.[35] This does not mean the Central Committee decided to take the side of the Siberian Pravdists against the Bolsheviks in the united organization, however, for there is no evidence that they ever repudiated it. There is a very good chance that the Bolshevik Central Committee recognized the authority of all the united committees in Siberia, despite their obvious rejection of Leninist principles of organization. Hence, it is difficult to assess just where the Central Committee stood in relation to the conflict between the Pravdists and the majority of Krasnoiarsk Bolsheviks. Obviously, it decided to encourage the former group, but there is little reason to suspect that it wished to antagonize the latter before it fully understood the situation.

Meanwhile, the Siberian Pravdists went ahead with their own plans to unite all other Leninists and left Bolsheviks under their own authority by calling for a con-

ference of all who supported *Pravda*. Actually, they were
successful in organizing support within Eniseisk gubernia, from the cities of Achinsk and Eniseisk. The purpose of the conference, which lasted from April 10th to
the 13th, was to rival the forthcoming conference of
Siberian Social Democrats, which was to meet in Krasnoiarsk on April 22nd. Held prior to the publication of
Lenin's April theses (they did not appear in Siberian
newspapers until the 18th), this conference passed a
number of militant antiwar resolutions. It called for the
confiscation of land by the peasants and it denounced
the Provisional Government. The Siberian Bureau was
created, which included I. I. Belopol'skii, F. K. Vrublevskii, A. N. Gretsov, E. F. Dymov, A. G. Rogov, and B.
Z. Shumiatskii.[36]

It is interesting that a number of Mensheviks within
the united party organization began to protest against
the actions of the Bolshevik Pravdists who were, theoret-
ically, members of the organization. They accused the
Pravdists of creating an atmosphere of polemic, and that
they did not have the right to publish *Sibirskaia Pravda*
under the party title. This paper, incidentally, was published so as to create the impression that it spoke for the
entire party. At this point, a Bolshevik member of the
Krasnoiarsk Committee, who claimed to be "as hard as
stone," defended the viewpoint of the Mensheviks, pointing out that he did not see any difference between his
position and that of *Sibirskaia Pravda*. A number of
Pravdists lashed back in a manner that revealed the true
nature of the dispute among the Krasnoiarsk Bolsheviks.
They pointed out that the Krasnoiarsk Committee "sits
between two stools." It wants to serve, simultaneously,
both the right and the left tendencies within the party.
The Krasnoiarsk Committee "*considers itself to be Bolshevik, but it came out sharply against the basic principles of*

party structure as they were adopted and defended at the Second Party Congress" (italics added).[37] Here is one crucial aspect of the problem, and in the claim of the non-Pravdist Bolshevik that his position was the same as *Sibirskaia Pravda*, is the other.

A few days before the All-Siberian Conference of Social Democrats was to take place, the Krasnoiarsk Social Democrats held a general party meeting to discuss it. In trying to decide what the order of the day for the conference should be, it was agreed that the agrarian question would head the list. Reporting to the meeting on the question of land confiscations, Shlikhter pointed out that confiscations were the current moving force of the revolution. Social Democrats must, he said, recognize this revolutionary method of action of the peasants, especially since the bourgeoisie and the Socialist Revolutionaries oppose it. Opposing him, the left-wing Menshevik, Weinbaum, argued that such a sanction might create a vendee. "We must not connect ourselves too closely with the peasantry. Before us is the unfortunate example of the S.R.s, whose revolutionary force was spent throwing bombs. Now without them, they look like Kadets. The peasants are conservative. If they receive the land, they will become reactionary; therefore its confiscation before the Constituent Assembly is intolerable." He was supported in this by the Bolshevik-conciliator, Frumkin, but the left-wing Menshevik, Dubrovinskii, and the Bolshevik-conciliator, Okulov, both spoke in favor of Shlikhter, whose ideas in the form of a proposal won by a vote of 260 to 22.[38]

According to *Sibirskaia Pravda*, which reported on this debate in its May 1st issue, the majority of Krasnoiarsk Social Democrats agreed that the isolation of the workers' movement from the peasants' could only result in a repetition of the Paris Commune. In order to forestall this, the united organization resolved that it supported the confiscations and unlawful use of land and called for the establishment of soviets of peasants and agricultural workers to take charge of these revolutionary actions. This step would not only connect the urban and rural revolutions, but it would also undermine the peasants' confidence in the Socialist Revolutionaries. The Krasnoiarsk Social Democrats wanted to capitalize on the S.R.'s policy of asking for the peasants to wait for the convening of the Constituent Assembly.[39] On the agrarian question, then, the united Krasnoiarsk Social Democrats took the same position as the Bolshevik Pravdists.

One other area in which the Bolshevik Pravdists had been critical of the united organization was concerning its attitude toward the Provisional Government. On May 5th, after the news of the April crisis in Petrograd became known, the united organization recalled its own delegates to the local organ of government, the Krasnoiarsk Committee of Public Safety. At the same time, it called for the gathering of all democratic forces around the soviets. Then, on May 16th, a general meeting of the organization voted a formal protest against the inclusion of Social Democrats in a coalition ministry. More important, this time the party organization passed a resolution calling for all democratic forces to rally around the Soviets *with the aim of taking power* (italics added).[40]

But despite this narrowing of the gap on the most important revolutionary issues, the united organization of Krasnoiarsk Social Democrats continued to refuse to recognize the authority of the Central Committee. The main reason for this appears to be their unwillingness to adopt Leninist principles of party organization. The Bolshevik Pravdists continued to press the issue. On May 24th, in a lengthy article in *Sibirskaia Pravda*, the Siberian Bureau of the Central Committee laid out their differences with the united Social Democratic organization. The main issues, the article claimed, were relations to the Provisional Government, the transformation of the bourgeois revolution into a socialist one, and the non-recognition of the Central Committee. It called for all Pravdists to leave the united organization and to create an independent Bolshevik party on the basis of the party's decisions of 1908, 1910, and 1913.[41]

The response of the united organization to the Pravdist appeal in light of the party's stand on the agrarian question and its resolutions of May 5th and May 16th, reveals that the first two differences may have been somewhat contrived. After censuring the Siberian Pravdist group for "disruptive and wrecking tactics," a number of Krasnoiarsk Social Democrats disputed the Pravdists' claim that these issues divided them. It is interesting that the Bolshevik-conciliator Frumkin and the Menshevik-internationalist Dubrovinskii both argued that the Petrograd Bolsheviks, including Lenin, did not claim that it was possible to move immediately from the bourgeois to a socialist revolution. According to Shornikov, Frumkin leaned heavily on the arguments of Kamenev in pointing out that the productive forces in Russia could not support a socialist revolution.

In rebutting these arguments, however, the Pravdist Rogov then asked the crucial question: Why did the Krasnoiarsk Committee not recognize the authority of the Central Committee and fulfill the decisions of the April conference? According to Shornikov, he received no answer, but this seems inconceivable. A possible answer to Rogov's question might have been that the Krasnoiarsk Social Democrats were awaiting the outcome of the attempt of Bolsheviks and internationalists to unify in Petrograd. After censuring the Siberian Pravdists, the Krasnoiarsk Committee decided to get in touch with the Organizational Commission, which was set up by the Central Committee, the Interdistrictites, and the Menshevik-internationalists to try to convene a congress to reunite the party. Unfortunately, the source omits the reason. Probably the Krasnoiarsk Committee was operating under the erroneous assumption that there would be unity among the Social Democratic internationalists.[42] They could not know that while Lenin wanted to unify all the internationalist forces of the party, he wanted to do so on his terms. And whether or not the Siberian Pravdists were aware of the true state of relations between the Bolsheviks and the most Menshevik-internationalists in the capital, they walked out of the united organization in Krasnoiarsk on May 30th.[43]

WESTERN SIBERIA

After Krasnoiarsk, Omsk had the largest and most influential Social Democratic organization in Siberia.[44] It, too, seemed to be under the control of a large bloc of Menshevik-internationalists and Bolshevik-conciliators, who were united on a platform of Zimmerwald internationalism and a refusal to break ranks over organizational principles. Influential from the beginning in both the Soviet and the trade-union movement, the Social Democrats only reluctantly cooperated with the Coalition Committee that functioned as the organ of government.

The Omsk Committee of the R.S.D.R.P. had been formed late in 1916 and was able to organize itself very quickly during the first weeks in March.[45] By the 17th, the party had created three district organizations, each with its own committee. In one of the districts, the right bank, the Bolsheviks were in control, headed by Z. I.

Lobkov. The remaining two districts were primarily under the influence of Menshevik-internationalists; one of them was the all-important railroad district.[46]

Evidently, each district committee was free to organize and recruit party forces as it saw fit, and the Right Bank Collective, as it was called, set to work immediately, not only in the factories, but also among the soldiers. By the 17th, the Social Democrats had already created party cells in nineteen regiments and had elected a Social Democratic Regimental Collective. Before adjourning, the seven-man committee assigned specific areas to each member-party organization in the district, which included the areas of organizing soldiers, propaganda, trade unions, and finances.[47]

During March and April, the Omsk Social Democratic party grew by leaps and bounds. This suggests that the rules for admission to membership were rather loose. And there is no evidence to indicate that questions of admission to the party were bones of contention. On April 17th, *Sibirskaia Pravda* reported that the united party organization in Omsk had about 1,000 members, published its own daily newspaper, *Rabochii*, and generally followed the lead of the Petrograd Soviet on the issues of war and relations to the Provisional Government.[48] This, of course, is not at all odd, since the majority of Social Democrats, including Bolsheviks, took this position until the return of Lenin and the All-Russian April party conference in Petrograd.

In Omsk, there is evidence that suggests the united Committee did consider itself under the authority of the Central Committee, at least until the Petrograd April conference. On March 23rd, they sent a letter to the Central Committee in Petrograd outlining their party strength, the basis of their mass support, and their influence among the soldiers and workers.[49] It is quite probable that the Omsk Social Democrats, who were typical of Siberian Social Democrats in general, expected that the powerful trend toward unity throughout Russian Social Democracy would be reflected in the Central Committee.

The basis for this unity in Omsk seems to have been the compromise on an agrarian strategy and on principles of organization. During the first weeks of the February revolution, on the initiative of the Right Bank District Committee, the united Committee created a Party Bureau to conduct work among the peasants. This Bureau came out of a mid-April meeting of the Right Bank District, held to discuss the necessary tactics to combat the influence of Socialist Revolutionaries and the "bourgeois" parties in the countryside. While researchers do not have the protocols of the united Committee meeting that decided to create this Bureau, it can be assumed that its function was to organize lectures and discussions to explain the party's agrarian program to the peasants.[50] The fact that the united Committee, controlled by Menshevik-internationalists, followed the lead of the Bolsheviks on this question is further proof that both sides were willing to bend in the interests of party unity.

Elsewhere in Siberia, in Tomsk and Novonikolaevsk, it is very difficult to reconstruct the activities of the united party organizations during March and April. According to a newspaper account of its activities, published on April 2nd, it appears that the Tomsk organization had no fractional or organizational disputes during March. The members were far too busily engaged in the practical tasks of revolution and were not particularly involved in the larger issues of war and revolution in Petrograd. Much of their efforts went toward organizing the coal miners in the Sudzhensk and Anzhersk regions.[51]

This period of ideological tranquility between the Bolsheviks and the Mensheviks in Tomsk came to an end when I. L. Nakhanovich returned from Petrograd on April 19th. He informed the Tomsk Social Democrats of the strongly antiwar mood of the Petrograd workers and the ground swell of hostility toward the Provisional Government. He also pointed out that a majority of antiwar Social Democrats did not support it. His report generated the first sharp fight between the Bolsheviks and Mensheviks in the united organization, but there was no result.[52] Meanwhile, news of the April crisis reached the city and the Bolsheviks began to work to strengthen their influence in the Tomsk Soldiers' Soviet, which passed a resolution condemning the Provisional Government on April 29th.[53]

In Novonikolaevsk, however, there was no movement whatsoever, although it is almost certain that the Tomsk Bolsheviks informed the Novonikolaevsk Bolsheviks of the situation in the capital. But in Novonikolaevsk, the Bolsheviks were far less numerous in the united organizations than the Mensheviks and the Social Democrats had far less influence in the city than the Socialist Revolutionaries. Under these conditions it would have been foolish for the Bolsheviks to have broken ranks with the Mensheviks, especially since the majority of workers and soldiers in the city did not appear to share the hostility toward the Provisional Government of the Tomsk garrison.[54]

THE APRIL CONFERENCE OF SIBERIAN SOCIAL DEMOCRATS

Despite the scanty evidence for party history during the spring of 1917, the brief outline of its development above suggests a plausible hypothesis for understanding the reluctance of the Siberian Bolsheviks to follow the resolutions of the party at the Seventh All-Russian April conference.

As Rex Wade has shown, the majority of Social Democratic leaders in Russia adhered to the formulations of Siberian Zimmerwaldism until the return of Lenin and his three-week battle for control of the party in April. Most of the Bolshevik leadership, including Stalin, Kamenev, and Muranov were in exile in Eniseisk gubernia at the time the ideological formulations of Tsereteli and Dan were worked out. Social Democratic exiles in the Narym region of Tomsk gubernia and in Transbaikalia were closely in touch with each other and, indeed, hammered out ideological differences by mail. Serov, for example, was in close contact with Tsereteli. Sverdlov, whose thinking paralleled that of Lenin, took an ultraleft stand but his views were shared only by the small minority of Krasnoiarsk Bolsheviks. In light of this and the impression gained from *Pravda*, many of the Social Democrats remaining in Siberia had every reason to expect that the party was on the road to genuine unity.

A second and perhaps more compelling reason for the tendency toward unity was the situation of the Social Democrats relative to the Socialist Revolutionaries. Everyone knew that the Socialist Revolutionaries were solidly entrenched in the countryside. And they were also far more influential in the urban areas than most Soviet historians care to admit. If, as everyone assumed, the two major parties would fight it out in the ballot box and at the Constituent Assembly, the Socialist Revolutionaries would swamp the Social Democrats, either collectively or in individual factions. It was essential, from the Social Democratic standpoint, to undermine the S.R. influence with the peasantry, for unlike the agrarian socialists, the majority of Bolsheviks and Menshevik-internationalists, who wanted to transform the bourgeois revolution into a socialist revolution, believed this could be accomplished only if the Russian conflict sparked a proletarian revolution in the West. If S.R. influence went unchallenged in the countryside, the peasants would surely turn conservative and perhaps dampen the revolutionary fires in Russia before the conflagration in Europe had been ignited.

The Social Democrats also had to oppose the Socialist Revolutionaries on the war issue. The majority S.R. position on the war was tantamount to out-and-out patriotism. The formulations of Siberian Zimmerwaldism were designed only to keep Russia in the war to prevent a triumph of German militarism that would surely eliminate the possibility of successful proletarian revolution in Europe. The crucial questions for the Siberian Social Democrats, therefore, concerned how the Bolsheviks and Mensheviks could overcome old organizational and ideological differences and cut into S.R. influence among the peasants.

In light of this situation, as seen from the standpoint of the revolution in Siberia during the spring, the Social Democrats faced a similar problem in dealing with the Socialist Revolutionaries and in maintaining party unity. The majority of Bolsheviks and Mensheviks recognized the necessity for compromises. Historically, Bolshevism as a revolutionary formulation addressed itself to the problem of the peasantry far more seriously than did Menshevism. Most Menshevik-internationalists believed, along with Trotsky, that giving the land to the Russian peasantry before the proletarian revolution broke out in the West would be a disaster. But the Bolsheviks, following Lenin's analysis, believed that the capitalist differentiation in the countryside had given rise to a whole class of poor peasants and agricultural laborers, who would make an alliance with the Russian workers. This meant that the party must conceive of a carefully worked out agrarian policy that would split off the revolutionary peasants from the conservatives. And in 1917, one tactic was to try to unite peasants, workers, and soldiers into joint soviets. Evidently, the Menshevik-internationalists found this formulation convincing, and were able to make the compromise.

On the Bolshevik side, as suggested above, the compromise came on the issue of party structure and organization. One can surmise that the old Bolshevik views on party organization, over which the party split in 1903, had relatively little appeal under the revolutionary conditions. Many Bolsheviks, even during the underground days, never shared Lenin's views on party organization and they had less reason to do so now. Between 1905 and 1914 the party was virtually torn apart by the conciliationist movement, and there is good reason to believe that the hard-liners were increasingly in the minority. Soviet historians tend to mask this phenomenon, but the history of the party in 1917 would be incomprehensible if this were not the case. Consequently, the majority of Bolsheviks in Siberia were already prepared for a compromise with the Mensheviks on the issue. In short, each side was able and willing to give primarily what the other wanted.

It becomes quite clear that the Bolsheviks in Siberia followed Lenin's general viewpoint in every respect except on Leninist principles of party organization. The fact that Soviet scholars have published very little on the All-Siberian Conference of April 22nd is a good indication of this. Attending the conference were one representative from Irkutsk, two from Omsk, one from Novonikolaevsk, one from Barnaul, four from Krasnoiarsk, and three from the Anzhersk and Sudzhensk mines. The Transbaikalia Social Democrats did not send representatives, for they had not even yet begun to organize themselves regionally. A good indication of the strength of Bolsheviks in the united organizations is seen in the elections to the Central Siberian Regional Bureau of the R.S.D.R.P., created by the conference. All its members were Bolsheviks, with the exception of Dubrovinskii from Krasnoiarsk. Besides him there was N. N. Yakovlev from Tomsk, Chuchin from the mines, and Shlikhter and Okulov from Krasnoiarsk. Frumkin and Teodorovich, also from Krasnoiarsk, were elected as candidates.[55]

The role of this bureau in guiding party activities in Siberia is a matter scarcely dealt with by Soviet historians, although most of the party's top leadership was active in it. Shornikov, as has been noted above, has devoted the bulk of his monograph to proving that the Siberian Regional Bureau of the Central Committee, formed by the Bolshevik Pravdists in Krasnoiarsk, was the leading Bolshevik party organ in Siberia. But, fortunately, he has not ignored evidence contrary to this view, even though he chooses to discount it.

According to him, his issue was discussed publicly in 1933 and 1934 by a society of old Siberian Bolsheviks. Apparently F. Chuchin published a pamphlet or handwritten account entitled, "Revolution and Counter-Revolution in Siberia," which challenged the claims of Shumiatskii, Rogov, and other Pravdists that their bureau was responsible for the creation of independent Bolshevik organizations in Siberia.

Paraphrasing Chuchin's argument that conditions in Siberia dictated party unity, Shornikov writes:

All this inevitably led to the creation of a broad democratic coalition, since the reserves for creating an army for the socialist revolution were extremely weak. The party line, naturally, had to be the unification of all Social Democrats. F. G. Chuchin praises the existence in Siberia of united Social Democratic organizations. All those who came out for the creation of independent Bolshevik organizations, Chuchin declares to be "disorganizers," "careerists," "sectarians," who wanted "to break the united front." His main blows were directed against the Siberian Bureau of the Central Committee (he uses the term *Krasnoiarsk Pravdists*), who are characterized by him as a narrow group who nobody knew and who were unrecognized persons (left communists), whose main desire was "to receive a mandate from the Central Committee, in order to command the party masses, and not to render them assurance and moral support." Chuchin characterized the Siberian Regional Bureau as a "secretly self-constituted staff, without an army."[56]

It is interesting that Shornikov reports that Chuchin denied that the bureau formed at the April 22nd conference was a leading party organ. Neither it, nor the Pravdist Siberian Regional Bureau, were acting under the guidance of the Central Committee.

Scholars do know, however, that the Pravdist bureau was confirmed by the Central Committee on or about April 13th. It is entirely possible that it was confirmed as the Central Siberian Regional Bureau of the Central Committee, since, as Shornikov records, a number of its documents were signed in this way.[57] And since the April 22nd conference was officially called the *Western Siberian Conference of Social Democrats*, it is possible that it, too, was recognized by the Central Committee, at least unofficially. This would make sense, for between the time Sverdlov allegedly helped to create the Siberian Regional Bureau of the Central Committee in Krasnoiarsk, a relatively large number of Siberian Bolsheviks were in direct contact with the Central Committee in late March and early April, as has been seen.

Judging from the available resolutions of the April 22nd conference, the Social Democrats in Siberia shared Lenin's appraisal on all-important matters, except the desirability of splitting with the Menshevik-defensists. With respect to the Provisional Government the conference resolved:

1) that the further widening and deepening of the Russian revolution requires the elimination of the Provisional Government.

2) that its removal both in the center and in the localities can be accomplished by transferring power into the hands of the soviets of workers', soldiers', and peasants' deputies.

3) that the slogan calling for the overthrow of the Provisional Government will organize the forces of revolutionary democracy around the soviets and introduce planning and consciousness into the spontaneous movement to seize power now taking place in the localities; a seizure of power naturally guarantees the satisfaction of the basic demands of the proletariat and revolutionary peasantry for securing the results of the revolution in the Constituent Assembly.

4) that the transfer of power into the hands of the most revolutionary democracy makes it possible now to take measures, which will shift the burdens connected with the war and economic disorganization, from the backs of the people to the backs of the possessing classes by means of an immediate confiscation of treasury, appanage, cabinet, monastery, church, and landlords' lands; the establishment of a single, high progressive income tax, the taxation of defense profits, the confiscation of illegal profits of speculators—this will inevitably lead to a closing up and organizing of the forces of democracy into a single force, which guarantees the further development of the revolution until the satisfaction of the basic demands of the revolutionary peasantry.

The vote on this resolution was ten to two with two abstentions. On its next resolution it logically proceeded to develop the notion that the war could only end when the prowar Provisional Government was eliminated. It also declared that "Russian Social Democracy must support and strengthen the international unity of the proletariat, constantly working for the creation of a new, active third international." The vote on the antiwar resolution was eleven in favor with five abstentions. This means that the majority of Siberian Social Democrats at the conference agreed with Lenin on this extreme left point.

The issue of party unity also reflected the Leninist view, with the exception that these Bolsheviks genuinely believed that party unity was both possible and desirable. The resolution on the question was as follows:

Discussing the organizational question, the Western Siberian Conference of the R.S.D.R.P. affirms that Social Democracy will strive to realize under all conditions its aim to organize the proletariat into an independent class party in all nonparty organizations (soviets, professional unions, cooperatives, and citizens committees), striving to keep Social Democratic factions separate for the disciplined carrying out of defined class policies.

It declares

1) welcome decisions of the All-Russian meeting about calling for a unity congress

2) that representatives of local organizations, who take part in All-Russian Fractional meetings must come out with the demand for party unity

3) it will recognize as the foremost and urgent task the uniting of all Social Democratic forces under the banner of the party, not tolerating the possibility of including into the party clearly opportunistic elements

4) it will recognize the basic signs of party opportunism, a reconciliation with which is impossible:

a) the tendency of social patriots, who smooth over the imperialist character of the war as it is conducted in all countries

b) the tendency of those same social patriots, not to allow during the course of the war, an economic struggle of the working class and the preaching of class peace.[58]

Unfortunately, Soviet scholars have not published the resolution on the agrarian question. Now if the conference had taken an incorrect line on this, there is good reason to assume that it might have been published. But if it passed a resolution on the agrarian question similar to the one passed by the Krasnoiarsk organization on April 16th, there would have been little to differentiate the Bolshevik-conciliators from the Pravdists, except the latter's insistence on Leninist principles of party organization, which even Lenin was not insisting upon at this time.

In the first months after the February revolution, the primary operating assumption of most Bolsheviks in Siberia was that the party should be united on the basis of Zimmerwald internationalism. Until mid-April, when Lenin's April theses were published in Siberian newspapers and the April crisis and the decision of the party conference became known, most Siberian Bolsheviks continued to adhere to the formulations worked out during the war. And in May, even though it became clearer that the policies of the Central Committee were different from their own, they stubbornly refused to fall in line. This, of course, was due in large part to the fact that there was nothing in the revolutionary experience of most of them to help them understand the profound changes that were taking place in the revolution in Petrograd.

By May, however, the issues of war and revolution were becoming clearer, even in Siberia, and increasingly the radicalism building up in the capital was mirrored in the cities along the Trans-Siberian railroad. Soon the process of polarization that resulted in the creation of the Communist party began to affect the life of the revolution in Siberia. This, as shall be demonstrated in the following chapter, came in the form of a series of crises, from late April to August, that began to split the united party organizations, result in the creation of an independent Bolshevik party, and increase their influence in the Soviets, among the soldiers, and in the unions.

5

The Formation of an Independent Bolshevik Party in Siberia

During the summer, in the wake of the Kerensky offensive, the July days, and the Kornilov affair, the revolution in Siberia began to polarize. The ugly realities of war, economic disorganization, and social disintegration, which had shaped the character of the revolution in Petrograd from the outset, began to have a more serious impact in Central and Western Siberia. The soviets became more militantly antiwar and antigovernment. Increasingly, Bolsheviks were elected to soviet executive committees, the city dumas, and the popular assemblies in Tomsk gubernia. More important, the unity of Siberian Social Democracy began to break down and an independent Bolshevik party began to form.

In contrast to the spring, many Bolsheviks in Siberia

no longer subordinated ideological differences over the war and the character of the revolution to the practical tasks of reorganizing political life. Then it was no longer necessary. In principle, the majority of Social Democrats already shared Lenin's appraisal of the revolution. Their unwillingness to break with the Mensheviks was a tactic geared to the realities of political life in the three major regions of Siberia. With the increasing polarization, these realities were beginning to correspond to the revolutionary situation in Petrograd.

But still, Siberia was not Petrograd. The impact of the polarization on the masses in many areas lagged behind the impact in the capital and in Krasnoiarsk. In many cities, the Mensheviks and Socialist Revolutionaries were still influential among the workers and soldiers. In Omsk and in Transbaikalia, the Menshevik-internationalists were as radical as the Bolsheviks and had mass support among the railroad workers. In Irkutsk, there were few Bolsheviks and a very small working class. A premature split of the united Social Democratic parties in these cities might easily damage Bolshevik influence in the revolutionary infrastructure and result in a weakening of the prosoviet forces. And finally, the forces of counter-revolution were stronger and developed more quickly in Siberia than in European Russia.

Consequently, the Bolshevik leadership in Siberia, moved very cautiously in building its own organization. They recognized that throughout Siberia the Bolsheviks were engaged in three separate, but interrelated struggles. First, together with the Mensheviks and the Socialist Revolutionaries, they waged a common struggle against the then politically active Kadets, conservatives, and military officers. Second, together with the Menshevik-internationalists and left Socialist Rev-

olutionaries, they battled the right Socialist Revolutionaries and Menshevik-defensists for control of the
political infrastructure. Third, they worked within the
united organizations to force out the defensists and to
win the Menshevik internationalists over to the Central
Committee.

While their overall strategy in forming the Bolshevik
party in Siberia was shaped by developments in the
party in Petrograd, their tactics were still geared to political realities in the three major regions. Hence, it was
necessary to move with great skill and the proper sense
of timing. In regions where the sentiment toward party
unity was strongest, a premature break with the
Menshevik-defensists might well have meant a break
with the Menshevik-internationalists. In others, precipi-
tate behavior might force the Menshevik-defensists and
right Socialist Revolutionaries to the side of the Kadets.
Consequently, the Bolsheviks moved to create their own
party organizations only in areas where they had already
captured the major soviets, or where the Menshevik-
internationalists were most predisposed to recognize the
authority of the Central Committee. Elsewhere they remained within the united organizations to carry on the
struggle until October, when, apparently in preparation
for the coup d'etat, they were ordered by the Central
Committee to form their own organizations.[1]

Prior to the October revolution, the Bolsheviks were
successful in creating their own party and in winning
control of the soviets only in Central and Western
Siberia. But this was sufficient to guarantee their victory
in the October revolution. In Eniseisk gubernia, where
the soviets had been in Bolshevik hands from the beginning, the party organized during June and July. The
July conference of Social Democratic internationalists in

Eniseisk gubernia created a powerful party center in Siberia, around which a regional party organization began to develop.

During August, September, and October, the stage was set for the unification of all Social Democratic internationalists from Omsk to Chita. On August 12th, a Central Siberian Regional Conference of Social Democratic Internationalists created a Central Siberian Regional Bureau of the R.S.D.R.P.(b), which became the highest party authority for Altaisk, Tomsk, Eniseisk, and Irkutsk gubernias. Unfortunately for the Bolsheviks, however, large numbers of Menshevik-internationalists in Omsk and Chita balked at the idea of recognizing the authority of the Central Committee. In Tomsk, very few of them decided to go into the Bolshevik organization, which was created as soon as the results of the Sixth Party Congress became known in Siberia. In Omsk and Irkutsk, the Bolsheviks remained within the united organizations until the second week in October, when it became clear that the majority of Menshevik-internationalists could not be won over to the Central Committee. In Transbaikalia, the Bolsheviks remained united with the Menshevik-internationalists until February 1918. Consequently, it is clear that the Bolshevik policy of remaining within the united committees to win over the Menshevik-internationalists was not much more successful in Siberia than Lenin's attempt to win over Martov in Petrograd.

THE ROLE OF THE CENTRAL COMMITTEE

The formation of the Bolshevik party in Siberia during 1917 was but part of a nationwide phenomenon, which was the creation of the Communist party and the destruction of Russian Social Democracy. While the history of Bolshevism up till 1917 was a key factor in the party's development, the impact of the revolution was far more significant. So much so, in fact, that one can argue that the Bolshevik party that came to power in October took its basic form only at the Sixth Party Congress in August.

Until the Congress, the legal status of the Central Committee was questionable for a large number of Bolsheviks and Menshevik-internationalists in the provincial organizations. In Siberia, where the sentiment for party unification was strongest, the authority of the Central Committee over party affairs was not generally recognized until after the Party Congress. Yet the majority of united committees in Western and Central Siberia were connected with the Central Committee since April. The majority of Bolsheviks, moreover, oriented themselves ideologically and tactically by *Pravda*, the organ of the Central Committee.

This seeming contradiction, however, was more apparent than real, since *Pravda* and the Central Committee reflected the vicissitudes of the complex process of party formation at the party center. Between March and July, it changed its policies on party unity several times, although once Lenin gained ascendancy in the last two weeks of April it consistently maintained that unification with the Menshevik-defensists was not possible.[2]

Until mid-March, under the influence of Molotov, A. G. Shlyapnikov, and P. A. Zalutsky, it originally took a line in favor of a decisive break of the Bolsheviks with all forms of revolutionary defensism. In Siberia, this view was shared only by a small group of left-wing Bolsheviks in Krasnoiarsk. Even Sverdlov and Shumiatskii did not think it desirable for the Bolsheviks to break immediately with the Menshevik-defensists. Ideologically, both the left-wing Bolsheviks in Petrograd and in Krasnoiarsk were in agreement with the Leninists. As Shlyapnikov put it: "The fundamental task of the revolutionary Social Democracy, is, as before, the struggle for the transformation of the present antipopular war into a civil war of the peoples against their oppressors, the ruling classes." For this it would be necessary to unify only the revolutionary, internationalist elements of Russian Social Democracy.[3] The left-wing Bolsheviks did not have the tactical flexibility of Lenin and his followers, nor did they have the stature within the party to retain control of the Central Committee.

Before Lenin returned to take control, the Central Committee passed into the hands of Kamenev, Stalin, and Muranov, who returned from Siberian exile in mid-March. They immediately based party policy on the formulations of Siberian Zimmerwaldism, which meant approval of the Siberian Bolsheviks' policy of remaining within the united committees.[4] Ironically, at the very moment Lenin returned and waged his struggle for control of the Central Committee during the second and third weeks in April, the Siberian Bolsheviks had shifted their ideological ground, as has been seen in the previous chapter.

Once again the thinking of the Siberian Bolsheviks was in tune with the thinking of the Central Committee, but then on the basis of Lenin's appraisal of the revolution. The ideological congruence of the resolutions of the April 22nd All-Siberian conference of Social Democrats with those of the Seventh All-Russian Bolshevik party conference, however, did not mean that the Siberian Bolsheviks were then ready to fall in line with the Central Committee on the question of party unity. But with Lenin in command and Sverdlov as party secretary, it did mean that the Central Committee would begin to play a more active role in local party affairs.[5]

THE FIRST STAGES OF PARTY FORMATION IN SIBERIA

From mid-April until September when Lenin began to think in terms of armed insurrection, the policy was to unify the internationalist elements of the party under the banner of the Central Committee. It was to be done in a way that would not leave the Bolsheviks open to the charge of party wreckers. This was particularly important if they were to have any chance of drawing Martov's internationalists into the party.[6] At the same time, however, it was necessary to break the back of conciliationist and rightist tendencies among Bolsheviks. The slogan "party unity, no matter what" was completely inconsistent with the resolutions of the April party conference. Hence, maximum pressure had to be put on the Siberian Bolsheviks to engineer a split between the Menshevik-internationalists and the Menshevik-defensists.

The first concrete connections between the Siberian Bolsheviks and the then Leninist Central Committee were established during the Seventh All-Russian Bolshevik Party Conference at the end of April. Attending from Siberia were B. Z. Shumiatskii, as a delegate from the Siberian Regional Bureau of the Central Committee,[7] and I. V. Prisiagin from Barnaul.[8] Both men met with Lenin and filled him in on the situation of the party in Siberia. Evidently they convinced him that the time was right for the creation of an independent organization in Siberia.[9] Shumiatskii must have made a good impression on Lenin. He was appointed an agent of the Central Committee and the Siberian Regional Bureau of the Central Committee was confirmed as an official party organ.[10] On May 5th, he was sent off to Krasnoiarsk to begin his work.

During May, a number of other representatives were

sent off to other Siberian cities to stimulate the formation of the party. Prisiagin was sent back to Barnaul. Tarasov-Rodianov was sent to Omsk.[11] M. K. Aleksandrov carried a letter to the Tomsk Bolsheviks, recommending "an immediate split with the Mensheviks and the formation of a Bolshevik organization."[12] A representative was also sent to Novonikolaevsk.[13]

Unfortunately, what these representatives may have told the Bolsheviks in Siberia is not available in the published sources. It can be assumed from what subsequently happened that their mission was to make the local Bolsheviks aware of party developments in Petrograd and to stimulate a break with the Menshevik defensists. It is probable that their mission was also related to the negotiations between the Bolsheviks and Interdistrictites.[14] Most likely, the Bolsheviks in Siberia were told to go ahead with the creation of Social Democratic internationalist organizations if there was a good chance of winning over the Menshevik-internationalists. And there probably was little pressure to force recognition of the Central Committee since the issue would be resolved at the Sixty Party Congress. The manner and timing, however, were left in the hands of the local party leaders.

In Krasnoiarsk, the campaign to form an independent Bolshevik organization began immediately upon Shumiatskii's return to the city. To publicize the resolutions of the April conference, he published a brochure entitled, "What the Social Democratic Bolsheviks Want."[15] Then, on May 15th, a group of Pravdists organized the Red Guard, apparently in an effort to prepare the workers for the creation of an independent Bolshevik organization in the city.[16] On May 26th, the Pravdists held a meeting to plan for preparing all their supporters in the factories, workshops, and barracks.[17]

Finally, on May 29th, the Siberian Regional Bureau of

the Central Committee, "in its own name, and in the name of the Central Committee," published an open letter in *Sibirskaia Pravda* "to all who supported the newspaper." Citing the failure of the Krasnoiarsk Social Democratic organization to recognize the authority of the Central Committee and to expel "all revolutionary defensists, social chauvinists, social patriots, and social utopians," the letter called for its supporters to form a new Bolshevik party organization. The basis of the new organization was to be:

1) recognition of the Central Committee,
2) recognition of the party decisions of 1908, 1910, 1912, and 1913,
3) a decisive break *with all forms* of opportunism (Zimmerwald-Kienthal),
4) recognition of the democratic-centralist form of organization.

The letter also set the time and place for the organizational meeting.[18]

The quick and angry response of the Krasnoiarsk organization came the next day at a general meeting attended by about 350 members. Frumkin made a report that argued that the Siberian Pravdists deviated not only from the views of the majority of Krasnoiarsk Bolsheviks, but also from those of Lenin and *Pravda*. He argued that the Siberian Pravdists based their position on the possibility of a socialist revolution in Russia; Lenin and *Pravda*, he claimed, recognized its impossibility. The highly popular Dubrovinskii denied that there were serious political and tactical differences within the organization. He attributed the present struggle to a clash of personalities. At this point, a member named Kalashnikov rose to disagree. "The Pravidsts," he pointed out, "do consider the socialist revolution to be advancing. The question is serious. Mutual dissatisfactions, pettiness, disagreements in appraising the course of the revolution must be given a definitive answer."[19]

Thus, the Pravdist Rogov raised the crucial question:

Why did the Krasnoiarsk united organization refuse to recognize the authority of the Central Committee and fulfill the decisions of the April conference? Unfortunately, the available sources do not reveal the nature of the discussion that followed. The most likely explanation is that Shumiatskii had overstepped his mandate and the other Bolshevik leaders did not believe that the Central Committee meant for them to break with the Menshevik-internationalists at that time.[20] So far as is known, he did not, after all, have any specific orders from the Central Committee to force the break. Consequently, the meeting voted a resolution condemning the Siberian Pravdists for the disruptive and wrecking tactics.[21]

That evening, only 106 of the 2,300 member Krasnoiarsk united organization answered the call of *Sibirskaia Pravda*.[22] Most of these appear to have been ultraleft Bolsheviks. A number of Leninist Pravdists remained within the united organization.[23] These facts, however, did not weaken the resolve of Shumiatskii and his supporters. That evening, a city party-committee was elected that included the Pravdists V. N. Yakovlev, I. I. Belopol'skii, A. Rogov, S. Bal'batov, A Dzhorov, E. Dymov, and S. Bogachev.[24]

Thereafter, the then independent Bolshevik organization began to compete with the united organization for mass support. On June 1st, they held meetings in the barracks, calling on the soldiers to support the slogan "all power to the soviets."[25] A few days later *Sibirskaia Pravda* issued an open letter to "all Social Democrats, Pravdists, and those who sympathized with *Pravda,* explaining the need to create a Bolshevik Military Organization, on orders of the Central Committee of the R.S.D.R.P."[26] This was probably in connection with the All-Russian Bolshevik Military Congress of mid-June.

The fact that the letter was addressed both to Social Democrats and to those who sympathized with *Pravda*, indicates that the new Bolshevik organization was intent on establishing its claim to be the legitimate Social Democratic party in Krasnoiarsk.

On June 9th, the first meeting, attended by about 250 people, was held to create the military organization. This suggests that the Pravdists were achieving a certain amount of success in drawing support from the united committee.[27] Speeches were heard calling for the unity of the working class with the revolutionary army. The meeting decided to create the Military Organization immediately and charged it with conducting propaganda and the creation of cells in each company.[28] No doubt the efforts of the Bolshevik Pravdists among the soldiers was greatly facilitated by the rising tide of hostility generated by the orders, by then well known, to send garrison units off to the front for the Kerensky offensive.

Ironically, the success of the Pravdists in mobilizing mass support for their organization was a key factor in bringing the united organization around to their point of view.[29] Another was the impact of the offensive on the city. On June 23rd a mass organizational meeting of 1,500 members, called by the united committee, turned out to unanimously vote on a resolution protesting the offensive at the front.[30] Then, at a joint meeting of the Krasnoiarsk united Social Democratic organization, the Siberian Regional Bureau of the Central Committee, and the Krasnoiarsk Bolshevik Committee, the Krasnoiarsk Social Democrats voted to recognize the authority of the Central Committee on June 25th.[31] The Menshevik defensists, of course, walked out and created their own organization.

The only other independent Bolshevik party organization created during this period was in Barnaul. According to Shornikov's account, I. V. Prisiagin returned from the April party conference in Petrograd at the end of May and began to work for the creation of an independent organization. At the beginning of June, he reported to a large meeting of the united organization the results of the Bolshevik party conference and the changing mood among the workers and soldiers in Petrograd. Following his report, the Bolsheviks offered a resolution that the united party organization in Barnaul endorse the resolutions of the April conference and recognize the authority of the Central Committee. The meeting voted this proposal down and the fifteen Bolsheviks attending walked out. On June 5th, they held a meeting with part of the Menshevik-internationalists and created an independent organization of Social Democratic internationalists. Each group within the internationalist organization, however, retained its own factional identity, since the party committee was officially named the *Bolshevik-Internationalist Committee*. It was headed by I. V. Prisiagin.[32]

Prior to the Sixth Party Congress held in Petrograd at the end of July and early August, the united organizations in the five other major cities of Siberia—Omsk, Novonikolaevsk, Tomsk, Irkutsk, and Chita—remained united. Without evidence it is difficult to determine why, but a good possibility is that the Menshevik-internationalists in Omsk, Tomsk, and Chita were followers of Martov, while the Menshevik internationalist in Krasnoiarsk and Barnaul were primarily Interdistrictites. In Novonikolaevsk and Irkutsk, the Mensheviks were primarily followers of Tsereteli, hence, there were few Menshevik-internationalists with whom the Bolsheviks could form independent organizations. Certainly few of the followers of Martov in Siberia were predisposed to break with the Menshevik-defensists; and since they were influential among the railroad workers in Omsk and Chita, the Bolshevik policy was to proceed cautiously and to avoid taking actions to antagonize the Menshevik-internationalists. Nonetheless, Omsk, Tomsk, and Novonikolaevsk, where the Bolsheviks were strongest and the revolution most radical outside of Krasnoiarsk, they waged a vigorous campaign to rid the united organizations of defensists.

In Tomsk the first simulus to split with the Menshevik-defensists came in May, when Aleksandrovskii brought a letter from the Central Committee recommending an immediate split with defensism. The fact that the letter was carried and not sent indicates, perhaps, that they did not want the Mensheviks within the united organization to get wind of this policy, or of the fact that Tomsk Bolsheviks were in contact with the Central Committee. The Bolsheviks responded by creating an Organizational Commission within the united party organization, which reported on May 26th that it was necessary for the Tomsk Social Democrats to connect themselves with other organizations in Siberia and with the central institutions of the party.[33]

No action was taken on this report, but the Tomsk organization did decide to reorganize the party structure and to reelect the party Committee. The result of the reelection was a victory for the Bolsheviks and the Menshevik-internationalists. The Menshevik-defensists, however, remained within the united organization and both groups of Mensheviks were not predisposed to recognize the authority of the Bolshevik Central Committee.[34]

In mid-June, the Bolsheviks began to campaign more vigorously to push for the formation of an independent party organization in Tomsk gubernia. It is possible that the formation of independent organizations in Krasnoiarsk and Barnaul had something to do with their decision of June 16th to issue a call "to all comrades who shared the platform of the all-Russian conference of Social Democrats (Bolsheviks)," to join with their fellow Bolsheviks to form revolutionary, internationalist organizations. No doubt the decision was prompted by the upsurge of the party throughout the country in connection with the Kerensky offensive. It pointed out that it was obvious that the Provisional Government and its socialist ministers could not resolve the question of peace and save the country from ruin. Bolsheviks must break with the petit-bourgeois tendencies of those socialists "who have transformed themselves into official government parties." By implication this meant those Menshevik-defensists who remained in the united organization.

The call was also directed against the mistaken position of the Menshevik-internationalists, who refused to break with the defensists. To force them to break,

> it is necessary for the Bolsheviks to work persistently and perseveringly among the masses, explaining our slogans to them, attempting to organize them systematically to create a spontaneous movement which will strengthen revolutionary Social Democratic influence.

This meant that if the Menshevik-internationalists could not be brought around to the Bolshevik point of view, the task was to undermine their influence among the masses. For this it was necessary "to attempt to reveal clearly the internationalist form within the existing framework of the Social Democratic organization."[35]

The Bolsheviks of Novonikolaevsk, obviously under the influence of Tomsk, pursued the same policy during May and June. At a May 25th meeting, the Bolsheviks got into a heated debate with the Menshevik-defensists on the issue of a coalition ministry. The Menshevik-internationalists supported the Bolsheviks in the debates. At the next general meeting on May 28th, the fight continued. The Bolsheviks, led by the Latvian A. Klepper and the former conciliator G. Dronin, argued that the All-Russian April conference of Bolsheviks in Petrograd had taken the correct position on the coalition ministry. That is, the inclusion of socialists into the bourgeois Provisional Government injects the masses with the illusion of compromise. Klepper called for the transfer of all power to the soviets. In a test of strength, the Bolsheviks were able to cut off debate and to pass a resolution calling for no support of the coalition government, for class struggle, and warning against the illusion of a possible compromise between socialists and the bourgeoisie. The vote was 43 to 20, with 8 abstaining.[36]

In mid-June, following the lead of the Tomsk Bolsheviks, the Novonikolaevsk Bolsheviks pushed for the reorganization of the united organization and for new elections to the party Committee. These were held on June 20th. Three Bolsheviks and two Menshevik-internationalists were elected.

A similar situation developed within the united party organization in Omsk. Late in May, the Central Committee dispatched Tarasov-Rodionov to help the local Bolsheviks stimulate a split with the defensists. On June 5th, he sent a letter to the Central Committee reporting the results of his efforts:

I have only just left Omsk. The literature you have given me I have passed around. Two days after my arrival I appeared before a general organizational meeting (it is united, and includes a group of *edinsty* [Plekhanovites]). I gave the meeting the greeting of our Central Committee. The stormy applause of almost all present showed that a majority (mainly railroad workers) stood for our point of view. A split with the Plekhanovites and the defensists has become immanent and I have hastened it, despite their will power. The leader of the Plekhanovites, Gladishev, declared after my greetings that the Central Committee in whose name I spoke would not be supported or recognized by the Omsk organization. The workers answered this with hissing. Then Gladishev declared his intention of leaving the united party. I advise that the Omsk organization will be ours.

A few days later, on June 11th, a general meeting of 450 workers passed a strong antiwar resolution (apparently for the first time). It was obviously in response to the Kerensky offensive and it called for a decisive break with the bourgeoisie, in whose interest the war was begun and had continued. Following this, the Menshevik-defensists, headed by Vinogradov and Safonova, officially declared their resignation from the united organization.[37]

Just as in Tomsk and Novonikolaevsk, the Bolsheviks were still disinclined to press the issue of formal recognition of the Central Committee. They would not have been successful anyway since the majority of party members in Omsk were followers of Martov. Yet, they did believe that it would be possible to win them over to the Bolshevik point of view by reasoned arguments. In a letter sent to the Central Committee at the end of June, Ya. Anisimov, secretary of the Right Bank District Committee, which was entirely Bolshevik, reported that they were conducting an ongoing, theoretical debate with the Menshevik-internationalists concerning the appraisal of the character and course of the revolution. The Bolshevik point was that the revolution was becoming a socialist revolution. To help in this regard, he asked the Central Committee to send him theoretical materials. He also pointed out that "in spite of an almost complete lack of active Bolshevik workers, we are more and more winning positions within the united organization."[38]

Thus, by the end of June, the Bolsheviks were well on their way to bringing the united organizations in Western and Central Siberia around to the Leninist point of view on party unity. The policy appeared to have been to remain within the united organizations, to radicalize the mood among the workers and soldiers, to split off the defensists, but to delay separations until all the Menshevik-internationalists had been won over. In Irkutsk and Transbaikalia, however, the Menshevik-defensists who followed Tsereteli completely dominated the organizations and there was no movement toward the formation of an independent Bolshevik party. Consequently, the first stage of party formation in Siberia involved only the cities of Omsk, Tomsk, Barnaul, Novonikolaevsk, Krasnoiarsk, Kansk, Eniseisk, and Achinsk. And only in the cities of Eniseisk gubernia and in Barnaul was an independent Bolshevik party formed before the Sixth Party Congress, which opened at the end of July.

THE JULY DAYS AND ITS AFTERMATH

The first stages of party formation in Siberia were abruptly halted by the repression of the Bolshevik party in Petrograd and the rise of antisocialist, antisoviet, middle-class, and military opposition throughout Russia in the wake of the July days. When Kerensky became head of government on July 7th, he continued to conduct that repression of the Bolsheviks, begun by the first coalition government. *Pravda* was closed, the Central Committee was forced underground, and Lenin went into hiding. The Red Guards and a large number of military units were disarmed. Searches, arrests, and persecutions continued. In Sukhanov's words, "Every Bolshevik that could be found was seized and imprisoned. Kerensky and his military friends were definitely trying to wipe them from the face of the earth."

The military cadets who conducted the arrests not only moved against the Bolsheviks, but they also raided the headquarters of the Mensheviks. At the same time, the bourgeois and Socialist Revolutionary press attacked them. The Kadet press went even further. Sukhanov states that they "evidently considered that the Bolsheviks were done for. . . . the Kadet *Rech* and its gutter-press imitators began striking out more and more Rightwards: at Chernov, Tsereteli, the Mensheviks, and S.R.s, and at the Soviet generally." Sukhanov concludes that the essence of bourgeois policy was that "the Soviets . . . must be wiped off the face of the earth," since they "constituted the original sin of the revolution, the source of dual power. . . ."[39]

In Siberia, as in Petrograd, the defining characteristic of the revolution between July 5th and October 25th was the polarization of the revolution in terms of pro- and antisoviet coalitions. This could not fail to have had an impact on the Bolsheviks in Siberia. During July and August no united organizations split. In September only the Bolsheviks in Tomsk and Novonikolaevsk formed independent Bolshevik organizations, and they failed to bring the Menshevik-internationalists with them. In Omsk, they did not leave the united organization until October 13th, and again, they failed to win over the Menshevik-internationalists. But party politics in Siberia became progressively less important in the late summer and autumn. While it is true that the Bolsheviks failed to win the Menshevik wing of Russian Social Democracy to their point of view, increasing numbers of soldiers and workers supported the idea of soviet power. This meant that the entire coalition of left socialists in Siberia—Bolsheviks, Menshevik-internationalists, left and center Socialist Revolutionaries—moved to the left. Consequently, the Menshevik-defensists and the right Socialist Revolutionaries began to move toward the Kadets and the military.

The parting of the ways in Siberia, between those who supported the idea of a socialist revolution and those who did not, came in late June and in early July. The focal points were the garrisons in Omsk, Tomsk, and Krasnoiarsk, which were completely under Bolshevik and left Socialist Revolutionary influence.[40] In Tomsk, a huge mass meeting of soldiers had taken place on June 21st to protest the Kerensky offensive. At issue was the order for the garrison to march off to the front. It was clear that the majority, in fact almost all, simply wanted to go home to cultivate their fields, a policy that the garrison commander permitted on a rotating basis. Citing the fear that Tomsk gubernia would suffer from famine if they went to the front at that time, the meeting unanimously passed a Bolshevik and left Socialist Revolutionary resolution that categorically stated that they would not go. It was a profound psychological break, and it committed the soldiers, consciously or unconsciously, to the antiwar socialists who presided over the meeting.[41] Similar meetings were held in other Siberian cities with about the same result.[42]

When news of the July days reached Siberia during the second week in July, the Bolsheviks, Menshevik-internationalists, and left Socialist Revolutionaries in Omsk, Tomsk, Novonikolaevsk, and Krasnoiarsk organized large demonstrations of workers and soldiers in support of the workers and soldiers in Petrograd. The theme of the demonstrations was "down with the Provisional Government, and transfer power to the soviets." The demonstration took place in Krasnoiarsk on July

9th, when some 10,000 workers and soldiers peacefully protested the shooting of their comrades in Petrograd and marched under the banner proclaiming "all power to the soviets." The Novonikolaevsk march took place on July 11th, and in Tomsk it occurred on July 14th. In all cases, the right Socialist Revolutionaries and the Menshevik-defensists opposed the demonstrations and planned to move against the Bolsheviks.

In Omsk, the head of the Socialist Revolutionary party, Peter Derber, sent a telegram to the head of the Novonikolaevsk garrison asking if he could send troops against the Omsk Bolsheviks. The commander, Federov, agreed, but the garrison refused to move.[43] Similarly, the S.R. Krakovetskii, head of the Irkutsk garrison, was ordered by Kerensky to move against Bolsheviks in Krasnoiarsk, but those troops also refused to go.[44] Meanwhile, the Socialist Revolutionary and bourgeois press in all of the major cities were claiming that the Leninists were preparing to overthrow the government of revolutionary democracy. In Tomsk, *Birzhevye vedemosti*, in an account of the Tomsk demonstrations, reported that "nowhere else, with the possible exception of Kronstadt and other similar 'republics' is the power of Bolshevism as predominant as in Tomsk."[45]

In all cases, even in Krasnoiarsk, the Bolsheviks steadfastly denied charges by the right socialists and the Kadets that they were planning an armed insurrection. Although Soviet sources carefully prune out any reference to the Menshevik-internationalists or to the left Socialist Revolutionaries, with the exception of Krasnoiarsk where they split with the right Socialist Revolutionaries during the July days, it seems clear that the left socialist coalition supported the Bolsheviks. Whether the Bolsheviks were actually planning an armed insurrection is problematic.[46] In any event, the workers and the soldiers genuinely began to believe in the Bolshevik appraisal of the character and course of the revolution, and increasingly supported them in the soviets. Whether the left Socialist Revolutionaries and Menshevik-internationalists believed them made no real difference, since the masses were then running to the left and the forces of counterrevolution and reaction were beginning to strike out at all prosoviet socialists who supported the slogan "all power to the soviets." But, actually, only the Bolsheviks and left Socialist Revolutionaries were successful in winning mass support.

THE SIXTH PARTY CONGRESS

During the lull between the July days and the Kornilov affair, as Kerensky unsuccessfully attempted to establish himself as the strong man of the Russian revolution, the saviour of revolutionary democracy from the left and right extremes, the Bolshevik party in Russia slowly began to recover its momentum. In Siberia, the process toward party formation continued as the Bolsheviks prepared for the forthcoming party congress. The process was somewhat complicated by the fact that many Bolsheviks, especially in Omsk, Irkutsk, and Chita, were less predisposed than ever to break with the united party organizations, even though many of them still had Menshevik-defensist members. The reason had not so much to do with Social Democratic party politics this time, however, as with the emergence of a strong antisoviet, antisocialist coalition. To put it simply, the Bolsheviks, Menshevik-internationalists, and left Socialists in these cities needed each other. At this critical period, there was no reason for the Bolsheviks to run prematurely to create their own organizations in cities where no good could come of it. Consequently, between July and October, the Siberian Bolsheviks, apparently with the acquiescence of the Central Committee, moved to create independent Bolshevik organizations only in Eniseisk gubernia during July, Tomsk gubernia during September, and Altaisk gubernia in early October.

The process began in mid-July with the convening of an Eniseisk gubernia conference of Social Democratic internationalists "who stood on the platform of the April party conference." The conference included delegates from Krasnoiarsk, Kansk, Achinsk, Eniseisk, and several smaller towns along the railroad, including a few from Western Irkutsk gubernia. The purpose of the conference was to unite all Social Democrats who would make a decisive break with the defensists into a single organization connected to the Central Committee. It was also charged with working out a plan for the Bolshevik campaign to the Constituent Assembly elections. One of the planks in its campaign platform called for the broad regional independence of Siberia.

To coordinate the activities of local organizations, the conference created the Krasnoiarsk District Bureau of the R.S.D.R.P.(b). Shumiatskii, acting as the agent of the Central Committee, formally turned over to the new Bureau all of the functions of the Siberian Regional Bureau of the Central Committee and dissolved it. Then the conference elected the Bureau, which included Ya. F. Bograd, A. Pomerantseva, V. Yakovlev, F. Vrublevskii, and I. Teodorovich.[47]

It is important to note that the tone of the conference continued to reflect the sharp ideological and organizational differences that had split the Krasnoiarsk Bolsheviks in June. Shumiatskii accused the conciliator Bolsheviks of deviating from the policies of the Central Committee and defended the tactics of the Pravdists.

Dubrovinskii claimed the Krasnoiarsk Bolsheviks had been following the policies of the Central Committee, which had acknowledged the necessity of remaining within the united organization, "for tactical reasons."[48]

More serious were the ideological divisions among the Bolsheviks. There were essentially four points of view: the left-wing Bolshevik, represented by Shumiatskii and Vrublevskii; the Leninist, represented by A. Okulov and A. Rogov, and possibly, V. Yakovlev and Pomerantseva; the Trotskyite, represented by Bograd, Dubrovinskii, and G. Weinbaum; and the right-wing Bolshevik, represented by M. K. Frumkin. In general, the left-wing Bolsheviks and the Leninists argued for an immediate socialist revolution, while Frumkin and Weinbaum argued that Russia could not have a socialist revolution or a workers-peasant republic since the distribution of land to the peasantry would make them conservative and would result in the repetition of the revolution of 1848 in France or would lead to the fate of the Paris Commune. In other words, they were using the same arguments they used in April and May. The only difference was that the Leninist argument as put forth by Shumiatskii then carried the day. "The bourgeoisie can not possibly satisfy the basic demands of the peasantry," he said, "and this is why the party of the proletariat must advance such a program." More important, "it must advocate a government, which would guarantee these demands. This is a dictatorship of the peasants and the proletariat. Such a union guarantees and defends the progress of both classes in the revolution."[49]

Meanwhile, the Tomsk Social Democratic organization, which had not yet split with the Menshevik-defensists, but which was under the control of the Bolsheviks, began to organize all of Tomsk and Eniseisk gubernia. The Tomsk conference, which was attended by delegates of

Tomsk, Krasnoiarsk, Novonikolaevsk, Zmeinogorsk, Sudzhensk, Kemerovsk, and Anzhersk, was held on July 18th and 19th, concurrently with the Krasnoiarsk conference.[50]

The fact that the conferences were held concurrently arouses suspicions that it was created as a rival center to the Krasnoiarsk group, but, with the party in Tomsk gubernia under the influence of Yakovlev, this does not seem to have been the case. Rather, the Tomsk conference was called to inform those Bolsheviks in the united organizations that had not yet split with the Menshevik-defensists about the formation of a Central Siberian organization of Social Democratic internationalists. It was obviously designed to avoid antagonizing the Menshevik-internationalists. But it was entirely a Bolshevik affair, and probably had the approval of the Central Committee.

In its resolutions, the conference protested against the arrests and repressions of revolutionary Social Democrats and the attack on the freedom of the press. The struggle must be against the imperialistic bourgeoisie in the form of class war. "The most immediate demand must be for the calling of an extraordinary congress of soviets." Conspicuously absent is any reference to a dictatorship of the workers and peasants, and so forth. But the main theme of organizing to fight the bourgeois counterrevolution certainly fit the Bolshevik conception of what was necessary in Russia.[51]

Unfortunately, in the available documents, not a word is mentioned about the forthcoming Party Congress. It is entirely possible that the Tomsk conference was organized for that purpose, since it included delegates from both Tomsk and Eniseisk gubernia, including the Krasnoiarsk organization, which had already recognized the authority of the Central Committee. The only delegate to attend from Siberia was Boris Shumiatskii as a representative of the Central Siberian Regional Bureau of the R.S.D.R.P.(b). In his report to the congress, Shumiatskii refers to an organizational conference of Central Siberia. Soviet sources claim that he was referring to the Eniseisk gubernia conference, but this seems most unlikely because he would have attended the Party Congress as a delegate from the Krasnoiarsk District Bureau of the R.S.D.R.P.(b).[52] The most likely explanation is that the Tomsk conference organized a Central Siberian Bureau or at least planned to organize it and Shumiatskii was told to go to Petrograd as its representative. Soviet scholars, naturally, would not like to admit that Lenin and the Central Committee were tolerant of the Siberian Bolsheviks who continued to remain in the same organizations with the defensists.

Meanwhile plans went ahead for the convening of a more broadly inclusive conference of Social Democratic internationalists (Bolsheviks-internationalists), which met in Krasnoiarsk from August 6th through the 12th. Attending were delegates from Krasnoiarsk, Kansk, Znamensk, Nizhneudinsk, Barnaul, Sudzhensk, Anzhersk, Tomsk, and Kemerovsk, and also from the Krasnoiarsk District Bureau of the R.S.D.R.P.(b), which represented the smaller party organizations in Eniseisk gubernia.[53]

In its resolutions on the tasks of the party, the conference seemed to have reached a compromise on the various tendencies within the party, which reflected the resolutions of the Sixth Party Congress.[54] The nature of the revolution was linked to events in the West, yet the Leninist conception of a union of the proletariat and the poorer peasantry was of paramount importance. But in contrast to the resolutions of the Eniseisk gubernia conference, no mention was made of a dictatorship of

workers and peasants. The theme at the time was revolutionary democracy. The party would "persistently
explain that the satisfaction of the interest of the proletariat and the broad layers of revolutionary democracy
are possible only by the transfer of all state power into
the hands of the revolutionary people through the
soviets of workers, soldiers, and peasant deputies." The
soviets would become the mighty organs of popular
democracy in Russia, the only bulwark against bourgeois
reaction, the only power capable of calling the Constituent Assembly. They must, therefore, take power.
Thus, the party demanded "with all its strength that the
revolutionary proletariat be prevented from premature
uprisings, but concentrate all its energies and efforts toward a revolutionary uprising on an all-Russian scale."[55]

These resolutions contained something for everyone.
The Trotskyites, the Leninists, and right-wing and left-
wing Bolsheviks could all live with these formulations,
and there was nothing in them to prevent the
Menshevik-internationalist followers of Martov from
coming over. Unfortunately, the rules for the party organization are not given, but it is almost certain that they
adopted the rules of the Sixth Party Congress, to which
they sent a telegram of greetings on August 7th.[56]

Ironically, the Siberian Pravdists appear to have lost
influence at the meeting. On August 12th, a Central
Siberian Regional Bureau of the R.S.D.R.P.(b) was
created. Its members included Ya. F. Bograd, N. N.
Yakovlev, A. G. Rogov, Ya. F. Dubrovinskii, A. I.
Okulov, F. K. Vrublevskii, Ya. M. Pekazh, A. V. Pomerantseva. I. Teodorovich, and G. C. Weinbaum. With the
exception of Vrublevskii, whose factional orientation
is doubtful, there were no left-wing Bolsheviks in the
Bureau, and only one right-wing Bolshevik, I. Teodorovich. The rest were Interdistrictites and Leninists.

Located in Krasnoiarsk, the Central Siberian Regional Bureau of the R.S.D.R.P.(b) was the highest party organ in Siberia until mid-October, when an all-Siberian conference of Bolsheviks created an all-Siberian bureau. During September and early October, the Central Siberian Bureau began to organize all Bolsheviks in Tomsk and Altaisk gubernia under its aegis. On September 8th and 9th, a gubernia conference of Tomsk Social Democrats met to form a gubernia Bolshevik organization and a Gubernia Committee. They tried and failed to attract the Menshevik-internationalists into the Bolshevik organization.[57] The Tomsk Gubernia Bolshevik Committee included N. N. Yakovlev, V. M. Klipov, S. Konachikov, A. A. Azletskii, V. D. Vegman, F. P. Serebrennikov, I. N. Kudriavstev, and F. Sukhoverov,[58] A similar conference of Altai Social Democratic internationalists was held in Barnaul on October 2nd. It, too, formed a Gubernia Committee. Presumably, both the Tomsk-Altaisk gubernia committees and the Krasnoiarsk District Bureau made up the entire second-level party organs in Siberia. The Omsk and Irkutsk Bolsheviks did not split with the Mensheviks until October 13th and 8th, respectively, and there is no evidence that they were connected with any central party organs before the October revolution.

THE IMPACT OF KORNILOV

News of the Kornilov affair had an electric effect upon the Siberian soviets. During September and October, the larger urban soviets became increasingly militant as a left coalition of Mensheviks, Bolsheviks, and left Socialist Revolutionaries gained control of all but Irkutsk and Novonikolaevsk. In September, the Bolsheviks gained control of several soviets outright, primarily because of a dramatic increase in their influence in the garrisons. From September through February 1918, Bolshevik party life became progressively less important because the best party workers devoted almost all of their time and energy to working in the soviets. The result was party control over the soviets that was to become the chief characteristic of the new Soviet state.

At the end of August, the militant soviets began to pass Bolshevik resolutions on the contemporary course of the revolution. On August 30th, a general meeting of the military section of the Barnaul Soviet and the garrisons' Regimental and Company committees demanded the convening of a peoples' court to deal with Kornilov, the transfer of all state power to the soviets, the immediate calling of an all-Russian Congress of Soviets, and disbanding of the State Duma.[59] On August 31st, the Second Congress of Western Siberian Soviets meeting in Omsk passed resolutions calling for an immediate end to the war, transfer of all land to the peasantry, and for the convening of a new Congress of Soviets. A large number of Bolsheviks and left Socialist Revolutionaries were elected to the Central Executive Committee of the congress, including N. N. Yakovlev, who chaired it.[60] Similar resolutions were passed by all of the major soviets, including Novonikolaevsk.[61]

Typical of the Bolshevik inspired resolutions was the declaration of the Tomsk Soldiers' Soviet, passed on September 2nd.

> The Soldiers' Soviet of the Tomsk garrison stands completely opposed to any compromise not only with General Kornilov, but also with those classes and agents who, it seems, are with the counterrevolutionary bourgeoisie.[62]

This, of course, was a direct reference to the right Socialist Revolutionaries and Menshevik-defensists, whose continuing support of the Provisional Government was seen as objectively counterrevolutionary by the Bolsheviks.

Another example of the response to Kornilov can be seen in the resolutions of the Verkhneudinsk Soviet on September 1st. V. M. Serov gave an analysis of the Kornilov affair that became the basis for the resolutions of the Menshevik-Socialist Revolutionary dominated soviet. He pointed out that

> without a doubt the adventure of Kornilov was nourished and supported by the monarchist and bourgeois elements of Russian society, who were grouped around the relic of the old regime: the Fourth State Duma and the State Council. The bourgeoisie in the Provisional Government participated in the conspiracy. Now a new government must be organized on the basis of purely democratic beginnings. The bourgeoisie can no longer be in the wrong places. The slogan 'all power to the soviets,' which for a long time was advanced by the Petrograd proletariat, must, at last, be realized. The new government must be organized as a central organ of the Soviets, for only they will support it in the struggle against counterrevolution.

Following his report, the Soviet passed a resolution calling for the creation of an all-socialist government, which would be shielded by the power of the soviets and which, as a matter of common sense, would play a leading role.[63]

In Central Siberia, where a soviet revolution had, in effect, already taken place, the entire gubernia mobilized for the transfer of power to the soviets on a formal basis. On September 7th, the First Gubernia Congress of Eniseisk Soviets met in Krasnoiarsk, entirely under the control of the Bolsheviks. It claimed to represent 200,000 workers, soldiers and peasants in Eniseisk gubernia—almost twenty-five percent of the adult male population. Its resolutions called for the transfer of all power to the soviets, workers' control over industry and supply, all land to the peasantry, and the most draconian measures to stamp out speculation and profiteering.[64]

PRELUDE TO THE OCTOBER REVOLUTION

During September and October, the revolution in Siberia began to polarize sharply, and the tide began to run swiftly in favor of the Bolsheviks. Their increasing popularity in the militant urban soviets, no doubt, reflected their willingness to take decisive action to extract Russia from the war and to deal with the threatening economic catastrophe. It is not entirely impossible that the Bolshevik-controlled Eniseisk gubernia served as an attractive model to the workers and soldiers elsewhere in Siberia; and to the middle classes, it was a warning of what would happen if the Bolsheviks came to power in Russia.

With the onset of winter, food and fuel shortages were becoming critical. Inflation, speculation, bootlegging, and hoarding were increasing. During the first half of October, food riots had broken out in Omsk and spread to Irkutsk.[65] Disorders in the garrisons, in many cases under the instigation of the Anarchists, resulted in the disarming of many soldiers in Irkutsk and other cities.[66] Criminal acts and drunkenness were becoming commonplace. The poor blamed the bourgeoisie for the war, the shortages, and the rising prices. They, in turn, blamed the poor and the Bolsheviks for the public disorders. In the bourgeois and right Socialist Revolutionary press, all left-wing socialists were tarred with the brush of Bolshevism that had then become a label of opprobrium on the right. The workers, soldiers, and poorer peasants turned to the Bolsheviks and left Socialist Revolutionaries for economic justice and decisive action, while the middle classes looked to the Kadets and the military officers for the restoration of order and the preservation of property. The only holdouts to the Bolshevik tide were the Menshevik and Socialist Revolutionaries in Irkutsk and Novonikolaevsk, who controlled the urban soviets and the peasant soviets in Eastern and Western Siberia. The right Socialist Revolutionaries, who actually controlled these soviets, worked during September and October to support the Provisional Government and to undermine the influence of the Bolsheviks. On October 10th, they convened a Second Congress of Eastern Siberian Soviets in Irkutsk, but even here the Bolsheviks had made inroads. Of 115 delegates, 32 were Bolsheviks and 15 were left Socialist Revolutionaries. According to the account of Maksakov, the only source, the Bolsheviks and the left Socialist Revolutionaries boycotted the congress after a right Socialist Revolutionary orator delivered a scathing attack on the Bolsheviks, which the majority of delegates obviously enjoyed.[67]

Apparently realizing the futility of trying to win over the right Socialist Revolutionary-controlled peasant soviets and Eastern Siberian Regional Bureau of soviets created by the Congress, the Bolsheviks decided to organize an All-Siberian Congress of Soviets. It was called by the Krasnoiarsk Soviet, on orders of the Central Siberian Bureau of the R.S.D.R.P.(b).[68] It was probably done at the instigation of the Central Committee, which, since September, had begun to reestablish its connections with the Siberian organizations. By October, it had appointed N. N. Yakovlev agent of the Central Committee in Western Siberia, V. N. Yakovlev in Western Siberia, and B. Z. Shumiatskii in Eastern Siberia.[69]

According to Shornikov's account, both N. N. Yakovlev and B. Z. Shumiatskii were ordered by the Central Committee to prepare the party for the overthrow of the Provisional Government and to win control of the soviets to support the action of the soviets in Petrograd.[70] Undoubtedly, the calling of an All-Siberian Congress of Soviets was a step in this regard. The Bolsheviks knew that together with the left Socialist Revolutionaries they could control the Congress and win control of the Central Executive Committee. They also knew that this Congress would play a supportive role to the all-Russian Congress of Soviets due to meet in Petrograd.

Whether they actually knew that the party planned an armed insurrection to seize power itself is difficult to document, but it is inconceivable that they did not. Since mid-September, Lenin's desire for the Bolsheviks to take power was an open secret in Russia. In early October, Kamenev and Zinoviev gave the plan away. Boris Shumiatskii was in Petrograd until about October 10th. It is very likely that he informed the party in Siberia of the plans at the First all-Siberian Conference of Bolsheviks, which had been called to coincide with the First Congress of Siberian Soviets. This, of course, ensured that the Bolsheviks would not only be able to coordinate their actions throughout Siberia, but also gave them a heavy representation at the Congress.

Without access to archival materials, it is impossible to determine what the Bolshevik plans were in Siberia, but one may guess that the best they could hope for was to win control of the Central Executive Committee of Soviets and claim authority over all Siberian soviets, including those controlled by the right Socialist Revolutionaries. They knew that their party forces in Siberia were too weak to take power by themselves and that the Menshevik-internationalists and left Socialist Revolutionaries would oppose the idea of a Bolshevik party dictatorship.[71] But if the central Soviet government was entirely in the hands of the Bolsheviks, all that was necessary was to support it by proclaiming the local soviets as organs of the new soviet power.

The First Siberian Congress of Soviets, with delegates from sixty-nine soviets from Cheliabinsk to Vladivostok, more than fulfilled Bolshevik expectations.[72] Of 129 delegates, 64 were Bolsheviks, 35 were left Socialist Revolutionaries, 11 were Menshevik-defensists, 10 were Menshevik-internationalists, and the rest were right and center Socialist Revolutionaries. The right Socialist Revolutionaries stayed at the congress only long enough to declare it illegal, pointing out that the Central Committee of the Peasant Soviets in Petrograd had refused to take part in the Second All-Russian Congress of Soviets that was also illegal. Then, according to Shornikov, they threw their mandate cards at the speakers' table and walked out.

Without the right Socialist Revolutionaries, the congress went rather smoothly, although the Menshevik-defensists and center Socialist Revolutionaries who remained were given no seats on the Central Executive Committee (*Centrosibir*). Shumiatskii was chosen to head Centrosibir, which included two other Bolsheviks, Weinbaum and Okulov, and two left Socialist Revolutionaries. Its resolutions were entirely Bolshevik.

> Any compromise with the bourgeoisie must be decisively refused. The all-Russian Congress of Soviets must immediately take power and the local soviets must follow suit. Only the power of the Soviets guarantees peace, the transfer of land to the peasants, workers' control over industry, and the confiscation of capital.

These resolutions were adopted by a vote of 98 to 63.[73]

Thus the stage was set for the October revolution in Siberia and for the victory of the Bolsheviks. During the summer and early autumn, they created a small but powerful organization in Central and Western Siberia, which suffered only a minor setback during the July days and their aftermath. Connections with the Central Committee were once again tightened and the party was in the hands of two capable leaders in Siberia— Shumiatskii and Yakovlev—both of whom enjoyed both Lenin's and Sverdlov's confidence. Increasingly, Bolshevik slogans were adopted by the urban soviets, which were then controlled by a powerful left-socialist coalition, in which the Bolsheviks were senior partners. All that remained was to follow the lead of Petrograd.

6

The Victory of the Bolsheviks in Siberia

The victory of the Bolsheviks in the October revolution in Siberia was the result of a prolonged and complex process that was not essentially completed until February 1918.[1] In contrast to March, the character of the October revolution in Siberia and the behavior of the Bolsheviks was directly related to the revolution in Petrograd, since the conflicts among the socialists in European Russia had a profound impact upon the socialists in Siberia. From the moment the Bolsheviks in the capital overthrew the Provisional Government on October 25th, they faced significant opposition from the Mensheviks and Socialist Revolutionaries. The right socialists moved closer to the Kadets, conservatives, and the military, and opposed the Bolsheviks by armed force. More significantly, with respect to Siberia, deep divisions appeared within the left-socialist coalition that controlled the Second All-Russian Congress of Soviets.

Not only the Menshevik-internationalists and Left-Socialist Revolutionaries, but also a number of leading Bolsheviks were opposed to the idea of an all-Bolshevik government that the Leninists foisted upon the congress. These divisions widened precipitously when the Bolshevik majority on the Central Executive Committee supported the Sovnarkom (The Peoples' Council of Commissars) decree of October 27th, which, in effect, abolished the freedom of the press.[2] Three Bolshevik Commissars, including the Siberian I. Teodorovich, resigned from Sovnarkom. The Left-Socialist Revolutionaries resigned from the Central Executive Committee of Soviets.[3] Then, Vikzhel (The Central Executive Committee of the All-Russian Railwaymens' Union) issued an ultimatum threatening a general strike if the fighting did not stop and if negotiations did not begin toward the creation of an all-socialist government. This ultimatum was sent to all the major railroad centers in Russia via the railway telegraph system. This was not taken over by the Bolshevik government until December 8th, when the Military Revolutionary Committee occupied it with a company of soldiers.[4]

The fact that Vikzhel controlled the railway telegraph system from October 25th through December 8th was of considerable importance in the provincial cities. The entire country was made aware of the socialist opposition to the self-constituted Bolshevik government. The Bolsheviks, however, controlled the regular telegraph and telephone system. This meant that the new government was not entirely cut off from the provincial cities and could announce to the country the bold steps it was taking to deal with the national catastrophe. As a result, the telegraph wires throughout Russia buzzed with conflicting reports, resolutions of various groups, rumors, as well as the decrees of Sovnarkom.

Because of the news from Petrograd, the Bolsheviks in Siberia were immediately faced with the same constellation of opposing forces as the Bolsheviks in Petrograd. The Menshevik-internationalists and Left-Socialist Revolutionaries opposed them within the executive committees of the soviets. The Menshevik-defensists and right Socialist Revolutionaries opposed them in the soviets, the cooperatives, the city dumas, and all other public institutions. The Kadets, conservatives, military officers, and some right Socialist Revolutionaries formed secret military organizations and planned armed insurrections. To compound the difficulty, the Siberian regionalist movement gained momentum and blossomed into a full-blown movement toward Siberian autonomy.

For about four weeks, just about the time interval that the Left-Socialist Revolutionaries refused to enter into the new government, this constellation of opposing forces was sufficient to forestall the Bolshevik victory in Western and Eastern Siberia. It was able to do so in Transbaikalia until mid-February. But, it was a futile attempt.

Despite their numerical weakness, the balance of forces in Siberia favored the Bolsheviks. First and foremost, their party had created a national Soviet government that was taking vigorous measures to deal with the three most crucial issues of the revolution: bread, land, and peace. Although the dictatorial habits of the Bolshevik government immediately alienated it from most of Russian "society," its vigor and dynamism won it the support of the workers, soldiers, and poorer peasants throughout Russia.[5] It was, after all, a genuine Soviet government. During the crucial months of

November and December in Siberia, the support of the workers, soldiers, and the poorer peasantry was transformed into allegiance, with the important result that the Soviet government was able to muster more armed force in its behalf than any of its opponents.

Thus, the sheer fact that the Soviet government had been created and established itself in Petrograd proved to be disastrous for all those who opposed the Bolsheviks in Siberia. The opposition of the Menshevik-internationalists and Left-Socialist Revolutionaries undermined their own positions within the soviets. To the workers and soldiers, their reversal on the issue of soviet power must have been incomprehensible. Most had little understanding of the political issues that divided the left socialists. If the Mensheviks and Socialist Revolutionaries failed to go into the Soviet government, it reflected badly upon them, not on the Bolsheviks. And it is not inconceivable that the outright opposition to soviet rule by the Menshevik-defensists and right Socialist Revolutionaries contributed to the political difficulties of the non-Bolshevik left socialists.

The opposition of the Menshevik-defensists and right Socialist Revolutionaries was even more futile. The association of a number of Right-Socialist Revolutionaries with the Kadets and military officers earned the label of counterrevolutionary for the entire group. As supporters of the Provisional Government, they opposed the concept of soviet power, which was then synonymous with the further development of the revolution. They could only succeed if a non-Soviet government emerged out of the political turmoil in Petrograd. In any case, the workers and soldiers responded to Menshevik and Socialist Revolutionary opposition by electing Bolshevik delegates to the soviets during November.

While loss of mass support for the Mensheviks and

Socialist Revolutionaries was an important factor in the Bolshevik victory in Siberia, a large measure of credit must go to the Bolsheviks themselves. Between March and October they not only imbedded themselves deeply into the revolutionary infrastructure—that is, the soviets, unions, city dumas, and so forth—but they also organized themselves hierarchically in tight party formations in Central Siberia, with closer connections to their Central Committee than the other parties had with their central institutions. They also succeeded in bringing a number of influential Menshevik-internationalists into the organizations with them.

Because they were so well organized, at least in comparison with their political rivals, the Bolsheviks alone in Siberia were able to gear their tactics and strategy to the realities of political life in Siberia, and at the same time to be guided in their actions by the policies of the Central Committee at the national revolutionary center. They also seem to have had a higher caliber of leadership than the Mensheviks and Socialist Revolutionaries. Men like N. N. Yakovlev knew when to ignore certain party policies, without losing sight of the main objectives of the party. This high degree of political flexibility of the leaders, combined with good organization, enabled the Bolsheviks to coordinate their actions in the October revolution in a way that maximized their strengths and minimized their weaknesses.

While there is no documentary evidence that the Siberian Bolsheviks had a definite plan of action, the pattern of events during the October revolution and a good deal of circumstantial evidence leaves a strong impression that they did.[6] It is possible, moreover, that their tactics and strategy had the approval of the Central Committee, and may have been based upon Lenin's instructions. According to M. M. Shornikov, the Central Committee sent

Boris Shumiatskii back to Siberia in mid-October "to guarantee the victory of the socialist revolution and to render practical help in mobilizing the masses."[7] He also claims that the Central Committee sent directives to N. N. Yakovlev, ordering him to prepare the party and the soviets for the overthrow of the Provisional Government. Since it was not a secret in Petrograd that Lenin meant for the Bolsheviks to take power alone, and since both Yakovlev and Shumiatskii were Leninists, at least on the issue of Bolshevik power, they were probably given instructions to prepare the party for the armed insurrection.[8]

The news of the impending coup d'etat was probably passed along by Yakovlev and Shumiatskii at the first meeting of Siberian Bolsheviks from Cheliabinsk to Vladivostok, during the First All-Siberian Congress of Soviets in October. The mandate was "prepare the party," but in Siberia, with the exception of Eniseisk gubernia, it was not yet strong enough to hold power. The Mensheviks and Socialist Revolutionaries still controlled several of the larger urban soviets—Omsk, Novonikolaevsk, Irkutsk, Verkhneudinsk, and Chita. The Bolsheviks had only Tomsk, Barnaul, and Krasnoiarsk. Apart from Krasnoiarsk, there were no Bolshevik Military Organizations in Siberia. There were Red Guards, but they were just becoming organized. More important, the Bolsheviks had no idea of how much armed strength they could muster. While it was clear that the workers and soldiers in the major cities would support soviet power, no one knew if they would fight for Bolshevik power.

Consequently, the Bolsheviks planned and prepared for the armed insurrection by establishing soviet rule immediately in Central Siberia, by maintaining a popular front with the left-socialists in Western Siberia, by waging struggles for the control of the soviets in Western and Eastern Siberia, and by planning for a coordinated Bolshevik takeover of Siberia once they had gained control of the major soviets.[9] To accomplish these tasks party members were sent from one region to another, emissaries and personnel were sent from Petrograd, and strong efforts were made to discredit the Mensheviks and Socialist Revolutionaries among the workers and soldiers.

CENTRAL SIBERIA

The victory of the Bolsheviks in Eniseisk gubernia was accomplished peacefully during the last four days of October. Actually, it was little more than the formalization of what had occurred during the summer and autumn. Upon hearing the news of the revolution in Petrograd on October 26th, the Krasnoiarsk soviet held a special session and decided to act immediately to establish a Soviet government. A committee of six was formed to take immediate control of the telegraph. Delegates from the Executive Committee of the Soviet were sent to all the reliable companies and a military command staff was organized, headed by the Left-Socialist Revolutionary Sergei Lazo.[10]

A decision was made to strengthen and to arm the Red Guard. A Military Commissar was appointed to head the staff of the Red Guard, and the head of the garrison was advised to turn over to the organization 700 rifles and 21,000 shells.[11] Evidently, although the Krasnoiarsk garrison was sympathetic to the Soviet, the Bolsheviks preferred to rely upon armed workers for military muscle.

Next, the Soviet turned its attention to taking over the

gubernia administration by creating a special Peoples' Commissariat within the Soviet. The creation of this institution paralleled the creation of Sovnarkom by the Central Executive Committee of Soviets in Petrograd. This Commissariat claimed for itself all political and economic power in the gubernia. And to finance it, the Soviet Executive Committee established a commission for working out a tax levy.[12]

On the 27th, more information was received from Petrograd, including the telegram from Vikzhel. Immediately, the Menshevik-defensist newspaper *Golos Naroda* and the Socialist Revolutionary *Svobodnaia Sibir'* published articles calling for opposition to the Bolsheviks, and informing the population about what was happening in Petrograd. A special meeting of the Executive Committee was called to discuss the telegram and the opposition views in the newspapers. It was decided to warn the editors to cease publishing any materials hostile to Soviet power or to face closing. Armed with Sovnarkom's decree on the press, October 27th, the Menshevik and Socialist Revolutionaries' papers were closed in Krasnoiarsk on October 28th, when they apparently refused to knuckle under to the Bolshevik-controlled Soviet Executive Committee.[13]

On the 28th and 29th, the Soviet Executive Committee took further steps to consolidate Soviet rule in the gubernia. It sent a number of delegates to Kansk, Achinsk, and Eniseisk, and established close connections with the Bolshevik-controlled Centrosibir' in Irkutsk. It purged the telegraph offices of unreliable elements and somehow cowed the striking government employees to return to their jobs. It formalized its control over the garrison and it sent armed guards to the banks and other public institutions. It also moved to establish labor conscription.[14]

The success of the Bolsheviks in Krasnoiarsk, of course, reflected the fact that they had no opposition whatsoever in the city. They controlled the City Duma, the Soviet, and all of the trade unions. They had long since intimidated the old gubernia administration. The right Socialist Revolutionaries and Menshevik-defensists had no support in the city and the Kadets and military officers did not dare to try to resist them openly.

Meanwhile, the news had already generated a similar response in Achinsk, Eniseisk, and Kansk. On the 27th, the Kansk soviet voted 110 to 16 to take power in the city. A Military Revolutionary Committee was created, which peacefully took into its own hands all power in the city during the next two days. Soviet rule in Achinsk and Eniseisk was established as easily by October 30th. Many delegates arrived from Krasnoiarsk in all three cities to help organize the Soviet administration.[15]

By October 31st, Soviet government had been effectively established in the towns and cities of Eniseisk gubernia. Already delegates were being sent out from the uezd centers to organize the Soviet administration in the countryside. The entire project, of course, was in the hands of the Bolsheviks, who were supported by the Left-Socialist Revolutionaries. All that remained at that time was to secure and to strengthen the new Soviet government, and the forces opposing the Bolsheviks in Siberia would be isolated from each other.

Consequently, the Eniseisk Gubernia Bolshevik Committee sent a request to the Bolshevik Committee in Tomsk to dispatch reliable machine-gun and artillery units from the Tomsk garrison. The fear was that the Mensheviks and Socialist Revolutionaries in Irkutsk might send a military expedition to Krasnoiarsk, which, at that time did not have machine guns and artillery. The detachments from Tomsk arrived in the city around midnight on November 4th and were greeted with wild enthusiasm. As *Krasnoiarsk rabochii* put it: "the arrival of the units from Tomsk is the first case in Siberia of armed active support of one revolutionary soviet by another. . . ."[16] This, undoubtedly, gave the workers and soldiers in Krasnoiarsk a great psychological lift.

WESTERN SIBERIA

The dramatic Bolshevik victory in Eniseisk gubernia during the last three days in October was unique in Siberia. Elsewhere they faced such significant opposition that they did not wish to break with the left-socialist coalition that controlled the soviets in all but Novonikolaevsk and Irkutsk. In Western Siberia, they faced an entirely different set of political realities than in Central Siberia and they adjusted their tactics accordingly. Here their primary task was to prevent the forces of counterrevolution from splitting the prosoviet coalition of left socialists or from winning popular support by creating a pogrom mood directed against the Bolsheviks.[17] Thus, in October and November, the Bolsheviks in Western Siberia followed a popular front policy until early December, when they had won all of the major soviets except Novonikolaevsk.

Tomsk Although the Bolsheviks controlled the Tomsk garrison and the Tomsk Soldiers' Soviet, and were closely connected with the Krasnoiarsk Soviet, they made no move to establish Soviet rule in the gubernia. Instead, upon hearing the news of the revolution in Petrograd on October 26th, they joined together with all other socialists in Tomsk to form the Tomsk Provisional Revolutionary Committee.[18]

Since the Tomsk Provisional Revolutionary Committee was created on the initiative of the Bolsheviks, it is safe to assume that this tactic was planned in advance. It is possible that a definite decision was made by the Central Committee or by the Siberian leaders not to move in Western Siberia until the Omsk Soviet had come under Bolshevik control. Western Siberia was a hotbed of counterrevolutionary activity. Under these conditions it was unnecessary and risky for the Siberian Bolsheviks to break ranks with the other socialists until it was certain that the Bolsheviks had made their gamble stick in Petrograd. Why risk sparking a civil war in Western Siberia prematurely? The formation of a Provisional Revolutionary Committee of socialists would hold together a pro-soviet coalition and would protect the Bolsheviks against the hostility of the Kadets, conservatives, and the military.

In its first instructions to the population on October 26th, the Provisional Revolutionary Committee outlined what was Bolshevik party policy in Western Siberia.

> For struggling with the approaching counterrevolution, which under the guise of struggling with Bolshevism, disperses soviets and other revolutionary organizations, the Provisional Revolutionary Committee declares to all the citizens of Tomsk that it will support the transfer of central power from the hands of Kishkin, Bagratunin, and company, into the hands of the true organs of revolutionary democracy—the Central Soviet of Workers, Soldiers, and Peasants.[19]

It omitted, however, any call for the local soviets to follow the example of the center. The main purpose of the overturn in Petrograd, the Committee declared, was to ensure the convocation of the Constituent Assembly, and to the majority of workers, soldiers, and peasants in

Western Siberia, this had great appeal. Here there would be no reason for the soviets to seize power, since the political revolution during the spring already put the power into the hands of the representatives of the people.

During the next few days, the Provisional Committee reconstituted itself as the Tomsk Revolutionary Committee and claimed authority throughout the gubernia. Into it went delegates from the Tomsk Committee of the R.S.D.R.P.(b), the Tomsk Soviet, the Central Bureau of Professional Unions, the Socialist Revolutionary Gubernia Committee,[20] the Menshevik-defensists, the Bund, and even representatives of the Soviet of military officers. A Belenets, chairman of the Tomsk City Committee of Bolsheviks, was elected chairman.[21]

Evidently, the plan was for the Tomsk Bolsheviks to play an active role in the all-socialist coalition, but at the same time to work to push the idea of Soviet power in the gubernia. In its first public declarations about the October revolution in the capital it expressed the idea in connection with the calling of the Constituent Assembly.

> The Tomsk organizations of Bolsheviks declares that it recognizes the government advanced by the Soviets of workers, soldiers, and peasants' deputies as the only government that can call the Constituent Assembly, immediately transfer the land to the peasants, and to conclude a peace.[22]

It also announced that it would put maximum pressure on the Tomsk Revolutionary Committee to take decisive measures against those who work to undermine the interests of the workers, soldiers, and poorest peasants. Meanwhile, the Bolsheviks worked in the barracks, factories, and workshops to build up steam for a Soviet seizure of power.

Their agitational and propaganda forces in Tomsk, however, were quite thin, since they sent the best of their Bolshevized military units to Krasnoiarsk and their best party workers to Omsk and to the mining districts in the Kuznets basin.[23] Nonetheless, the efforts in Tomsk began to have results. On October 30th, a meeting of soldiers from the 18th and 25th regiments passed a Bolshevik resolution calling for support of soviet power.[24] On the 6th of November, the 39th Siberian Rifle Reserve regiment passed a similar resolution.[25] On November 10th, a meeting of the 39th announced its approval of the decrees of the Second All-Russian Congress of Soviets.[26] This, undoubtedly, reflected Bolshevik attempts to win mass support in Tomsk for the C.E.C.'s action of November 7th, which granted the all-Bolshevik Sovnarkom the right to rule by decree.[27]

During the second week in November, much time was taken up with the elections to the Constituent Assembly. In Tomsk, the Bolsheviks won large margins in the garrison, but in the city, itself, they did not do as well. They polled 12,000 votes, but the Socialist Revolutionaries polled 7,000, the Kadets 6,000, the Siberian Regionalists 4,500, and the Mensheviks 1,000.[28] In the rest of the gubernia they did quite poorly.[29] They also bankrupted the Tomsk Gubernia Bolshevik Committee in the election campaign.[30]

But during the next two weeks, the atmosphere shifted rapidly in favor of the Bolsheviks. In the first place, the local organs of Provisional Government were themselves going bankrupt. On November 19th, N. N. Yakovlev presided over a meeting of the Town Popular Assembly, which discussed the economic catastrophe that was beginning to engulf the city. There were few commodities, little medicine, and scarce quantities of other basic necessities. The town treasury was almost empty and prices in the city were beginning to rise fantastically.[31] According to V. Vegman, a pogrom mood was developing and the Black Hundreds were beginning to agitate.[32]

By the last week in November, the political situation changed. On November 25th, following the news that Vikzhel was entering into negotiations with the Bolshevik government, the Tomsk Railroad Committee announced its support of the Petrograd government.[33] On the 30th, the peasant section of the Tomsk Soviet discussed carrying out the decree on land. It passed a resolution expression no confidence in the Gubernia Land Committee as a revolutionary organ to carry out the decrees. For this, "the peasant section declares that it was necessary to stress once again, that power must be put in the hands of the soviets and that all other organs must be subordinated to this power. . . ."[34]

With the Bolsheviks in control of the central government, a ripening fiscal and economic crisis in local government brought to the surface the question of Siberian autonomy. Either the soviets become the organs of local government, or Tomsk gubernia would get no funds from the central government. The Mensheviks and Socialist Revolutionaries thought that if a People's Commissariat were created by the Executive Committee of the Gubernia Popular Assembly they would be able to play a viable political role in the gubernia, but the Bolsheviks insisted that the Commissariate be created by the Soviets. During mid-November, they attempted to call a gubernia congress of soviets for this purpose, but the Mensheviks and Socialist Revolutionaries who controlled the Novonikolaevsk Soviet refused to take part.[35] At this point, the Tomsk Bolsheviks decided to wait for the Tomsk Soviet to take power in the city until the convening of the Third Congress of Western Siberian Soviets of

Workers and Soldiers, which was called to open in Omsk on December 2nd.

Omsk The Bolsheviks in Omsk followed a policy identical to the Bolsheviks in Tomsk. News of the coup in Petrograd reached Omsk on October 25th. On that day, the Bolsheviks, Left-Socialist Revolutionaries, and part of the Menshevik-internationalists formed a revolutionary committee calling for support of the workers and soldiers in Petrograd. The Western Siberian Executive Committee of Peasants' Soviets, which did not recognize the Second Congress of Soviets, passed a resolution calling for the support of the Provisional Government. The City Duma, which was controlled by the Mensheviks and Socialist Revolutionaries, passed a similar resolution and the left socialists who supported the idea of a soviet government walked out.[36]

The next day, the revolutionary committee was reorganized as the Western Siberian United Committee of Revolutionary Democracy.[37] On the 27th, it issued a declaration to all who support the socialist revolution:

> The die is cast. Either revolution or counterrevolution. Either with the rebels—toward the government of democracy, or with the Provisional Government through the blood and corpses of the rebels. There is no other choice.[38]

On the 28th, it declared that it recognized the Council of Peoples Commissars as the government.[39]

On the next day, a general meeting of the Omsk Soviet declared its support for the armed uprising of the Petrograd proletariat. It declared that all workers, soldiers, and peasants should rally around the soviets, "and to be prepared to stand up in active support of the workers and soldiers' rebellion. . . ." It also protested attempts by a number of City Duma deputies to represent the Petrograd uprising as "a family affair, as a usurpation of popular rights, as an affair of the Bolsheviks alone."[40] The Soviet, however, did not take any decisive action. Nor did it until after the Bolsheviks gained a clear majority in the Executive Committee on November 30th.[41]

Without access to documentary materials, one must surmise that the Menshevik-internationalists and the Left-Socialist Revolutionaries were able to prevent the Bolsheviks in the Omsk Soviet from forcing the issue of Soviet power. At the same time, as supporters of the concept of Soviet power, they could not sit back while the right socialists and the bourgeoisie tried to portray the entire episode as a Bolshevik affair. For their part, the Bolsheviks may not have attempted even to press the issue in the Omsk Soviet. Just as in Tomsk, the hostility from the right was primarily directed against the Bolsheviks. Therefore, it would have been unwise for them to become isolated from the left socialist coalition that controlled the Soviet.

By the end of October, the storm clouds of civil war were already gathering in the city. On the left, popular pressure began to build for a Soviet seizure of power. The Bolsheviks began to increase their following in the factory districts and in the garrison, aided by the arrival of a number of important party workers from Tomsk.[42] On October 29th, on the initiative of the Bolsheviks from Tomsk, the Omsk garrison held a military parade. Marching with the soldiers were 700 members of the Red Guard, whose numbers were then beginning to grow.[43]

On the right, the Kadets, conservatives, military officers, and a number of right Socialist Revolutionaries prepared to seize power in the city. According to Shornikov's account, an underground military staff was created to prepare an armed uprising. It included the two heads of the Kadets, Zhardetskii and Kargapolov, the Prosecutor of the Military-District Court, Mende, the Cossack Colonel Berezovskii, the right Socialist Revolutionary Nemchikov, the former Commissar of the Provisional Government, Lepko, and the Prosecutor of the Omsk District Court, Karshunov. Connections were established with the military cadets and plans were made for the seizure of the telegraph, telephone, for arrests, and so forth. The plan fell through when the military cadets moved prematurely to arrest the Commandant and the Military District Committee, and when the secret military staff was unable to attract any military support among the supposedly reliable troops.[44] The United Committee of Revolutionary Democracy put down the uprising and arrogated for itself all power in the city. Arrests were made and the Committee announced that it would deal severely with any attempts to generate a pogrom mood in the city.[45]

The most important result of the uprising was to completely discredit any attempt to oppose the Bolsheviks in the eyes of the workers and soldiers. First there was a complete reorganization of the committee structure in the Omsk garrison. Evidently, the Bolsheviks worked to get the Socialist Revolutionaries kicked out by the rank and file. A new Military-District Committee was elected that gave the majority of delegates to the Bolsheviks. According to V. Kosarev, a Bolshevik member of the Committee, its chairman became the de facto commander of the Omsk garrison.[46]

Simultaneously with the Bolshevization of the Omsk garrison, the Bolsheviks pushed the issue of workers' control of industry in the city. Prior to the arrival of the Tomsk Bolsheviks, the Omsk Bolsheviks were not particularly strong in the Omsk working-class districts. By

November 18th, the tide had clearly turned. On that day a conference of Omsk factory committees met to discuss their role in the revolution. Of 174 delegates, 74 were Bolsheviks, 23 were Menshevik-internationalists, 19 were Left-Socialist Revolutionaries, 4 were Right-Socialist Revolutionaries, and the majority of the rest were nonparty.[47]

Already, the results of the Bolshevization of the garrison during the first week in November generated pressure within the Omsk Soviet for new elections to the executive committee. No doubt, the Bolsheviks made the workers and soldiers aware that the Menshevik-internationalists and the Left-Socialist Revolutionary leadership were holding back the Soviet from taking power. On November 11, the Executive Committee agreed to hold new elections for the 17th, 18th, and 19th of November.[48] These were held and the Bolsheviks won, but reelections were held to the Executive Committee only on November 30th. The Bolsheviks gained a clear majority and V. Kosarev was elected president.[49]

In his letter of December 1st to Sverdlov, Kosarev reveals that the decision for the Soviet to take power in Omsk was made on November 30th. It was obviously timed to coincide with the opening of the Third Congress of Western Siberian Soviets of Workers and Peasants on December 2nd. The fact that the Bolsheviks in Petrograd may have had a hand in the planning is suggested by N. A. Avilov's trip to Omsk during mid-November. He discussed with Kosarev a whole range of problems pertaining to the creation of Soviet government in Siberia.[50] It was probably Avilov who directed the Tomsk Bolsheviks to try to convene a gubernia soviet congress and the Omsk Bolsheviks to call the Regional Congress. Clearly, the Soviet government for

Western Siberia, from the Urals to Eniseisk gubernia, was to be created at the regional conference.

On the eve of its opening, Omsk was in a worse economic condition than Tomsk. Despite the huge supplies of grain stored in the warehouses, the specter of starvation loomed over the city. The old Gubernia Supply Administration was rife with corruption. The owners of the grain were not willing to give it away without compensation. Thousands of bagmen and other disreputable types crowded in and around trains, stations, and warehouses looking for deals. Special petitions were received around the clock at the building that housed the Supply Administration. And, as in the case of Tomsk, medical supplies and other commodities were almost impossible to obtain.[51]

Given these conditions in Omsk, and in other Siberian cities at the beginning of December, the Third Congress of Soviets of Western Siberia met under conditions of great urgency. Attending its sessions were 103 delegates representing twenty-five soviets in Tomsk, Tobalsk, and Altaisk gubernias, and Akmolinsk oblast'. It was essentially dominated by the Bolsheviks and the Left-Socialist Revolutionaries from Omsk, Tomsk, Novonikolaevsk and Barnaul. By then, the Left-Socialist Revolutionaries had come over to the side of the Bolsheviks, perhaps in anticipation of their party's joining the Soviet government on December 10th. The Bolsheviks, however, gained control of the Central Executive Committee and N. N. Yakovlev was elected chairman of the Congress.[52]

The purpose of the Congress was to create a Soviet government for all of Western Siberia from the Urals to the Enisei River. In his initial report to the Congress, Yakovlev pointed out that ending the war was the most urgent task facing the new government in Petrograd.

The task of the Siberian soviets was to strengthen the authority of the central government. "The most we can do is to strengthen the authority of the soviets in the countryside. Delay means death."[53] In other words, Soviet government would be secure in the cities at that time and then had to be extended into the countryside to prevent rural Russia from becoming the staging area for a vendee. And this, it would seem, is exactly what the Right Socialist Revolutionaries had in mind.[54]

Among the more urgent tasks of a Soviet government in Western Siberia were the organizing of a regional administrative structure, dealing with the economic catastrophe, and funneling supplies back to Petrograd and Moscow. In its resolutions on the establishment of Soviet government in the region, the Congress made clear that the new administration would be an instrument of the Bolshevik dictatorship in Petrograd. It pointed out that the dictatorship of the bourgeoisie was then replaced with the dictatorship of the proletariat and the poorest peasantry. The demands of the dictatorship could be realized by the introduction of the following measures:

1) Reassurance to the population that peace negotiations will be conducted on the basis of no annexations and contributions,
2) transfer of lands to the peasantry without compensation,
3) introduction of workers' control over industry,
4) the democratic distribution of all products of prime need,
5) nationalization of all banks and important branches of industry,
6) a tax on the wealthy classes,
7) the introduction of labor conscription,
8) the democraticization of the courts and the army.[55]

As soon as these resolutions became public, the Omsk, Tomsk, Barnaul, and Novonikolaevsk Soviets took power. At the same time a Western Regional Soviet and Commissariate was set up, headed by N. N. Yakovlev.[56] Just before it closed, on December 8th, the congress sent a telegram to the Soviet government announcing the unanimous recognition by the congress of Sovnarkom.[57]

EASTERN SIBERIA

The Bolshevik victory in Eastern Siberia centered around the struggle for Irkutsk during November and December. On the eve of the October revolution, all power in the city—that is, the City Duma and the Irkutsk Soviet—was in the hands of the Socialist Revolutionaries and Mensheviks, although they had already begun to lose control of the garrison.[58] The Bolshevik forces in the city, however, were so thin that they were unable to channel the discontents within the garrison in a politically productive manner. Without leadership, the disgruntled masses of peasant-soldiers were more susceptible to anarchist influences than to those of the Bolsheviks. The Bolsheviks in Irkutsk were unable to win any influential positions in the revolutionary organs of power, except the Central Bureau of Professional Unions. But this was not sufficient to give them control of the two Soviets or the Executive Bureau of Soviets of Eastern Siberia.[59]

In a sense, the battle for Irkutsk was directed and carried on by the Krasnoiarsk Bolsheviks. The struggle began when the Bolsheviks, presumably with the concurrence or even the direction of the Central Committee, designated it to be the headquarters for Centrosibir'. During the summer, Lenin told Boris Shumiatskii that the Bolsheviks must win Irkutsk from the Mensheviks and Socialist Revolutionaries. If the Mensheviks and Socialist Revolutionaries were not beaten there, they would use it as a center from which to organize the peasants against the Bolsheviks in Western Siberia. This, of course, would effectively deny the capital much needed grain supplies.[60]

As students of 1848 and the Paris Commune, the Bolsheviks were almost certain that their socialist opponents, whom they considered petit-bourgeois, would try to help the bourgeoisie and the conservatives crush the urban revolution by organizing the wealthy and middle peasantry.

Consequently, the Bolsheviks decided to make Irkutsk the center for Soviet government in Siberia. This seemed to have been a deliberate attempt to undermine Socialist Revolutionary and Menshevik influence in the city. They knew that the right socialists would oppose the All-Siberian Congress of Soviets, as they had the Second All-Russian Congress of Soviets. They planned to use the Executive Bureau of Eastern Soviets to claim authority over the soviets in Eniseisk and Irkutsk gubernias and in Transbaikalia. But the Bolsheviks hoped that the Executive Committee set up by an all-Siberian Congress of Soviets would be recognized as the highest Soviet authority in Siberia. By leaving Centrosibir' in Irkutsk, the Bolsheviks hoped to undermine Socialist Revolutionary influence among the workers and soldiers within the city, and at the same time, to bring to the defense of Centrosibir' prosoviet forces from other parts of Siberia.

On October 29th, after Soviet government had been established in Eniseisk gubernia, the three Bolshevik members of Centrosibir'—Shumiatskii, Okulov, and Weinbaum—returned from Krasnoiarsk to begin the struggle for Irkutsk. Prior to their arrival the Socialist Revolutionaries who controlled the telegraph offices had managed to suppress news of the Bolshevik coup d'etat in Petrograd. With the arrival of these three Bolsheviks, the news was quickly spread around the city.

Their first act upon arriving in the city was to organize support for Soviet power in the garrison and among the workers. That afternoon they held a large meeting of representatives from the four infantry regiments and the 718th detachment. This was the first news that the troops had heard, but they immediately passed a resolution calling for the transfer of power to the Soviets.[61]

During the day, news spread to all areas of the city, prompting the Socialist Revolutionaries to organize a large meeting of the main public institutions. Late in the evening of October 29th, delegates from professional organizations, the Soviet of workers, the Soviet of soldiers, the City Duma, the socialist parties, and a large number of other public organizations met to discuss the situation. Speaking in the name of Centrosibir', Shumiatskii urged the meeting to transfer all power in the city to the Soviets. The leader of the Socialist Revolutionaries, Timofeev, made a long report about the complex political situation in the capital and called for the formation of a coalition government. He pointed out that the news reports indicated that the Bolshevik uprising had failed and that a dictatorship had been established.[62] The meeting refused to endorse the Bolshevik resolution offered by Shumiatskii.

During the next few days, the Socialist Revolutionary, Menshevik, and bourgeois press in the city began to publish fictitious telegrams and news reports about the battle against the Bolsheviks in the capital.[63] The Bolsheviks, who had no newspaper in Irkutsk, had to rely upon leaflets, newspapers from Krasnoiarsk, and agitational work among the soldiers and workers. They also worked to establish the authority of Centrosibir'.

On October 31st, amid the general confusion, Centrosibir' managed to send a telegram through the Socialist Revolutionary controlled telegraph office. It advised the Soviets in Siberia to take power without delay and to remove from positions of authority all agents of the Provisional Government, and not to allow disruptions to occur within the garrisons. It also called upon them to intensify their work on the elections to the Constituent Assembly.[64] According to Abov's account, Shumiatskii also managed to send another telegram that falsely reported that Soviet power had been established in Irkutsk but was overthrown by counterrevolutionary forces who supported the Provisional Government. This lie was plainly meant to reflect badly upon the Socialist Revolutionaries who already controlled the city,[65] and it was the last telegram they permitted Centrosibir' to send.

By October 31st, the Bolsheviks had begun to make great headway in organizing the workers and the soldiers. On that day a general meeting of factory workers adopted their resolution calling for reelections to the Irkutsk Workers' Soviet,[66] and on November 1st, they won a majority in the Soldiers' Soviet.[67] Meanwhile, the party had grown from about thirty members in early October to over 200.[68]

Without adequate documentation, it is difficult to determine what happened within the Workers' and Soldiers' Soviets between November 1st and November 15th, when the Bolsheviks appear to have won a majority. It appears that the split of the Socialist Revolutionaries and the inclusion of the Left-Socialist Revolutionaries in the Council of Peoples Commissars might have had a good deal to do with the situation in Irkutsk. By the second week in November the political atmosphere was extremely tense, as the pro- and antisoviet forces began to take shape. On the left were the Bolsheviks and Left-Socialist Revolutionaries who were supported by the entire garrison. But these soldiers were poorly armed, and it was problematic how many would actually fight. The

Red Guard was just beginning to take shape. On the right were the Right-Socialist Revolutionaries, the Mensheviks, three military schools, three companies of Cossacks, and a number of military officers. The antisoviet group was well armed with machine guns and mortars, and it was certain that the officers and cadets would put up a stiff fight.[69]

On November 8th, the Socialist Revolutionaries and Mensheviks organized a Committee to Save the Revolution and formed a Command Staff to coordinate the antisoviet forces in the city.[70] Within the Workers' and Soldiers' soviets they continued to resist the Bolsheviks, but it is clear that they were fighting a losing battle. Every day brought new Bolshevik delegates into the Soviets. on November 9th, a united meeting of the Soviets discussed the question of transferring power to themselves. A Bolshevik resolution narrowly lost by a vote of 111 to 121.[71] This vote was taken before the reelections were completed in the Workers' Soviet, but by November 15th, the Bolsheviks and the Left-Socialist Revolutionaries won a majority in the combined Soviet.[72]

Finally, on November 18th, the joint Executive Committees of the Soviets adopted a Bolshevik resolution calling for the transfer of power to the Soviet and for the creation of a Military Revolutionary Committee to effect the change. It also called for strengthening the Red Guard. Immediately upon passage of the resolution, the Mensheviks and the Right-Socialist Revolutionaries left the meeting.[73] The Military Revolutionary Committee, created on November 20th, included three Bolsheviks and two Left-Socialist Revolutionaries. It was decided that this Committee would take over all power in the gubernia until the formation of a Gubernia Peoples Commissariate.[74] The fact that the Left-Socialist Revolutionaries had two seats on the Military Revolutionary

Committee indicates that they probably gave the Bolsheviks control of the Soviets on November 15th.

Meanwhile, the Mensheviks and Right-Socialist Revolutionaries began to organize anti-Bolshevik support in the garrisons and in the working-class districts. On November 25th, they appear to have won back control of the joint Soviets. What happened, apparently, is that on November 24th an all-Siberian conference of Socialist Revolutionaries met in Irkutsk, and they may have packed the Irkutsk Soviets with delegates. On that day, the Military Revolutionary Committee arrested all the high-ranking officers of the garrison, but on the 25th they were freed by the Soviets.[75] The Bolsheviks declared that the meeting of Soviets called by the Mensheviks and the Socialist Revolutionaries was illegal because it did not reflect the mood of the masses. They demanded that the present Executive Committee of the Soviets turn over all its functions to the Military Revolutionary Committee, the Garrison Military Committee, and the Central Bureau of Trade Unions. When the meeting refused, the Bolsheviks left and presumably the Left-Socialist Revolutionaries did, also.[76]

Once again, the Bolsheviks went back to organize mass support to take control of the Soviets. On November 29th, a general meeting of the entire garrison's representatives adopted a resolution calling for the full support of Sovnarkom and for the activities of the Military Revolutionary Committee. It pledged to place the strength of the garrison at the committee's disposal.[77] Finally, on December 4th, the Bolsheviks won control of the executive committees of the Soviets and of the Regional Bureau of Eastern Siberian Soviets.[78] On that day, the Military Revolutionary Committee sent its Commissars to the post, the telegraph, the Supply Committee, the state bank, the Military-District Headquarters, and to the offices of the gubernia administration.[79] On De-

cember 8th, a joint meeting of the then merged Irkutsk
Soviet of Workers' and Soldiers' Deputies and the Regional Bureau of Eastern Siberian Soviets decided to dis-
arm the junkers in the military academies. The decision
was immediately passed on to the schools. The response
of the cadets was to pour out of the schools and to oc-
cupy the central part of the city.[80] This began an armed
uprising of anti-Bolshevik forces that lasted for eight
days.

After a fierce and bloody series of street battles in
which over 1,000 people were killed and wounded and
several hundred houses were destroyed, the contending
forces entered into peace negotiations on December
17th. It was decided to create a new coalition government in the city consisting of representatives of the
Military Revolutionary Committee, the Committee to
Save the Revolution, the postal-telegraph workers'
union, and the railroad workers' union. On the 19th, however, prosoviet forces arrived in Irkutsk from Kansk,
Achinsk, Krasnoiarsk, and Chemerovsk. The military
cadets were immediately disarmed and they left for
Harbin. The same day the Bolshevik-controlled Regional
Bureau of Eastern Siberian Soviets declared the coalition
government defunct and formally transferred all power
in the city to the Irkutsk Soviet.[81]

By that time, however, delegations from Transbaikalia
and Irkutsk gubernia began to arrive in Irkutsk to try
"to reconcile both sides of democracy." The Chita delegation was sent packing by the Irkutsk Soviet, which
claimed that it did not want any meddling in its affairs.[82]
The Bolsheviks were in complete control of the city and
they clearly did not wish to share power with anyone,
least of all the Mensheviks and the Socialist Revolutionaries. According to the French commercial agent
Jeandreau, "Shumiatskii is the complete master of Irkutsk," and ruled the city with a reign of terror.[83]

Thus, by the end of December, Bolshevik-controlled soviets had successfully seized power from Omsk to Irkutsk. The Socialist Revolutionaries in Omsk, Tomsk, and Irkutsk had tried and failed to oppose the Bolsheviks by military force. Their next strategy, as has been seen in Irkutsk, was to try to go into a coalition with the Bolsheviks and to work to organize Peoples' Soviets, which would be popularly elected organs of self-government. This political development greatly complicated the establishment of Soviet government in Siberia, since the Bolsheviks clearly did not want to share power with anyone, except the Left-Socialist Revolutionaries.

In Tomsk, on December 26th, an All-Siberian Extraordinary Congress of Delegates from Public Organizations, the Socialist Revolutionaries, the Mensheviks, the Popular Socialists, and many other groups created a Siberian Regional Soviet that was the executive organ of a Siberian Regional Duma created by the Congress. The Siberian Duma was to be the supreme power in Siberia until the convening of an All-Siberian Constituent Assembly in March 1918. The Siberian Regional Duma tried and failed to constitute itself as a non-Bolshevik Soviet governmental authority in Siberia in December 1917 and January 1918. On January 26th, the Bolsheviks dispersed it and arrested many of its leading members.

TRANSBAIKALIA

During December and January, there were two rival Soviet centers in Siberia. The Tomsk Regional Soviet of the Siberian Duma and the Central Executive Committee of the First All-Siberian Congress of Soviets. The Socialist Revolutionaries and Mensheviks who were behind the Siberian Duma were banking upon the strong regionalist sentiment in Siberia to wean away popular support from the Bolsheviks. The Bolsheviks were then in the awkward position of attempting to establish the authority of a dictatorial national government, a position that was bound to erode their initial popularity in Siberia. More important, there is a good possibility that a number of Bolsheviks began to chaff at the dictatorial and terroristic policies of Shumiatskii, who was then head of Centrosbir'.

Unfortunately, the available sources for much of Siberia shed no light on the attitudes of the rank-and-file Bolsheviks during this period, but in Transbaikalia, where there is some evidence, it appears that the local Bolsheviks supported the idea of an all-socialist coalition. On November 15th, the Verkhneudinsk Soviet, which was headed by the Bolsheviks V. M. Serov and A. Buiko, passed a resolution denouncing the defunct Provisional Government for failing to convene the Constituent Assembly. At the same time, it condemned "the seizure of power by one political party as intolerable and deeply harmful" to the revolution. The vote of this resolution was 82 in favor, 15 abstaining, and one opposed.[84] This meant that the Bolsheviks either voted for the resolution or abstained. Since the Social Democratic internationalists came out publically on November 17th against the Bolshevik action,[85] one can surmise that the Bolsheviks in Transbaikalia were against their own party's position. In light of Kamenev's and Zinoviev's behavior this is not at all surprising. Moreover, the Bolsheviks, like everyone else in Transbaikalia, were primarily concerned that nothing should disrupt the forthcoming Constituent Assembly.

Following the bloody battle of Irkutsk, however, it became apparent that the Soviet seizure of power under Bolshevik auspices was successful not only in European

Russia, but also in many Siberian cities as well. They also became aware in Transbaikalia of the strong trend toward the formation of coalition soviets and of the work of the Tomsk Congress of Regionalists. In response to these developments, a Third Regional Conference of Social Democratic internationalists met in Chita on December 10th, and recognized the inevitability and necessity of transferring power to the Soviets in the interests of realizing immediate peace and to lay the basis for the work of the Constituent Assembly.[86]

The Socialist Revolutionary-dominated Chita and Verkhneudinsk Soviets did not adopt this position. Instead, the socialists, working together, decided to organize the entire territory to ensure that all segments of the population would be represented in a new soviet government. On December 28th, three Congresses met in Chita to resolve the issues presented by the Bolshevik seizure of power and by the threat of counterrevolution gathering in Manchuria. Of primary concern was the threat to the revolution from the right.

In August 1917, a half-Buriat Cossack, Captain Gregory Semenov, had arrived in Verkhneudinsk seeking to recruit a volunteer force for the Russian army. He had been commissioned to do so by both the Provisional Government and the Petrograd Soviet. During the autumn he managed to collect a small force of 51 officers, three former Tsarist officials, 300 Buriat-Mongols, 80 Mongolians, and 135 Cossacks. When the Bolsheviks captured the Irkutsk Soviet in November, Semenov and his force went to Chita, and then to Manchuria. There he was joined by the officers who left Irkutsk after the battle in December. Late in December, he began to raid villages in Transbaikalia, at the very time the Congresses were meeting in Chita to reorganize the government of the territory.[87]

The three Regional Congresses that met on December 28th were the second Transbaikalia Regional Congress of Village Deputies, the Transbaikalia Regional Congress of City Dumas and the Committees of Public Safety, and the First Transbaikalia Congress of Soviets. At a joint meeting of the Congresses, a new supreme territorial authority was established: the Transbaikalia Peoples' Soviet.[88]

The Peoples' Soviet included thirty delegates from the village population, fifteen from the soviets, and five from the town self-governments.[89] Its Executive Committee included the Menshevik Vaksburg as president, the Bolshevik V. Sokolov as first vice-president, and the Socialist Revolutionary Flegontov as second vice-president.[90] This government represented the kind of compromise among the socialists that the Bolsheviks in Centrosibir' did not want, yet in Transbaikalia it seemed necessary for two reasons. In the first place, during early January a Cossack division returned from the front to Verkhneudinsk, which supported the Peoples' Soviet. The Bolsheviks, who went into the Soviet for tactical reasons, had been organizing and arming the Red Guard in Chita and they were disarmed by these troops. Second, the Tomsk Siberian Duma had formed a Siberian Soviet, which the Bolsheviks in Western Siberia did not challenge until the end of January.[91] On December 22nd, it sent telegrams to all local soviets in Siberia advising them to send delegates to the Siberian Regional Duma, which was to open in January. In addition, there was the very real threat of Semenov.

Consequently, the formation of the Peoples' Soviet at the end of December represented a compromise among the socialists of Transbaikalia based upon their understanding of an extremely confusing political situation. The nature of the compromise was embodied in the

Soviet's initial declaration that it would obey the laws of
the Siberian Duma in Tomsk and those of the Peoples
Commissars in Petrograd, only when they did not conflict with their own.[92] They also passed a resolution declaring Semenov to be a counterrevolutionary and called
for his arrest.[93]

But time was running out in Siberia for compromises.
During January more and more troops began to return
from the front. The majority of these troops were
strongly influenced by the Bolsheviks and the Anarchists. By the end of January, Centrosibir' felt strong
enough to order the arrests of the members of the Siberian Regional Duma in Tomsk, accusing it of organizing
an antisoviet front and inviting foreign intervention to
crush soviet government in Siberia.[94] These arrests were
carried out on January 24th, but a large number of
Duma delegates managed to get away.

Finally, in mid-February, two Cossack divisions accompanied by Bolshevik Commissars returned to Chita
and to Verkhneudinsk, thus effecting a formal soviet
seizure of power in Transbaikalia under Bolshevik auspices.[95] The Peoples' Soviet was prodded into oblivion
by Bolshevik bayonets, paralleling the dispersion of the
Constituent Assembly upon which the Socialist Revolutionaries had pinned their hopes. At that time, the
Bolsheviks controlled all of the major cities in Siberia
from Omsk to Chita.

THE ROLE OF THE PARTY

One of the great ironies of the Bolshevik victory in
Siberia during the winter of 1917–1918 is that the party
organizations played little or no role. All of the leading
Bolsheviks in Siberia were too busy in the soviets. Dur-

ing the turmoil, party connections with the Central Committee seem to have broken down. On January 11th, the Omsk Committee sent a letter to the Secretariat of the Central Committee complaining that the party situation in Western Siberia was most unsatisfactory. At the time of the letter, there had been no movement toward the regional unification of Bolsheviks. There was no guidance or help at all from the party center. All of the Bolshevik party workers were completely involved in the soviets and other public organizations.[96]

This, it would seem, was the policy of the Central Committee. In 1918, the main interest of Lenin and the Central Committee in Siberia was the shipment of grain to Moscow and Petrograd and the extension of Soviet authority into the countryside to prevent counterrevolution. To emphasize party life at this point in the revolution would have been pointless from a Leninist point of view. The main thing was to hold out in European Russia until the development of the socialist revolution in the West. Thus, the whole point of creating a Soviet administration in Siberia was to smash the forces of counterrevolution on the one hand, and to insure the flow of supplies to the workers and soldiers in European Russia on the other.

Another reason, perhaps, for deemphasizing party life in Siberia was the unreliability of the Siberian Bolsheviks from a Leninist point of view. What was needed then were ruthless types who would take any measures whatsoever to move the supplies. This meant the suppression of all opponents in Siberia, including the Menshevik-internationalists in Omsk who controlled part of the railroad workers' union. It is not difficult to imagine that Lenin would not trust the party organizations in Siberia to do the kind of dirty work necessary.

On December 1st, V. Kosarev hinted about the unreliability of the local Bolsheviks in a letter to Y. Sverdlov:

> The supplies question is of the greatest importance for 'Peter' and Moscow. We have much grain. But it is in the hands of the cooperatives, the defensists, and other enemies of democracy. Send a train or two, some good competent workers, and we will send you millions of poods of grain and it's good-bye hunger.

Then he added, somewhat sarcastically, that if he could not send the party workers, send 100 million rubles and carloads of manufactured goods and organize to guard the freight in European Russia. Evidently, the party had already dispatched some sailors to Omsk, but what was needed was something else. "It is a pity," Kosarev writes, "that you didn't send them with some leaders who understand what is necessary here to push the supplies."[97]

Fortunately for the party in European Russia, Lenin and Sverdlov knew exactly what to do to move the grain. On January 13th, a delegation from the Regional Soviet reached Petrograd with a shipment of grain from Omsk. They informed Lenin personally that 1,000 carloads of grain remained in Omsk, because the Omsk railwaymen refused to dispatch it. Lenin instructed that detachments of Cheka were to accompany the representatives back to Siberia, and that forty to sixty people were to be stationed in key locations along the shipping routes. He sent a note to the Commissariat of Supplies saying that the most revolutionary measures must be taken to move the carloads of grain from Siberia to Petrograd.[98]

Between December 1917 and March 1918, the effectiveness of the Cheka units in Omsk began to show. During December, 889,000 poods had been shipped from Omsk to Petrograd. In January, when the Mensheviks

and Socialist Revolutionaries began to energetically
sabotage the effort, only 587,000 poods were shipped.
During February, however, the amount skyrocketed to
1,867,000 poods and in March it went to 3,309,000. February and March obviously reflect the work of the
Cheka units.[99] Naturally, the Soviet sources are reluctant
to reveal much about the activities of the Cheka units in
Siberia during the winter of 1918, but it is safe to assume that they were instrumental in consolidating Bolshevik rule. It is not beyond possibility that their work
included the suppression and perhaps even the liquida-
tion of recalcitrant Bolsheviks.

By the end of February, the entire Soviet structure in
Siberia was in the hands of reliable Bolsheviks and all in-
ternal opposition to the regime had been forced to go
underground. During the second week in February, the
Second All-Siberian Congress of Soviets met in Irkutsk.
A new Central Executive Committee was elected that replaced Shumiatskii as president with N. N. Yakovlev.
The selection of Yakovlev was made by the Central
Committee in Petrograd on the advice of V. Kosarev.
The replacement of Shumiatskii by Yakovlev resulted
from a split among the Siberian Bolsheviks on the question of the Brest-Litovsk peace. Shumiatskii and many of
the original Krasnoiarsk Pravdists were left Communists
and they opposed Lenin. Kosarev and Yakovlev seem to
have been the most consistent Leninists in Siberia
throughout 1917 and were far more valuable to head
the consolidating phases of the new Soviet government
in Siberia than the more radical left-wing Bolsheviks and
former Menshevik-internationalists. And only they, it
would seem, had the ideological flexibility to follow the
Leninist path, which had then turned in the direction of
Socialism. The task at that time was to make an effective

and viable Soviet regime in Siberia and to protect it against the forces of counterrevolution.[100] This, unfortunately, proved to have been impossible, not because the Bolsheviks were not able to put down internal challenges to Soviet authority, but because of the tragic and unnecessary foreign intervention in the spring of 1918.

Epilogue

During January and February, under the leadership of Centrosibir', headed by Boris Shumiatskii, the Bolsheviks struggled to consolidate soviet power in the cities and to extend it into the countryside. Their primary tasks, as they understood them, were to continue the shipment of foodstuffs to European Russia, to prevent Siberia from becoming a staging area for the forces of counterrevolution, and to halt the descent into anarchy. To carry out these tasks, they attempted to create an effective Soviet administrative apparatus, to socialize the economy, and to lay the foundation for a socialist culture.

Underlying their activities in Siberia during January and February was the widespread belief that the outbreak of socialist revolution in Western Europe was imminent. Hence, it made sense to try to create socialism immediately in Siberia, even though the productive base was nowhere near sufficient for the development of a socialist economy. It also made sense to prepare Siberia for political autonomy, because in the new socialist society all regions would be united on a federated basis. This meant that the Bolsheviks in Siberia did not have to go against the strong sentiment for autonomy at a time when they were taking the most ruthless measures to put into effect the decrees of Sovnarkom and to suppress all forms of political opposition.

During the winter and early spring, the actual process of creating a socialist order in the cities and villages of Siberia was accompanied by a good deal of force and violence. Some of it was deliberately directed by the Cheka units against the middle classes, the cooperatives, and the Socialist Revolutionaries, but much of it resulted from the descent into anarchy and the severe food and fuel shortages. Following the signing of the treaty of Brest-Litovsk on March 3rd, large numbers of soldiers began to return home from the front to establish a new revolutionary order. Many of them were embittered by their experiences; many felt cheated by the fact that the peasants divided the land before they had got there. Many used the occasion to settle old scores and to deprive the richer peasants of their land and personal belongings. In some areas, armed bands roamed the railroad zone, stopping trains, murdering guards, and looting nearby settlements.

In the cities, where the spectre of starvation loomed, the Bolsheviks took the most drastic measures to deal with speculators, hoarders, and bagmen, but they were too few to be effective. Revolutionary tribunals were set up to deal with offenders who were caught, and Cheka units often dispensed summary justice on the spot. Nothing, however, could stop the crimes of violence, the lootings, the robberies, and general lawlessness that often made life intolerable even for those who had initially supported the Bolsheviks. And for the middle classes, life was becoming hell. The term *bourzhui* was synonymous with *leper* to the workers and soldiers who controlled the streets of the larger cities. Anyone who had property, money, and, often, merely an adequate living was subject to rough treatment. In January 1918, the mood in Irkutsk was vividly expressed by the French Counsul in Irkutsk, Henry Bourgeois who wrote to the French Ambassador that having the name *Bourgeois* in Irkutsk at that time was like having the name *Aristocrat* in Paris in 1793.

As might be expected, the anarchy, ruthlessness of the Bolsheviks, and ineffectuality of Soviet administration greatly strengthened the forces of counterrevolution. In Transbaikalia, under the leadership of the Cossack Atman Gregory Semenov, a strong force of Cossacks and army officers had been conducting military operations against the Bolsheviks since December. They were financed and armed by the Japanese who were preparing to intervene militarily to annex Eastern Siberia. During February, the most reliable workers and soldiers from Western and Central Siberia were formed into Red Army units and sent to Transbaikalia under the command of Sergei Lazo. This, in turn, greatly weakened the Bolsheviks' ability to deal with the quickening pace of counterrevolution.

In November 1917, following the suppression of the armed attempts in Omsk, a Captain Kirilov formed an underground organization of officers called the *White Legion*. In January 1918, three more military organizations came into being. One was formed by the Socialist Revolutionary A. Pepeliaev and the conservative Sumarokov in Tomsk. Another was formed by Captain Ivanov-Rinov in Omsk, and the third was a Cossack group in the Far East. There was no attempt to unite these groups, however, until March 1918, when the anti-Bolshevik political forces in Siberia managed to settle their differences long enough to coordinate them.

The focal point of anti-Bolshevik opposition in Siberia until the Czech uprisings at the end of May 1918 was the Siberian Regional Duma that met in Tomsk from January 7th until the 26th, when it was dispersed by the Bolsheviks and sixteen of its members were arrested. Prior to the arrests, the more conservative wing of the Siberian regionalist movement headed by Gregory Potanin had left the Congress that formed the Duma, charging it with being too willing to cooperate with the Bolsheviks. The arrests of January 26th, however, temporarily removed the Regionalists' objections to the left tendencies of many of the delegates.

The purpose of the Siberian Regional Duma was to work out plans for a Provisional Siberian Government and, despite the bickerings between the Potanin group and the Socialist Revolutionaries led by Peter Derber, the foundation had been laid during January. In mid-January, an all-Siberian congress of cooperatives met in Novonikolaevsk and passed a resolution declaring its nonrecognition of Sovnarkom and for the recognition of Siberia's complete autonomy. A loan was worked out for the Provisional Siberian Government and a scale was worked out for the introduction of a new currency.

The Provisional Siberian Government was created by forty members of the Siberian Regional Duma, who met in secret immediately following the arrests of sixteen of their fellow delegates. Among the members of the new government were several of the former Gubernia Commissars of the Provisional Government, including V. M. Krutovskii, the former head of Congress of Western Siberian Peasants, Peter Derber, and the former Commander of the Irkutsk Military district, the Socialist Revolutionary Krakovetskii. Declaring itself to be the sole government in Siberia, the Siberian Provisional Government divided itself into two parts: the West-Siberian Commissariat, which went to Novonikolaevsk, and the Autonomous Siberian Provisional Government headed by Derber, which went to Harbin. A member of the government also went to Moscow to make connections with the Central Committee of the Socialist Revolutionary party and with the Union to Save the Fatherland led by General Kornilov.

On February 28th, General Flug, head of the newly formed Siberian section of the Union to Save the Fatherland, arrived in Novonikolaevsk to coordinate the political and military opposition to Bolshevism. There he met with Gregory Potanin and together they worked out a plan to merge the nonparty military units with those being formed by the Socialist Revolutionaries, which was the major party in the new Siberian government. In March, the West-Siberian Commissariate in Novonikolaevsk created a Central Staff to take command of the military units west of Lake Baikal.

There were then over 7,000 anti-Bolshevik troops in Siberia. In Omsk, there were 3,000 members under the command of Colonel Ivanov-Rinov; in Tomsk there were about 1,500 under the command of Sumarokov and Pepeliav; there were 600 in Novonikolaevsk; and over 1,000 in Irkutsk.

In May, plans were made for a coordinated uprising against the Bolsheviks that involved the Czechs, agents of the French Military Mission in Russia, as well as the Whites, the Socialist Revolutionaries, and the representatives of the Siberian Provisional Government. On May 14th, General Flug laid out his plan for the uprisings at a meeting between representatives of the Central Staff and the Czech command. The actual uprisings took place during the last week in May, under the command of Colonel Ivanov-Rinov.

Because the best troops of the new Soviet regime in Siberia were engaged fighting Semenov in Transbaikalia, the White military units were able to overthrow soviet power with virtually little opposition. In those cities where the soviets were able to muster armed force in their behalf, the Czechoslovaks were easily able to dispatch them. By the end of the first week in June, Soviet power in all areas of Siberia except Transbaikalia was overthrown and immediately political infighting among anti-Bolshevik forces began. Ominously, the most conservatively minded military officers gained the upper hand in dealing with the Bolsheviks.

During June, the White units in all of the major cities along the Trans-Siberian railroad rounded up all members of the soviets they could lay their hands on and exterminated the Bolshevik leadership in Siberia. They did the same thing in Transbaikalia following the defeat of the Soviet forces in late August 1918. Almost forty percent of the party's top leaders were shot, including N. N. Yakovlev, Ya. F. Bograd, Ya. F. Dubrovinskii, V. N. Yakovlev, N. L. Nakhanovich, G. C. Weinbaum, I. V. Prisiagin, and V. N. Serov. Many who went into the underground were captured and killed during 1919 and 1920. Sergei Lazo, for example, met a particularly horrible death in 1920 at the hands of the Japanese. He was thrown alive into the furnace of a locomotive. Such atrocities, of course, were common during the civil war.

The impact of the politics of extermination on the Bolshevik party in Siberia drastically changed its character. A large percentage of party members, whose roots were to be found in the cultural and intellectual milieu of the 1890s, were replaced by a different kind of party member—one who very often was far more indifferent and callous toward human suffering and misery. Frequently they were young men who had been brutalized, and to a great extent dehumanized, by their experiences at the front. These men were as dedicated to the party as were those who perished at the hands of the Whites, but it was of a different order. They were cruder, not so flexible, more likely to grasp the letter and not the spirit of Lenin's laws. These were, of course, the very men who would give Joseph Stalin his iron control of the party.

Notes

INTRODUCTION

1. Two especially useful works on the Bolsheviks during 1917 are Robert
V. Daniels, *The Conscience of the Revolution, Communist Opposition in Soviet Russia*
(Cambridge, Massachusetts: Harvard University Press, 1960); and Alexander
F. Rabinovich, *Prelude to Revolution: The Petrograd Bolsheviks in the July 1917
Uprising* (Bloomington, Indiana: Indiana University Press, 1968).

2. Robert V. Daniels, "Review of Revolutionary Russia," Richard Pipes,
ed., *Slavic Review* 28 (March 1969): 139. A significant exception to this viewpoint, which Daniels accepts, is E. H. Carr, *The Bolshevik Revolution 1917–1923*,
3 vols. (New York: Macmillan, 1950–1952).

3. See *Istoriia Kommunisticheskoi Partii Sovietskogo Soiuza*, 4 vols. (Moscow:
1964–), vol. 3.

4. Ronald G. Suny, *The Baku Commune, 1917–1919: Class and Nationality in
the Russian Revolution* (Princeton, New Jersey: Princeton University Press,
1972).

5. Boris Z. Shumiatskii, *Sibir' na putiakh k Otiabriu* (Moscow: 1927), p. 34.

6. *See*, for example, V. V. Riabikov, *N. N. Yakovlev–predstavitel' Tsentrosibiri*
(Novosibirsk, U.S.S.R.: 1955).

7. For a discussion of published Soviet primary and secondary sources on
the revolution in Siberia *see Istoriografiia Sovietskoi Sibiri, 1917–1945gg.*
(Novosibirsk, U.S.S.R.: 1968), pp. 5–31.

8. M. M. Shornikov, *Bol'sheviki Sibiri v bor'be za pobedu Oktiabr'skoi revoliutsii* (Novosibirsk, U.S.S.R.: 1963).

9. V. P. Safronov, *Oktiabr' v Sibiri* (Krasnoiarsk, U.S.S.R.: 1962).

10. Shornikov, *Bol'sheviki Sibiri*, p. 254.

11. Ibid., p. 255.

12. D. M. Zol'nikov, *Rabochee dvizhenie v Sibiri v 1917g.* (Novosibirsk, U.S.S.R.: 1969), p. 110.

13. Ibid., p. 112.

CHAPTER 1

1. *See*, for example, M. M. Shornikov, *Bol'sheviki Sibiri v bor'be za pobedu Oktiabr'skoi revoliutsii* (Novosibirsk, U.S.S.R.: 1963); V. P. Safronov, *Oktiabr' v Sibiri* (Krasnoiarsk, U.S.S.R.: 1962); *Istoriia Sibiri*, 5 vols. (Leningrad: 1968–1969), vol. 3.

2. By far the most useful work is Donald W. Treadgold, *The Great Siberian Migrations* (Princeton, New Jersey: Princeton University Press, 1957).

3. Ibid., pp. 34–35.

4. Compiled from: Glavnoe Upravlenie Zemleustroistva i Zemledeliia, *Aziatskaia Rossii*, vol. *1: Liudi i poriadki za Uralom* (Saint Petersburg: 1914): 86; Shornikov, *Bol'sheviki Sibiri*, p. 84; Tsentralnoye Statisticheskoe Upravlenie, *Pouezdnye itogi Vserossiiskoi sel'skokhoziastvennoi i pozemel'noi perepisi 1917 goda po 57 guberniiami i oblastiam* (Moscow: 1923), pp. 148–68.

5. *Aziatskaia Rossii*, 1: 293; Shornikov, *Bol'sheviki Sibiri*, p. 83; A. I. Petrov, "Perepis' gorod'skogo naseleniia Sibiri," *Severnaia Aziia*, no. 3 (1927), pp. 37–42.

6. *Aziatskaia Rossii*, vol. 1: 82–85.

7. Glavnoe Upravlenie Zemleustroistva i Zemledeliia, *Atlas' Aziatskoi Rossii* (Saint Petersburg: 1914).

8. *Ekonomicheskoe polozhenie Rossii nakanune Velikoi Oktiabr'skoi sotsialisticheskoi revoliutsii. Dokumenty i materialy*, 3 vols. (Leningrad: 1967), vol. 3: 158–59.

9. Safronov, p. 64, Shornikov, *Bol'sheviki Sibiri*, p. 122.

10. *See* note 7 above.

11. Treadgold, p. 179, 228.

12. Shornikov, *Bol'sheviki Sibiri*, pp. 121–22.

13. Ibid.

14. *Pouezdnye itogi*, pp. 148–68; Shornikov, *Bol'sheviki Sibiri*, pp. 142–43.

15. *Istoriia Sibiri*, 3: 324–25.

16. Ibid.

17. *Pouezdnye itogi*, pp. 148–68; *Istoriia Buriat-Mongol'skoi A.S.S.R.* 2 vols. (Ulan Ude, U.S.S.R.: 1954), 1: 169.

18. All the Soviet scholars cited in this study implicitly or explicitly accept Lenin's conception of rural class differentiation as he worked it out in *The Development of Capitalism*.

19. M. S. Alferov, *Krest'ianstvo Sibiri v 1917 godu* (Novosibirsk, U.S.S.R.: 1958), p. 14; Safronov, p. 91.

20. P. Kayden and N. Antiserov, *The Russian Cooperative Movement during the War* (Stanford, California: Stanford University Press, 1929), p. 20.

21. Shornikov, *Bol'sheviki Sibiri*, p. 136.

22. M. Korndonskaia, "Sibirskoe krest'ianstvo v dni Oktiabr'skoi revoliutsii," *Proletarskaia revoliutsiia*, no. 10 (1928), p. 54.

23. Tsentralnoye Statisticheskoe Upravlenie, *Rossiia v mirovoi voine, 1914–1918gg. (v. tsifrakh)* (Moscow: 1925), p. 49.

24. Some scholars argue that the Russian army, between 1914–1918, suffered almost 8 million casualties in a total of 15 million men called up. *See*, for example, Nicholas A. Golovine, *The Russian Army in the World War* (New Haven, Connecticut: Yale University Press, 1931).

25. Safronov, p. 51; *Bor'ba za vlast' Sovietov v Buriat-Mongolii (1917–1918gg.). Sbornik dokumentov* (Ulan Ude, U.S.S.R.: 1957), p. 288.

26. D. M. Zol'nikov, *Rabochee dvizhenie v Sibiri v 1917g.* (Novosibirsk, U.S.S.R.: 1969), p. 53.

27. Ibid., p. 86.

28. V. P. Girchenko, *Etapy revoliutsionnogo dvizheniia v. Buriatii, 1917–1918gg.* (Verkhneudinsk, U.S.S.R.: 1927), p. 22.

29. Zol'nikov, p. 53.

30. Ibid., pp. 55–61.

31. Richardson L. Wright and Bassett Digby, *Through Siberia, an Empire in the Making* (New York: McBride, Nast and Co., 1913).

32. Henry G. Read, "Siberia, Its Industrial and Commercial Resources," *Cassier's Magazine* 36 (September 1909): 407.

33. For an interesting account of the early exploration of Siberia *see* Raymond H. Fisher, *The Russian Fur Trade* (Stanford, California: Stanford University Press, 1943).

34. The following material is drawn from *Aziatskaia Rossii*, 1: 45–63, passim, and *Atlas' Aziatskoi Rossii*.

35. B. Z. Shumiatskii, *Sibir' na putiakh k Oktiabriu* (Moscow: 1927), p. 36.

36. Safronov, p. 51.

37. Zol'nikov, p. 82.

38. Ibid., p. 53.

39. Safronov, p. 40.

40. Zol'nikov, p. 95.

41. *Za vlast' Sovietov. (Sbornik statei napechatannykh v gazete Krasnoiarskii rabochii k 40=letiiu Velikogo Oktiabria.)* (Krasnoiarsk, U.S.S.R.: 1958), p. 7.

42. Ibid., p. 8.

43. Ibid., p. 7.

44. Shornikov, *Bol'sheviki Sibiri*, p. 47.

45. *Rossiiskaia Kommunisticheskaia partiia (Bol'shevikov). V rezoliutsiiakh ee s'ezdov i konferentsii (1898–1921)* (Moscow: 1922).

46. So far as I know, there have been no in-depth studies of the impact of the war on Russian Social Democracy. Admittedly, the discussion here merely

attempts to touch upon the highlights and is barely adequate.

47. Irakli Tsereteli, *Vospominaniia o Fevral'skoi revoliutsii*, 2 vols. (Paris: Mouton, 1963), 1: 10. Naturally, the early formulations of the Tsereteli circle were not Zimmerwaldist, since they began to work out their views before the conference was held. Only later, when the congruence of their formulations and the declarations of the conference emerged, did the term *Siberian Zimmerwaldism* become meaningful.

48. I. Vardin, "Politicheskaia ssylka nakanune revoliutsiia," *Proletarskaia revoliutsiia*, no. 5 (1922), pp. 93–118, passim.

49. W. S. Woitinsky, *Stormy Passage* (New York: Vanguard Press, 1961), p. 225.

50. Tsereteli, 1: 8.

51. For an analysis of Siberian Zimmerwaldism *see* Rex A. Wade, *The Russian Search for Peace, February–October 1917* (Stanford, California: Stanford University Press, 1969): Wade, "Irakli Tsereteli and Siberian Zimmerwaldism," *Journal of Modern History* 39 (December 1967): 425—31.

52. V. Vel'man, "Fevral'skaia revoliutsiia v Sibiri," *Proletarskaia revoliutsiia*, no. 38 (1925), p. 174.

53. Ibid.

54. V. Ya. Gurevich, "Fevral'skaia revoliutsiia v Krasnoiarske," *Volnaia Sibir'*, no. 2 (1927) 1: 112–14.

55. *Vospominaniia o revoliutsionnom Novonikolaevske (1904–1920gg.)* (Novosibirsk, U.S.S.R.: 1959), p. 37.

56. I. N. Smirnov, "Nakanune revoliutsii, Iz istorii Sotsialist-icheskogo Voennogo Soiuza," *Byloe Sibiri*, no. 2 (1922), p. 2.

57. V. Kosarev, "Voenno-sotsialisticheskii soiuz," *Sibirskie ogni*, no. 1 (1922), pp. 65–66.

58. Shornikov, *Bol'sheviki Sibiri*, p. 12.

59. Kosarev, p. 67.

60. Ibid., p. 68.

61. Riabikov, p. 39.

62. Kosarev, p. 68.

CHAPTER 2

1. The earliest date that can be established is March 1st, when the Bublikov telegram arrived in the city. It is obvious from various memoir accounts that several telegrams were received in Siberian cities during the first week in March informing about events in Petrograd. But what they contained or who read them can not be determined but for the few exceptions cited below (note 20). There is no direct evidence, for example, that the rank and file of the garrisons knew of Army order no. 1. Yet, there was an immediate deterioration of discipline in the garrisons as soon as the news of the revolution in Pet-

rograd became known. One can deduce from this that either the knowledge of Army order no. 1 was so well known that no one bothered to comment on it, or, and this I suspect is more likely, that the disorders were spontaneous and arose out of conditions similar to those in the Petrograd garrison. The demands of the soldiers in Siberia were for an easing of discipline, politeness from the officers, full civilian rights when not on duty, and the replacement of unpopular officers. *See Krasnoiarskii Soviet, mart 1917–iiun' 1918g. (Protokely i postanovleniia s'ezdov Sovietov, plenumov, i otdelov).* Sbornik dokumentov (Krasnoiarsk, U.S.S.R.: 1960), p. 39; *Bor'ba za vlast' Sovietov v Buriat-Mongolii*, p. 27; Woitinsky, pp. 244–45.

2. The Kadets play virtually no role in the February Revolution.

3. This work will deal exclusively with the role of the Social Democrats, especially those who were or who became Bolsheviks, in the larger cities. Until the return of "Bolshevized" troops during the winter of 1917–1918, their role in the countryside was rather limited except in the mining areas and in Central Siberia where the peasantry was relatively poor.

4. Shornikov, *Bol'sheviki Sibiri*, p. 201.

5. The Provisional Government sent I. P. Laptev to Omsk, E. L. Zubashev to Tomsk and Krasnoiarsk, P. I. Preobrazhenskii to Irkutsk, and . . . Rusanov to Transbaikalia and the Far East. *See* chapter 4.

6. A Siberian Social Democrat, possibly I. L. Nakhanovich from Tomsk, attended a meeting of the Petersburg Committee on March 18th. E. M. Yaroslavskii, "Bol'sheviki v fevral'skie-martovskie dni 1917," *Proletarskaia revoliutsiia*, nos. 2–3 (1927), p. 53.

7. The first evidence of a connection between Siberian Bolsheviks and the Central Committee was an April 10th meeting of the Central Committee that took up a dispute among the Krasnoiarsk Bolsheviks. *See* chapter 5.

8. A. F. Ivanov (1881–1918), Bolshevik. Member of the R.S.D.R.P. since 1903. Head of city consumer cooperative. After October revolution was Commissar of Tomsk Militia; Chairman of the City Supply Administration. Shot by Whites in 1918. (Zol'nikov, p. 328.)

9. A. V. Shotman (Danilov), Bolshevik. Left Tomsk in May 1917.

10. B. M. Gan. Nonparty Social Democratic sympathizer. He became a Bolshevik after the October revolution.

11. He has been identified as a Menshevik defensist.

12. *Bor'ba za vlast' Sovietov v Tomskoi gubernii (1917–1919gg). Sbornik dokumental'nykh materialov* (Tomsk, U.S.S.R.: 1957), p. 5.

13. Ibid., pp. 6–7.

14. A. Shotman, "Fevral'skaia revoliutsiia v Tomske," *Proletarskaia revoliutsiia*, nos. 61–62 (1927), p. 262.

15. One of these was N. N. Yakovlev (1886–1918), Bolshevik. Member of the R.S.D.R.P. since 1905. Leading Bolshevik in Western and Central Siberia. Appointed agent of the Central Committee late in 1917. Became Chairman of Centrosibir', the highest level Soviet governmental organ in Siberia after the October revolution. Killed by the Whites, September 1918. *See* V. V. Riabikov.

16. Shotman, pp. 263–64.

17. B. M. Gan, "Fevral'skaia revoliutsiia v Tomskoi gubernii," *Severnaia Aziia*, no. 13 (1927), p. 14.

18. *See* chapter 4.

19. Shotman, p. 263.

20. *Vospominaniia o revoliutsionnom Novonikolaevske*, p. 43.

21. N. I. Teterin, "Novonikolaevsk v Fevral'skuiu revoliutsiiu," *Severnaia Aziia*, no. 13 (1927), p. 25.

22. Ibid., p. 26.

23. V. Nikolaev, "Fevral'skaia revoliutsiia na Altae," *Severnia Aziia*, no. 13 (1927), p. 30.

24. *Bol'sheviki Zapadnoi Sibiri v bor'be za Sotsialisticheskuiu revoliutsiiu (Mart 1917–mai 1918)*. *Sbornik dokumentov i materialov*. (Novosibirsk, U.S.S.R., 1957), p. 26.

25. *Omskie Bol'sheviki v period Oktiabr'skoi revoliutsii i uprocheniia Sovietskoi vlasti (Mart 1917g.–mai 1918g.)*. *Sbornik dokumental'nykh materialov* (Omsk, U.S.S.R.: 1958), p. 8.

26. Ibid., p. 33.

27. For example, *see* V. A. Solov'ieva, "Vozniknovenie i pervye mesiatsy dvoevlastiia v Sibiri (mart–aprel' 1917g.)," in *Sibir' period kapitalizma*. *Ekonomicheskoe i obshchestvenno-politicheskoe razvitie Sibiri v 1861–1917g.* (Novosibirsk, U.S.S.R.: 1968).

28. Gurevich, p. 115.

29. A. A. Baikalov. Menshevik defensist. Active in Krasnoiarsk since 1905.

30. Gurevich, p. 115.

31. M. I. Frumkin, "Fevral'–Oktiabr' 1917g. v Krasnoiarske," *Proletarskaia revoliutsiia*, no. 9 (1923), p. 140.

32. Gurevich, p. 118.

33. A. G. Shlikhter (1868–1940). Bolshevik. Member of the R.S.D.R.P. since 1897. Left Siberia in June. Became a member of Sovnarkom. Ambassador to Austria.

34. Frumkin, p. 140.

35. *Za vlast' Sovietov*, pp. 22–23.

36. Gurevich, p. 117.

37. *Velikaia Oktiabr'skaia sotsialisticheskaia revoliutsiia, Khronika sobytii*, 4 vols. (Moscow: 1957), *Fevralia–6 May 1917 goda*, 1: 68.

38. *Velikaia Oktiabr'skaia sotsialisticheskaia revoliutsiia, dokumenty i materialov*. *Revoliutsionnoe dvizhenie v Rossii v Aprele 1917 g., Aprel'skii krizis* (Moscow, 1958), p. 250.

39. P. Akimov, "Fevral'skii perevorot v Irkutske," *Katorga i ssylka*, no. 3 (1927), p. 155.

40. Ia. Papernikov, "Fevral'skaia revoliutsiia v Irkutske," *Katorga i ssylka*, no. 1 (1927), p. 94.

41. V. G. Arkhangel'skii, "Pervyi mesiats fevral'skoi revoliutsii 1917g. Irkutske," *Volnaia Sibir'*, no. 2 (1927), pp. 47–48.

42. Ibid., p. 49.

43. Woitinsky, p. 244; Papernikov, p. 95.

44. Arkhangel'skii, p. 50.

45. Ibid.

46. Tsereteli, 1: 18.

47. According to Papernikov, p. 93, there were about 2,000 exiles living legally and semilegally in and around Irkutsk at the time.

48. See Russell E. Snow, "The Russian Revolution in Transbaikalia, 1917–1918," Soviet Studies 23 (October 1971): 201–215; James Morely, "The Russian Revolution in the Amur Basin," Slavic Review 16 (December 1957): 450–61.

49. See V. N. Sokolov, "Fevral'skii perevorot' v Chita," Severnaia Aziia, no. 1 (1927), pp. 36–41.

50. These committees, as yet, did not control the gubernia administrative apparatus, nor did they have much influence, if any, over the country as far as we can tell. On the other hand, we simply do not know the extent to which peasants looked to the citizens' committees in the uezd centers for guidance.

51. Tsereteli, 1: 18–19.

52. I. N. Smirnov, "Fevral'skaia revoliutsiia v Tomske," Severnaia Aziia, no. 13 (1927), p. 8.

53. Bor'ba za vlast' Sovietov v Tomskoi gubernii, p. 10.

54. Ibid., p. 17.

55. Ibid., pp. 14–15.

56. Ibid., p. 23.

57. Ibid., p. 25.

58. Bol'sheviki Zapadnoi Sibiri, p. 36.

59. M. M. Shornikov, Bol'sheviki Novonikolaevska v period podgotovki i provedeniia Oktiabr'skoi revoliutsii (Novosibirsk, U.S.S.R.: 1963), p. 9.

60. Omskie Bol'sheviki, p. 8.

61. Bol'sheviki Zapadnoi Sibiri, p. 26.

62. Omskie Bol'sheviki, p. 36.

63. Almost every city soviet in Siberia sent telegrams of greetings and pledges of support to the Petrograd Soviet.

64. In other words, the soviets adopted a general policy reflecting the aims of the minimum program of the R.S.D.R.P., as we shall see in chapter 4. They also adopted the S.R. land program, which the Bolsheviks advocated in one form or another.

65. B. Z. Shumiatskii (1886–1943). Bolshevik. Joined the R.S.D.R.P. in 1903. Active in the revolution of 1905 in Krasnoiarsk; worked later in Chita. Appointed agent of the Central Committee in Siberia on April 14th. First chairman of Tsentrosibir', but was replaced by N. N. Yakovlev. (Zol'nikov, p. 332.)

66. V. M. Klipov (b. 1885). Member of the Tomsk Military-Socialist Union. Was in Krasnoiarsk at the time of the February revolution. Bolshevik. Member of the R.S.D.R.P. since 1906. Became Chairman of the workers' section of the Tomsk Soviet of Workers and Soldiers after they joined. (Zol'nikov, p. 328.)

67. Gurevich, p. 117.

68. Ya. F. Dubrovinskii (1882–1918). Menshevik internationalist. Became a

Bolshevik in June 1917. Chairman of Krasnoiarsk Soviet from its inception until his death in October 1918. Killed by the Whites.

69. A. I. Okulov (1880–1918). Bolshevik. Joined the R.S.D.R.P. in 1904. Born in Eniseisk gubernia. Member of the Executive Committee of the Eniseisk Gubernia Soviet. Killed by the Whites in 1918.

70. A. G. Rogov (1886–1957?). Bolshevik. Joined the R.S.D.R.P. in 1903. Native of Krasnoiarsk. Railroad worker. Head of the union of Tomsk railroad workers. Member of the Siberian regional bureau of the R.S.D.R.P.(b) in July 1917.

71. I. I. Belopol'skii (1884–1918). Bolshevik. Worker exile. President of the Krasnoiarsk Central Bureau of Professional Unions. Member of *Tsentrosibir'*. Killed by the Whites in 1918.

72. M. K. Frumkin. Bolshevik. Obviously a leading Bolshevik in Krasnoiarsk. Most likely a Kamenev supporter. Soviet scholars have just about obliterated his contribution to the revolution in Krasnoiarsk from the public record.

73. *Krasnoiarskii Soviet*, pp. 35–37.

74. Gurevich, p. 127.

75. The presidium of the Executive Committee included T. P. Markovskii and Shumiatskii as vice-chairmen, and two Socialist Revolutionaries and a Menshevik, M. K. Ivanov, as secretaries.

76. Gurevich, p. 132.

77. In Irkutsk, the Menshevik L. Goldman was elected Chairman of the Executive Committee, a post that he held until the October revolution. Unfortunately, I do not know who was the Chairman of the Chita Soviet Executive Committee.

78. V. M. Serov (1878–1918). Bolshevik. Joined the party in 1902. Delegate to the 1905 London Conference. Member of the Second State Duma. Killed by the Whites in 1918.

79. Girchenko, p. 26.

80. Sokolov, "Fevral'skii," p. 37.

81. Shornikov, *Bol'sheviki Sibiri*, p. 61.

82. This entire section is essentially a summary of Zol'nikov, pp. 151–67. His is the most thorough treatment of the subject available.

83. This section attempts to provide no more than a brief glimpse of the Social Democratic party as it emerged from the underground. Chapter 4 will provide an in-depth treatment of the party's growth and development between March and June with an emphasis upon the Bolsheviks and the issue of party unity.

84. A. Petrenko, "Fevral'skaia revoliutsiia v Tomske," *Proletarskaia revoliutsiia*, no. 49 (1926), p. 93.

85. Teterin, p. 27.

86. Nikolaev, p. 30.

87. Frumkin, p. 141.

88. Gurevich, p. 116.

89. *Za vlast' Sovietov*, p. 23.

90. Ibid., p. 10.
91. Shumiatskii, pp. 4–6.
92. Ibid., p. 7.
93. The role of the Siberian Pravdists in unifying the Bolsheviks in Siberia during 1917 is a major historiographical controversy in the Soviet Union. Shornikov makes the strongest case for the view that they were instrumental, but the evidence he presents fails to sustain it. The present work demonstrates that the Pravdists were largely ignored by the majority of Bolsheviks in Siberia and that although the Central Committee recognized the efforts of the Pravdists, it tacitly recognized that its own policies on party unification could not be applied to Siberia.
94. Shornikov, Bol'sheviki Sibiri, p. 571.
95. Frumkin, p. 155.
96. Vel'man, p. 193.
97. Sokolov, "Fevral'skii," p. 37.
98. This is exactly what happened in Irkutsk. Most of the new members joining the party were relatively prewar and quite moderate on social and economic issues. This greatly strengthened the defensist position within the united organization. Vel'man, p. 193.

CHAPTER 3

1. Western Siberia, which included Tomsk and Altirsk gubernias; Central Siberia, which includes Eniseisk and the westernmost part of Irkutsk gubernia; and Eastern Siberia, which included Irkutsk gubernia and Transbaikal territory.
2. A significant exception was Krasnoiarsk.
3. The fact that the Provisional Government was built upon the Tsarist governmental edifice accounted for much of its unpopularity in Siberia.
4. M. A. Gudoshnikov, Ocherki po grazhdanskoi voine v Sibiri (Irkutsk, U.S.S.R.: 1959), p. 6; and A. G. Lipkina, 1919 god v Sibiri (Leningrad: 1962), p. 16.
5. Zemstva were introduced in Siberia during the summer of 1917.
6. Robert P. Browder, ed., The Russian Provisional Government, 3 vols. (Stanford, California: Stanford University Press, 1961), 1: 242.
7. Frumkin, p. 140.
8. E. L. Zubashev, "Moia kommandirovka v Sibir," Volnaia Sibir', no. 2 (1927), p. 95.
9. Browder, 1: 243.
10. Vel'man, p. 191.
11. Ibid., p. 192.
12. Girchenko, p. 4.
13. Ibid., p. 5.

14. Ibid., p. 4.
15. Ibid., p. 8.
16. *Bor'ba za vlast' Sovietov v Buriat-Mongolii*, p. 288; A Buiko, "Rabota V. M. Serov v Pribaikal'e," in *Dal'istpart. R.K.P. Sbornik po istoriia revoliutsionnogo dvizhenie na Dal'nem Vostoke*, 3 vols. (Chita-Vladivostok, U.S.S.R.: 1923), 1: 10; *Istoria Buriat-Mongol'skoi A.S.S.R.*, 1: 44–45; Girchenko, p. 5.
17. Vel'man, p. 198.
18. V. V. Maksakov and A. Turnnov, eds., *Khronika grazhkonski voiny v Sibiri 1917–1918* (Moscow-Leningrad, 1966), p. 30.
19. Vel'man, p. 198.
20. *Velikaia. . . . Revoliutsionnoe dvizhenie v Rossii v Aprele 1917g.*, p. 859.
21. Vel'man, p. 198.
22. Shornikov, *Bol'sheviki Sibiri*, pp. 24–26.
23. R. B. Batuev, "K voprosu o politike Verkhneudinskogo Sovieta v period podgotovki i provedeniia Oktiabr'skoi revoliutsii," in *Iz istorii partiinoi organizatsii Buriatii* (Ulan Ude, U.S.S.R.: 1961), pp. 8–9.
24. A. Bonch-Osmolovskii, "Vneshnia torgovlia Dal'nego Vostok za vremia voiny i revoliutsii," *Novyi Vostok*, no. 5 (1924), p. 158.
25. Ibid., p. 157.
26. T. Hoshino, *Economic History of Manchuria* (Seoul: n.p., 1920), pp. 216–18.
27. I. A. Yakushev, "Fevral'skaia revoliutsiia i sibirskie oblastnye s'ezdy," *Volnaia Sibir'*, no. 2 (1927), p. 15.
28. Gan, p. 19.
29. Petrenko, p. 97.
30. Gan, p. 20.
31. Ibid., p. 21.
32. Zubashev, p. 101.
33. Ibid., p. 110.
34. Ibid., p. 108.
35. Shornikov, *Bol'sheviki Novonikolaevska*, p. 32.
36. This was especially the case in Tomsk, Omsk, and Irkutsk.
37. *Bor'ba za vlast' Sovietov v Tomskoi gubernii*, p. 49.
38. Yakushev, p. 20.
39. *Omskie Bol'sheviki*, p. 36.
40. Ibid., p. 234.
41. Ibid., p. 236.
42. Ibid., p. 235.
43. Ibid., p. 238.
44. *Krasnoiarsk Soviet*, p. 49.
45. Ibid., p. 50.
46. Ibid., pp. 51–59.
47. Ibid., p. 49.
48. Ibid., p. 50.
49. Ibid., pp. 51–59.
50. Ibid., pp. 77–80; 85–86; 105–107; 113–14.

51. Ibid., pp. 102–104.
52. Ibid., p. 84.
53. *Velikaia. . . . Revoliutsionnoe dvizhenie v Rossii v Aprele 1917g.*, p. 250.
54. *Pravda*, 28 April 1917.
55. *Velikaia. . . . Revoliutsionnoe dvizhenie v Rossii v Aprele 1917g.*, p. 281
56. *Krasnoiarskii Soviet*, p. 96.
57. *Velikaia. . . . Revoliutsionnoe dvizhenie v Rossii v Aprele 1917g.*, p. 449.
58. *Krasnoiarskii Soviet*, pp. 115–16.
59. Ibid., p. 126.
60. Shornikov, *Bol'sheviki Sibiri*, p. 73.

CHAPTER 4

1. See J. L. H. Keep, *The Rise of Russian Social Democracy* (Oxford: Oxford University Press, 1963).
2. Yaroslavskii, p. 52.
3. Ibid., p. 53.
4. *Velikaia Oktiabr'skaia sotsialisticheskaia revoliutsiia. Kokumenty i materialov. Revoliutsionnoe dvizhenie v Rossii posle sverzheniia samoderzhaviia* (Moscow: 1957), pp. 156–57.
5. Yaroslavskii, pp. 53–54.
6. *Pravda*, 28 March 1917.
7. Ibid., 8 April 1917.
8. Ibid., 2 May 1917.
9. Ibid., 18 May 1917.
10. Daniels, *The Conscience of Revolution*, p. 29.
11. *Bol'sheviki Zapadnoi Sibiri*, p. 24.
12. This is discussed below.
13. Vel'man, pp. 193–94.
14. Ibid., p. 199; *Velikaia. . . . Khronika sobytii*, 2: 628.
15. P. Okuntsov, "1917–1918gg. v g. Nerchinske i ego uezde," in *Dal'istpart*, 1: 121.
16. Girchenko, p. 5.
17. Ibid., p. 18; Okuntsov, *Dal'istpart*, 1: 122.
18. Batuev, *Iz istorii*, p. 18.
19. Ibid.
20. Frumkin, p. 142.
21. Gurevich, p. 118.
22. Shumiatskii, pp. 5–6.
23. Ibid., p. 7.
24. Ibid., p. 8.
25. Maksakov and Turunov, p. 32.
26. See *Velikaia. . . . Khronika sobytii*, 1: 168.
27. Ibid., p. 179.

28. Ibid., p. 210.

29. Shumiatskii, p. 18.

30. *Velikaia. . . . Khronika sobytii*, 1: 253.

31. In most of the communications of the Central Committee to the local organizations in Siberia during the autumn, the primary concern was the forthcoming elections to the Constituent Assembly. *See Perepiska Sekretariata TsK RSDRP(b) s mestynymi partiinymi organizatsiiami (mart–oktiabr' 1917g.). Sbornik dokumentov* (Moscow: 1957), p. 18.

32. M. M. Shornikov, *God semnadtsatyi, Bol'sheviki Sibiri v bor'be za pobedu Oktabr'skoi sotsialisticheskoi revoliutsii* (Novosibirsk, U.S.S.R.: 1967), p. 18.

33. *Velikaia. . . . Khronika sobytii*, 1: 423.

34. B. B. Anikeev, ed., *Deiatel'nost' TsK RSDRP(b) v 1917 godu* (Moscow: 1969), p. 66.

35. Ibid., p. 67.

36. *Velikaia. . . . Khronika sobytii*, 1: 431; *Bol'sheviki Zapadnoi Sibiri*, pp. 28–35.

37. Cited in *Velikaia. . . . Revoliutsionnoe dvizhenie v Rossii v Aprele 1917g.*, p. 92.

38. Ibid., pp. 120–121.

39. *Bol'sheviki Zapadnoi Sibiri*, p. 46.

40. Maksakov and Turunov, p. 36.

41. *Velikaia. . . . Khronika sobytii*, 2: 157.

42. Ibid., p. 194.

43. Maksakov and Turunov, p. 36.

44. According to Shornikov, *Bol'sheviki Sibiri*, pp. 566–78, membership of the united organizations in Western and Central Siberia were as follows: Omsk—350 in March, 1,650 in June; Tomsk—200 in April, 540 in June; Krasnoiarsk—2,500 in June; Novonikolaevsk—300 in April, 400 in June.

45. *Omskie Bol'sheviki*, p. 34.

46. Ibid., p. 234.

47. Ibid., p. 38.

48. *Velikaia. . . . Khronika sobytii*, 1: 493.

49. *Perepiska Sekretariata TsK . . . (mart–oktiabr' 1917g.)*, p. 108.

50. *Omski Bol'sheviki*, p. 49.

51. *Bor'ba za vlast' Sovietov v Tomskoi gubernii*, p. 33.

52. Shornikov, *Bol'sheviki Sibiri*, p. 227.

53. *Bor'ba za vlast' Sovietov v Tomskoi gubernii*, p. 30.

54. Shornikov, *Bol'sheviki Novonikolaevska*, p. 27.

55. Maksakov and Turunov, p. 46.

56. Shornikov, *Bol'sheviki Sibiri*, p. 178.

57. Ibid., p. 176.

58. *Bor'ba za vlast' Sovietov v Tomskoi gubernii*, pp. 53–55.

CHAPTER 5

1. This can only be inferred from N. N. Yakovlev's letter to Sverdlov, dated 20 October 1917 (*see Perepiska Sekretariatia TsK . . . (mart–oktiabr' 1917g.)*,

p. 391 and from the fact that the Bolsheviks in Omsk, Irkutsk, and Verkh-neudinsk all left the united organizations at the same time—right before the October coup d'etat.

2. This complex period of party history between Lenin's return to Petrograd on April 4th and the Seventh All-Russian Bolshevik Party conference has yet to be studied by non-Soviet scholars.

3. Daniels, *Conscience of the Revolution*, p. 41.

4. Ibid.

5. Sverdlov is the key figure connecting the local party organizations with the center. All information went through him. As one who was most closely in tune with Lenin's thinking, his influence over the local organizations was almost synonymous with Lenin's. He could easily provide a Leninist interpretation of party life in Petrograd for the provincial organizations.

6. Martov had been deeply scarred by the split of the Social Democrats in 1903, especially by the unscrupulous tactics of Lenin, and the history of the party between 1903 and 1917 could hardly have given him encouragement. If Lenin was to have any chance at all of attracting him into a unified party of internationalists, he would have to be very careful to avoid appearing to use the party splitting tactics and habits of the underground days. Yet, Lenin was bound and determined to rid the united party of all traces of defensism and Zimmerwaldism.

7. Shumiatskii, p. 34.

8. Shornikov, *Bol'sheviki Sibiri*, p. 223.

9. According to Shumiatskii, p. 34, Lenin was quite anxious for the Bolsheviks to gain influence in Irkutsk where he knew that the Mensheviks and Socialist Revolutionaries were strong.

10. Anikeev, pp. 101–102.

11. *Omskie Bol'sheviki*, p. 53.

12. Shornikov, *Bol'sheviki Sibiri*, p. 243.

13. *Vospominaniia o revoliutsionnom v Novonikolaevske*, p. 48.

14. "On May 10th, the Bolsheviks and Mezhraiontsy [Interdistrictites] met to discuss unification. . . . Lenin gave the Mezhraiontsy an unconditional invitation to join the Bolshevik party. . . . Certain tactical considerations, as well as the old organizational discords, contributed to the delay of the merger. Both Lenin and the Mezhraiontsy hoped that, if they proceeded slowly, all internationalist Mensheviks, particularly Martov and his following, could be brought into the Bolshevik camp." (Daniels, *Conscience of the Revolution*, p. 48.)

15. Shornikov, *Bol'sheviki Sibiri*, p. 226.

16. Maksakov and Turunov, p. 36.

17. Shornikov, *Bol'sheviki Sibiri*, p. 230.

18. *Bol'sheviki Zapadnoi Sibiri*, pp. 59–60.

19. Shornikov, *Bol'sheviki Sibiri*, pp. 234–235.

20. According to Safronov, p. 181, this is exactly what would have happened. Both Dubrovinskii and Weinbaum, leaders of the Menshevik internationalists, called for the retention of the united organization. They were, however, highly critical of the Menshevik defensists.

21. Shornikov, *Bol'sheviki Sibiri*, p. 236.
22. Shornikov, *God semnadtsatyi*, p. 49.
23. Frumkin, p. 155.
24. Shornikov, *God semnadtsatyi*, p. 49.
25. *Velikaia. . . . Khroniki sobytii*, 2: 227.
26. Shornikov, *Bol'sheviki Sibiri*, p. 237.
27. Ibid., p. 238.
28. Shornikov, *God semnadtsatyi*, p. 95.
29. This does not mean that the tactics of the Pravdists necessarily had the sanction of the Central Committee. It simply meant the more radical the revolutionary leaders in Krasnoiarsk, the more responsive were the workers and soldiers. It was a vindication of the Leninist point of view.
30. *Velikaia. . . . Khronika sobytii*, 2: 398.
31. Shornikov, *God semnadtsatyi*, p. 59.
32. Shornikov, *Bol'sheviki Sibiri*, pp. 242–43.
33. Riabikov, p. 46.
34. *Bol'sheviki Zapadnoi Sibiri*, p. 75.
35. Ibid., p. 88.
36. Shornikov, *Bol'sheviki Novonikolaevska*, pp. 20–24.
37. *Omskie Bol'sheviki*, p. 53.
38. Ibid., p. 55.
39. N. Sukhanov, *The Russian Revolution 1917, A Personal Record*, ed. and trans. Joel Carmichael (London: Oxford University Press, 1955), p. 487.
40. Although the Socialist Revolutionaries had not yet split formally, the left wing of the party was already called *Left-Socialist Revolutionary*.
41. *Bor'ba za vlast' Sovietov v Tomskoi gubernii*, p. 74.
42. Shornikov, *Bol'sheviki Sibiri*, pp. 302–24. Significant exceptions were the garrisons at Irkutsk and Novonikolaevsk, which were controlled by the Socialist Revolutionaries. But neither garrison was predisposed to fight for anybody or any cause. In Irkutsk, the anarchists were busy within the garrison, but they, of course, were not much interested in organizing the garrison, since they believed in spontaneous actions.
43. Shornikov, *Bol'sheviki Novonikolaevska*, p. 45.
44. Shornikov, *Bol'sheviki Sibiri*, p. 343.
45. *Bor'ba za vlast' Sovietov v Tomskoi gubernii*, p. 91.
46. This question has been thoroughly investigated by Alexander Rabinovich. He concludes that the Bolsheviks did not plan the uprising nor did they have a plan to take power at the time. Their main problem was to decide whether or not to place themselves at the head of the movement. This they did, and in the bargain, earned for themselves the accusation by the moderate socialists that they had planned the whole affair. Yet, the way in which the party began to mobilize its forces in Siberia during June raises the faint suspicion that they might have been planning some kind of action. No doubt further study of the party in the provincial centers might cast light on the question.
47. *Velikaia Oktiabr'skaia sotsialisticheskaia revoliutsiia. Dokumenty i materialov.*

Revoliutsionnoe dvizhenie v Rossii v iiule 1917g. (Moscow: 1959), pp. 192–98. These protocols are heavily edited to give the impression that the Siberian Pravdists played an all-important role at the conference.

48. Ibid., p. 194.

49. Ibid., p. 559.

50. *Bor'ba za vlast' Sovietov v Tomskoi gubernii*, pp. 89–90.

51. Ibid., p. 90.

52. *Shestoi s'ezd RSDRP (Bol'shevikov) August 1917 goda. Protokoly* (Moscow: 1958), p. 81.

53. *Velikaia Oktiabr'skaia sotsialisticheskaia revoliutsiia. Dokumenty i materialov. Revoliutsionnoe dvizhenie v Rossii v Avguste 1917g. Razgrom Kornilovskogo miatezha* (Moscow: 1959), p. 14.

54. See *Rossiiskaia Kommunisticheskaia partiia (Bol'shevikov). V resoliutsiiakh ee s'ezdov: Konferentsii (1899–1921)* (Moscow: 1922), pp. 202–205. This is quite remarkable since the resolutions of the Sixth Congress did not become known in Siberia until mid-August.

55. *Bol'sheviki Zapadnoi Sibiri*, pp. 127–28.

56. *Shestoi s'ezd*, p. 292. According to statute 7, "Members of the party are all those who recognize the party program, who go into one of its organizations, and who support all of its declarations and who pay dues. New members will join a local party organization on the recommendation of two members and will be confirmed at the next general meeting." *Rossiiskaia Kommunisticheskaia partiia*, p. 197.

57. *Bor'ba za vlast' Sovietov v Tomskoi gubernii*, pp. 114–20; Maksakov and Turunov, p. 44.

58. Shornikov, *Bol'sheviki Sibiri*, p. 427.

59. *Velikaia. . . . Khronika sobytii* 3: 386.

60. *Bol'sheviki Zapadnoi Sibiri*, pp. 139–43.

61. *Perepiska Sekretariata TsK . . . (mart–oktiabr' 1917g.)*, pp. 215–16.

62. *Bor'ba za vlast' Sovietov v Tomskoi gubernii*, p. 108.

63. *Bor'ba za vlast' Sovietov v Buriat-Mongolii*, p. 125.

64. *Bol'sheviki Zapadnoi Sibiri*, p. 156.

65. Maksakov and Turunov, p. 51.

66. James T. Bunyan and H. H. Fisher, *The Bolshevik Revolution, 1917–1918, Documents and Materials* (Stanford, California: Stanford University Press, 1934), p. 27.

67. Maksakov and Turunov, p. 46.

68. Shornikov, *Bol'sheviki Sibiri*, p. 459.

69. *Istoriia Sibiri*, 4: 43.

70. Shornikov, *Bol'sheviki Sibiri*, p. 482.

71. According to Shornikov, *Bol'sheviki Sibiri*, pp. 566–89, the Bolsheviks had about 8,000 party members in Siberia on the eve of the October revolution. Over 2,500, however, were in Krasnoiarsk alone. Another 1,000 were concentrated in the mining districts of Anzhersk and Sudzhensk. In Omsk, there were not more than 250, in Tomsk 500, in Novonikoalevsk 400, in Barnaul 50-100, and about 30 in Irkutsk. The Bolsheviks in Transbaikalia did not

split with the Menshevik internationalists until after the October revolution.

72. A. Abov, "Oktiabr' v Vostochnoi Sibiri (*Otryvki iz vospominanii*)," *Sibirskie ogni*, no. 4 (September–October 1924), p. 115. Abov, who attended the congress, reports that the minutes of the congress were burned during the eight-day battle for Irkutsk in December.

73. Ibid., p. 117.

CHAPTER 6

1. Transbaikalia was the last region in Siberia to come under Bolshevik control in mid-February 1918.

2. *Dekrety Sovietskoi vlasti*, 3 vols. (Moscow: 1963), 1: 24.

3. On October 27th, the Left Socialist Revolutionaries issued the following statement: "The resolution on the press just passed by the majority of the Central Committee is a clear and sharp expression of the system of political terror and a kindling of civil war. The Socialist Revolutionaries who remain in the Central Executive Committee . . . to protect the interests of the workers and the peasants . . . refuse to assume responsibility for the baneful system of terror and recall their representatives from the Military Revolutionary Committee, the Staff, and other responsible posts." Bunyan and Fisher, p. 203.

4. Ibid., p. 230.

5. The Bolshevik dictatorship in Russia was established on November 7th when the Central Executive Committee of the Second Congress of Soviets gave Sovnarkom the right to rule by decree. The vote was 29 to 23. Robert V. Daniels, *Red October* (New York: Charles Scribner's Sons, 1967), p. 212.

6. The fact that the Soviet sources for Siberia eliminate almost all party materials for October, November, and December from the documentary collections makes it necessary to reconstruct the plan ex post facto. It is quite possible that the Leninist Bolsheviks faced significant opposition from the (right-wing) Bolsheviks and had to adjust their tactics and strategy accordingly. Without documentation the best one can do on these crucial points is to make educated guesses.

7. Shornikov, *Bol'sheviki Sibiri*, p. 482.

8. Interestingly, Soviet sources provide no documents for these instructions. While this might suggest to some that no instructions may have been given, it seems more plausible to assume that they were given and that their contents, if revealed, would undermine the central thesis of Soviet historians of the "triumphal march of soviet power, under the guiding hand of the Bolsheviks and the Central Committee." *See*, for example, *Triumfal'noe shestvie sovietskoi vlasti*, 2 vols. (Moscow: 1963).

9. The fact that the Omsk and Tomsk soviets took power on December 6th, Barnaul on December 7th, Irkutsk on December 8th, and Novonikolaevsk on the 13th, could not have been coincidence. Nor could the fact that the uprisings took place while the Third Western Siberian Congress

of (Workers' and Soldiers') Soviets was meeting in Omsk. There is no evidence that the Bolsheviks in both the Tomsk and Barnaul soviets pushed very hard to get them to take power in October. Obviously, they were waiting until they gained control of the Omsk and Irkutsk soviets. The decision to move in December may have had something to do with the fact that the Socialist Revolutionaries and Mensheviks were moving to create an anti-Bolshevik soviet government in Tomsk at the Extraordinary Congress of Siberian Delegates, which created a Siberian Soviet and a Siberian Duma.

10. *Krasnoiarskii Soviet*, p. 228.

11. Ibid., p. 229.

12. Ibid., p. 233.

13. Ibid., pp. 232, 234.

14. Ibid., p. 233.

15. *Za vlast' Sovietov*, p. 235.

16. Shornikov, *Bol'sheviki Sibiri*, p. 489.

17. Fear of pogroms is a prevalent theme in much of the literature of this period. Anti-Semitism had been quite virulent in Siberia during the war and the Black Hundreds in 1917 did not fail to make the connection between the Bolsheviks and the Jews.

18. *Bor'ba za vlast' Sovietov v Tomskoi gubernii*, p. 158.

19. Shornikov, *Bol'sheviki Sibiri*, p. 492 dates the formation of the committee as November 4th, but this is a mistake. November 4th appears to have been the date that the Provisional Committee took over the gubernia administration.

20. In all of Siberia, except Krasnoiarsk, the Socialist Revolutionaries had not yet split. The organization as a whole seems to have been somewhat more to the left than the Socialist Revolutionaries in Irkutsk or Novonikolaevsk.

21. Shornikov, *Bol'sheviki Sibiri*, p. 495.

22. *Bor'ba za vlast' Sovietov v Tomskoi gubernii*, p. 162.

23. *Perepiska Sekretariata TsK . . .* (noiabr' 1917g.–fevral' 1918g.), p. 336. The Central Committee also dispatched a number of sailors to help the party in Omsk, but they were not very effective because they were poorly led.

24. *Bor'ba za vlast' Sovietov v Tomskoi gubernii*, p. 163.

25. Ibid., p. 165.

26. Ibid., p. 166.

27. Until November 15th, the Left-Socialist Revolutionaries in Petrograd refused to go into the new government. This, undoubtedly, had an impact in Siberia, where the Bolsheviks were allied with them and the Menshevik-internationalists. Together, the Menshevik-internationalists and the Left-Socialist Revolutionaries were strong enough to prevent the Bolsheviks from seizing power in many Siberian cities. After November 15th, the Bolsheviks and the Left-Socialist Revolutionaries were powerful enough to control all of the urban soviets and all of the regional congresses.

28. Riabikov, p. 67.

29. The poor showing in the gubernia, and in rural Russia generally, forced the Siberian Bolsheviks to take a new tack. Now they began to express

the need for reelections to the Constituent Assembly because the peasants did not know from the election lists whether they were voting for Right- or Left-Socialist Revolutionaries. This, of course, was the Leninist line on the Constituent Assembly in November.

They were also disturbed by the showing of the regionalists. Unfortunately, the question of Siberian regionalism has yet to be adequately investigated. By the autumn of 1917, it had grown substantially in Tomsk, Irkutsk, and in Transbaikalia, and during the winter it became a focal point of anti-Soviet opposition. See V. Vegman, "Oblastnicheskie illiuzii rasseianye revoliutsiei," *Sibirskie ogni*, no. 3 (May–June 1923), pp. 89–113; G. V. Krusser, *Sibirskie oblastiniki. (Ot 1864 g. do epokhi Kolchaka).* (Novovibirsk, U.S.S.R.: 1931).

30. *Bor'ba za vlast' Sovietov v Tomskoi gubernii*, p. 168.
31. Riabikov, p. 68.
32. Vegman, p. 94.
33. *Bolsheviki Zapadnoi Sibiri*, p. 207.
34. *Bor'ba za vlast' Sovietov v Tomskoi gubernii*, p. 171.
35. Ibid., p. 168.
36. *Bol'sheviki Zapadnoi Sibiri*, p. 178.
37. Shornikov, *Bol'sheviki Sibiri*, p. 492, claims that the Committee was also created on the initiative of the Bolsheviks. Again, he is mistaken on the date, which he pinpoints as November 4th.
38. *Bol'sheviki Zapadnoi Sibiri*, p. 179.
39. Maksakov and Turunov, p. 48.
40. *Omskie Bol'sheviki*, p. 83.
41. The Bolsheviks gained a majority in the soviet in the elections of November 16th, 17th, and 18th. Unfortunately, it is not possible, from the available sources, to determine why it took so long to reelect the Executive Committee.
42. These included V. Kosarev, A. A. Zvezdov, and Klipov. Zvezdov was a member of the Central Executive Committee of the Second All-Russian Congress of Soviets. All three had been in the Military-Socialist Union with N. N. Yakovlev, who was then agent of the Central Committee for Western Siberia. Riabikov, p. 69.
43. *Omskie Bol'sheviki*, pp. 84–85.
44. Shornikov, *Bol'sheviki Sibiri*, p. 490.
45. *Omskie Bol'sheviki*, p. 93.
46. *Perepiska Sekretariata TsK . . . (noiabr' 1917g.–fevral' 1918g.)*, p. 337.
47. *Omskie Bol'sheviki*, p. 87.
48. Ibid., p. 86.
49. Ibid., pp. 96–97. The Bolsheviks received nine seats on the executive committee, the Menshevik-internationalists received three, the Left-Socialist Revolutionaries two.
50. N. A. Avilov was the Commissar of Posts and Telegraph in the Soviet government. He was sent to Siberia to help organize soviet government. A number of emissaries were sent from Petrograd to the provinces with specific instructions of Sovnarkom "to call meetings of gubernia soviet executive

committees to report on the new land law and to stimulate the calling of uezd and gubernia soviet congresses." *Dekrety Sovietskoi Vlasti*, 1: 41.

51. Riabikov, p. 69.

52. See *Bor'ba za vlast Sovietov v Tomskoi gubernii*, p. 179; Shornikov, *Bol'sheviki Sibiri*, p. 497 ff.; Riabikov, pp. 69–70.

53. *Bol'sheviki Zapadnoi Sibiri*, p. 100.

54. See Oliver K. Radkey, *The Sickle Under the Hammer; The Socialist Revolutionaries in the Early Months of Soviet Rule* (New York: Columbia University Press, 1963).

55. *Bol'sheviki Zapadnoi Sibiri*, p. 100.

56. Riabikov, p. 70.

57. *Omski Bol'sheviki*, p. 100.

58. At the end of September, instigated by the Anarchists, "regiments of sharpshooters led by agitators removed the rifles from the arsenal and refused to obey their commanders. The Army Commander, Lieutenant Krakovetsky, . . . was placed under arrest . . . a detachment which remained loyal to the revolution succeeded in rescuing the commander. . . . The rebels were disarmed and arrested." Bunyan and Fisher, p. 27.

59. N. Alekseev, "Irkutsk v nachala Oktiabr'skoi revoliutsii v Sibiri," *Katorga i ssylka*, nos. 11–12 (1932), p. 296.

60. Shumiatskii, p. 37. From this account it seems clear that Lenin was thinking in terms of Bolshevik rule in Russia and the value of Siberian foodstuffs for the revolutionary proletariat in Petrograd and Moscow.

61. *Velikaia. . . . Khronika sobytii*, 4: 82.

62. Maksakov and Turunov, p. 48.

63. Abov, p. 119.

64. *Velikaia. . . . Khronika sobytii*, 4: 105.

65. Abov, p. 120.

66. *Velikaia. . . . Khronika sobytii*, 4: 106.

67. Ibid., p. 118.

68. Abov, p. 118.

69. *Bor'ba za vlast' Sovietov v Irkutskoi gubernii (oktiabr' 1917g.–iiul' 1918g.). Sbornik dokumentov* (Irkutsk, U.S.S.R.: 1957), p. 83.

70. Maksakov and Turunov, p. 49. This committee was created following news of the creation of a similar committee in Petrograd.

71. Ibid., p. 50.

72. Ibid., p. 52.

73. *Velikaia. . . . Khronika sobytii*, 4: 260.

74. *Bor'ba za vlast' Sovietov v Irkutskoi gubernii*, p. 110.

75. Maksakov and Turunov, p. 51.

76. *Bor'ba za vlast' Sovietov v Irkutskoi gubernii*, p. 117.

77. Ibid., p. 120.

78. Maksakov and Turunov, p. 52.

79. *Bor'ba za vlast' Sovietov v Irkutskoi gubernii*, p. 128.

80. Ibid., p. 128.

81. Maksakov and Turunov, p. 53.

82. Ibid.

83. Letter of December 23rd from the French agent in Irkutsk, Jeandreau, to the French Ambassdor in Petrograd. V. Maksakov, ed., "K istorii interventii v Sibiri," *Krasnyi Arkhiv*, 34 (1929), p. 153. The letters of Jeandreau, Henri Bourgeois, and Major Jean Pichon from Siberia paint a vivid picture of the first two months of Bolshevik rule in Siberia.

84. Batuev, *Iz istorii*, p. 25.

85. Ibid., p. 26.

86. According to Oliver K. Radkey, *The Elections to the Russian Constituent Assembly of 1917* (Cambridge, Massachusetts: Harvard University Press, 1950), the Socialist Revolutionaries received 107,220 votes and the Bolsheviks only 17,260.

87. Clarence A. Manning, *The Siberian Fiasco* (New York: Library Publishers, 1952), pp. 135–37.

88. Girchenko, p. 33.

89. Ibid., p. 34.

90. Maksakov and Turunov, p. 54.

91. Ibid., p. 57.

92. Girchenko, p. 33.

93. Ibid.

94. Maksakov and Turunov, p. 57.

95. V. N. Sokolov, "Oktiabr' za Baikalom. (Ianuar–fevral' 1918g.)" *Proletarskaia revoliutsiia*, no. 10 (1922), p. 390; Morely, pp. 465–66.

96. *Perepiska Sekretariata TsK . . . (noiabr' 1917g.–fevral' 1918g.)*, p. 380.

97. Ibid., pp. 336–37.

98. V. I. Lenin, *Polnoe Sobranie Sochinenii*, 5th ed., 53 vols. (Moscow: 1962–1966): 50: 28,411.

99. Riabikov, p. 73.

100. Ibid., p. 79.

Bibliography

A. DOCUMENTARY MATERIALS

Anikeev, V. V., ed. *Deiatel'nost' TsK R.S.D.R.P.(b) v 1917 godu.* Moscow: 1969.

Bol'sheviki Zapadnoi Sibiri v bor'be za sotsialistichskuiu revoliutsiiu (Mart–mai 1918). Sbornik dokumentov i materialov. Novosibirsk, U.S.S.R.: 1957.

Bor'ba za vlast' Sovietov v Buriat-Mongolii (1917–1918gg.). Sbornik dokumentov. Ulan Ude, U.S.S.R.: 1957.

Bor'ba za vlast' Sovietov v Irkutskoi gubernii (oktiabr' 1917g.–iiul' 1918g.). Sbornik dokumentov. Irkutsk, U.S.S.R.: 1957.

Bor'ba za vlast' Sovietov v Tomskoi gubernii (1917–1919). Sbornik dokumental'nykh materialov. Tomsk, U.S.S.R.: 1957.

Browder, Robert P., ed. *The Russian Provisional Government,*

251

1917; Documents, Selected and Edited by Robert Paul Browder and Alexander F. Kerensky. 3 vols. Stanford, California: Stanford University Press, 1961.

Bunyan, James T., and Fisher, H. H., eds. *The Bolshevik Revolution, 1917–1918, Documents and Materials.* Stanford, California: Stanford University Press, 1934.

Cummings, G. K., and Pettit, W. W., eds. *Russian-American Relations, March 1917–March 1920. Documents and Papers.* New York: Harcourt, Brace and Howe, 1920.

Dal'istpart. R.K.P. *Sbornik po istoriia revoliutsionnogo dvizhenie na Dal'nem Vostoke.* 3 vols. Chita-Vladivostok, U.S.S.R.: 1923.

Dekrety Sovietskoi vlasti. 3 vols. Moscow: 1963.

Ekonomicheskoe polozhenie Rossii nakanune Velikoi Oktiabr'skoi sotsialisticheskoi revoliutsii. Dokumenty i materialy. 3 vols. Moscow-Leningrad: 1957–1967.

Girchenko, V. P., ed. *Etapy revoliutsionnogo dvizheniia v. Buriatii, 1917–1918gg.* Verkhneudinsk, U.S.S.R.: 1927.

Glavnoe Upravlenie Zemleustroistva i Zemledeliia. *Atlas' Aziatskoi Rossii.* Saint Petersburg: 1914.

——— *Aziatskaia Rossii*, vol. 1: *Liudi i poriadki za Uralom.* Saint Petersburg: 1914.

Krasnoiarskii Soviet, mart 1917g.–iiun' 1918g. (Protokoly i postanovleniia s'ezdov Sovietov, plenumov, ispolkoma i otdelov). Sbornik dokumentov. Krasnoiarsk, U.S.S.R.: 1960.

Lenin, V. I. *Polnoe Sobranie Sochinenii*, 5th ed., 53 vols. Moscow: 1962–1966.

Maksakov, V., ed. "K istorii interventii v Sibiri," *Krasnyi arkhiv* 34 (1929): 126–65.

Maksakov, V., and Turunov, A., eds. *Khronika grazhdanskoi voiny v Sibiri 1917–1918.* Moscow-Leningrad: 1926.

Omskie Bol'sheviki v period Oktiabr'skoi revoliutsii i uprocheniia Sovietskoi vlasti (mart 1917g.–mai 1918g.). Sbornik dokumental'nykh materialov. Omsk, U.S.S.R.: 1958.

Perepiska Sekretariata TsK R.S.D.R.P.(b) s mestnymi partiinymi organizatsiiami (Mart–oktiabr' 1917g.). Sbornik dokumentov. Moscow: 1957.

Perepiska Sekretariata TsK R.S.D.R.P.(b) s mestnymi partiinymi organizatsiiami (Noiabr' 1917g.–fevral' 1918g.). Sbornik dokumentov. Moscow: 1957.

Rossiiskaia Kommunisticheskaia partiia (Bol'shevikov). V rezoliutsiiakh ee s'ezdov i konferentsii (1898–1921). Moscow: 1922.

Shestoi s'ezd R.S.D.R.P. (Bol'shevikov) Avgust 1917 goda. Protokoly. Moscow: 1958.

Tsentralnoye Statisticheskoe Upravlenie. *Pouezdnye itogi Vserossiiskoi sel'skokhoziastvennoi i pozemel'noi perepisi 1917 goda po 57 guberniiami i oblastiam.* Moscow: 1923.

——— *Rossiia v mirovoi voine, 1914–1918gg. (v tsifrakh).* Moscow: 1925.

Vardin, I. "Politicheskaia ssylka nakanune revoliutsiia," *Proletarskaia revoliutsiia*, no. 5 (1922), pp. 92–118.

Velikaia Oktiabr'skaia sotsialisticheskaia revoliutsiia. Dokumenty i materialy. Revoliutsionnoe dvizhenie v Rossii posle sverzheniia samoderzhaviia. Moscow: 1957.

Velikaia Oktiabr'skaia sotsialisticheskaia revoliutsiia. Dokumenty i materialy. Revoliutsionnoe dvizhenie v Rossii v Aprele 1917g. Aprel'skii krizis. Moscow: 1958.

Velikaia Oktiabr'skaia sotsialisticheskaia revoliutsiia. Dokumenty i materialy. Revoliutsionnoe dvizhenie v Rossii v Avguste 1917g. Razgrom Kornilovskogo miatezha. Moscow: 1959.

Velikaia Oktiabr'skaia sotsialisticheskaia revoliutsiia. Dokumenty i materialy. Revoliutsionnoe dvizhenie v Rossii v iiule 1917g. Iiul'skii krizis. Moscow: 1959.

Velikaia Oktiabr'skaia sotsialisticheskaia revoliutsiia. Dokumenty i materialy. Triumfal'noe shestvie sovietskoi vlasti. 2 vols. Moscow: 1963.

Velikaia Oktiabr'skaia sotsialisticheskaia revoliutsiia. Khronika sobytii. 4 vols. Moscow: 1957–1961.

Za vlast' Sovietov. (Sbornik statei napechatannykh v gazete Krasnoiarskii rabochii k 40=letuiu Velikogo Oktiabria.). Krasnoiarsk: 1958.

B. MEMOIRS

Abov, A. "Oktiabr' v Vostochnoi Sibiri (Otryvki iz vospominanii)," *Sibirskie ogni*, no. 4 (1924), pp. 107–21.

Akimov, P. I. "Fevral'skii perevorot v Irkutske," *Katorga i ssylka*, no. 3 (1927), pp. 156–57.

Alekseev, N. "Irkutsk v nachale Oktiabr'skoi revoliutsii," *Katorga i ssylka*, nos. 11–12 (1932), pp. 296–300.

Arkhangel'skii, V. G. "Pervyi mesiats fevral'skoi revoliutsii 1917g. v Irkutske," *Volnaia Sibir'*, no. 2 (1927), pp. 41–60.

Chuzhak-Nasimovich, N. F. "Razrushenie illiuzii. Oskolok Sibiri," *Katorga i ssylka*, no. 7 (1927), pp. 68–71.

Eideman, R. P. "Ulichnye boi vo vremia vosstaniia (Vospominaniia uchastnika dekabr'sikh dnei v Irkutske)," *Sibirskie ogni*, no. 6 (1927), pp. 85–98.

Frumkin, M. I. "Fevral'-oktiabr' 1917g. v Krasnoiarske," *Proletarskaia revoliutsiia*, no. 9 (1923), pp. 140–56.

Gan, B. M. "Fevral'skaia revoliutsiia v Tomskoi gubernii," *Severnaia Aziia*, no. 1 (1927), pp. 13–23.

Gurevich, V. Ya. "Fevral'skaia revoliutsiia v Krasnoiarske," *Volnaia Sibir'*, no. 2 (1927), pp. 112–32.

Kosarev, V. "Voenno=sotsialisticheskii soiuz," *Sibirskie ogni*, no. 1 (1922), pp. 65–70.

Kozhikov, I. "Bor'ba za Sovietskuiu vlast' u vorot Mongolii," *Proletarskaia revoliutsiia*, no. 11 (1926), pp. 156–206.

Nikolaev, V. "Fevral'skaia revoliutsiia na Altae," *Severnaia Aziia*, no. 1 (1927), pp. 29–35.

Novomeysky, M. A. *My Siberian Life*. Translated by Alec Brown. London: M. Parrish, 1956.

Papernikov, Ia. "Fevral'skaia revoliutsiia v Irkutske," *Katorga i ssylka*, no. 1 (1927), pp. 93–98.

Parfenov, P. S. "Predoktiabr'skie dni v Sibiri," *Sibirskie ogni*, no. 3 (1924), pp. 107–37.

Petrenko, A. I. "Fevral'skaia revoliutsiia v Tomske," *Proletarskaia revoliutsiia*, no. 2 (1926), pp. 91–100.

Shotman, A. "Fevral'skaia revoliutsiia v Tomske," *Proletarskaia revoliutsiia*, nos. 2–3 (1927), pp. 252–77.

Shumiatskii, Boris Z. *Sibiri na putiakh k Oktiabriu*. Moscow: 1927.

Smirnov, I. N. "Fevral'skaia revoliutsiia v Tomske," *Severnaia Aziia*, no. 1 (1927), pp. 8–12.

——— "Nakanune revoliutsii. Iz istorii 'Sotsialisticheskogo Voennogo Soiuza'," *Byloe Sibiri*, no. 2 (1922), p. 2.

Sokolov, V. N. "Fevral'skii 'perevorot' v Chite," *Severnaia Aziia*, no. 1 (1927), pp. 36–41.

——— "Oktiabr' za Baikalom. (Ianvar'–fevral' 1918g.)," *Proletarskaia revoliutsiia*, no. 10 (1922), pp. 389–99.

Steinman, E. "Na drugoi den' posle Fevral'skoi revoliutsii v Irkutskoi ssylke," *Proletarskaia revoliutsiia*, no. 1 (1923), pp. 247–50.

Sukhanov, N. *The Russian Revolution 1917, A Personal Record*. Edited and translated by Joel Charmichael. London: Oxford University Press, 1955.

Teterin, N. I. "Novonikolaevsk v Fevral'skuiu revoliutsiiu," *Severnaia Aziia*, no. 13 (1927), pp. 24–28.

Tsereteli, Irakli. *Vospominaniia o Fevral'skoi revoliutsii*. 2 vols. Paris: Mouton, 1963.

Ulianov, I. "Oktiabr'skaia revoliutsiia voennoplennye," *Proletarskaia revoliutsiia*, no. 90 (1929), pp. 95–110.

Vegman, V. "Oblastnicheskie illiuzii rasseliannye revoliutsiei," *Sibirskie ogni*, no. 3 (1923), pp. 89–113.

Vel'man, V. "Fevral'skaia revoliutsiia v Sibiri," *Proletarskaia revoliutsiia*, no. 38 (1925), pp. 167–200.

Vospominaniia o revoliutsionnom Novonikolaevske (1904–1920gg.). Novosibirsk, U.S.S.R.: 1959.

Woitinsky, W. S. *Stormy Passage*. New York: Vanguard Press, 1961.

Wright, Richardson L., and Digby, Bassett. *Through Siberia, an Empire in the Making.* New York: McBride, Nast and Co., 1913.

Yakushev, I. A. "Fevral'skaia revoliutsiia i sibirskie oblastnye s'ezdy," *Volnaia Sibir'*, no. 2 (1927), pp. 13–40.

Yaroslavskii, E. M. "Bol'sheviki v fevral'skie-martovskie dni 1917," *Proletarskaia revoliutsiia*, nos. 2–3 (1927), pp. 52–65.

Zubashev, E. L. "Moia kommandirovka v Sibiri," *Volnaia Sibir'*, no. 2 (1927), pp. 93–111.

C. SECONDARY SOURCES

Alferov, M. S. *Krest'ianstvo Sibiri v 1917 godu.* Novosibirsk, U.S.S.R.: 1958.

Bonch-Osmolovskii, A. "Vneshniaia torgovlia Dal'nego Vostok za vremia voiny i revoliutsii," *Novyi Vostok,* no. 5 (1924), pp. 156–64.

Bondarev, A. I. *Yakov Bograd; istoriko-biograficheskii ocherk.* Krasnoiarsk, U.S.S.R.: 1965.

Carr, Edward H. *The Bolshevik Revolution 1917–1923.* 3 vols. New York: Macmillan, 1950–1952.

Chamberlin, William H. *The Russian Revolution.* 2 vols. New York: Macmillan, 1935.

Daniels, Robert V. *The Conscience of the Revolution, Communist Opposition in Soviet Russia.* Cambridge, Massachusetts: Harvard University Press, 1960.

——— *Red October, The Bolshevik Revolution of 1917.* New York:

Charles Scribner's Sons, 1967.

———— "Review of Revolutionary Russia," *Slavic Review*, 28 (March 1969): 138–39.

Fisher, Raymond H. *The Russian Fur Trade*. Stanford, California: Stanford University Press, 1943.

Golovine, Nicholas A. *The Russian Army in the World War*. New Haven, Connecticut: Yale University Press, 1931.

Gudoshnikov, M. A. *Ocherki po grazhdanskoi voine v Sibiri*. Irkutsk, U.S.S.R.: 1959.

Hoshino, T. *Economic History of Manchuria*. Seoul: n.p., 1920.

Istoriia Buriat-Mongol'skoi A.S.S.R. 2 vols. Ulan Ude, U.S.S.R.: 1954–1959.

Istoriia Kommunisticheskoi Partii Sovietskogo Souiza, 4 vols. Moscow: 1964– .

Istoriia Sibiri. 5 vols. Leningrad: 1968–1969.

Istoriografiia Sovietskoi Sibiri, 1917–1945gg. Novosibirsk, U.S.S.R.: 1968.

Iz istorii partiinoi organizatsii Buriatii. Ulan Ude, U.S.S.R.: 1961.

Kayden, P., and Antiserov, N. *The Russian Cooperative Movement during the War*. Stanford, California: Stanford University Press, 1929.

Keep, J. L. H. *The Rise of Russian Social Democracy*. Oxford: Oxford University Press, 1963.

Korndonskaia, M. "Sibirskoe krest'ianstvo v dni Oktiabr'skoi revoliutsii," *Proletarskaia revoliutsiia*, no. 10 (1928), pp. 53–71.

Krusser, G. V. *Sibirskie oblastniki (ot 1864g. do epokhi Kolchaka)*. Novosibirsk, U.S.S.R.: 1931.

Lipkina, A. G. *1919 god v Sibiri*. Leningrad: 1962.

Manning, Clarence A. *The Siberian Fiasco*. New York: Library Publishers, 1952.

Morely, James W. "The Russian Revolution in the Amur Basin," *Slavic Review* 16 (December 1957): 450–71.

Petrov, A. T. "Perepis gorod'skogo naseleniia Sibiri," *Severnaia Aziia*, no. 3 (1927), pp. 37–42.

Rabinovich, Alexander F. *Prelude to Revolution: The Petrograd Bolsheviks in the July Uprising*. Bloomington, Indiana: Indiana University Press, 1968.

Radkey, Oliver K. *The Agrarian Foes of Bolshevism: Promise and Default of the Russian Socialist Revolutionaries, February to October, 1917*. New York: Columbia University Press, 1958.

—— *The Elections to the Russian Constituent Assembly of 1917*. Cambridge, Massachusetts: Harvard University Press, 1950.

—— *The Sickle Under the Hammer; The Socialist Revolutionaries in the Early Months of Soviet Rule*. New York: Columbia University Press, 1963.

Read, Henry G. "Siberia, Its Industrial and Commercial Resources," *Cassier's Magazine* 36 (September 1909): 387–407.

Riabikov, V. V. *N. N. Yakovlev—predstavitel' Tsentrosibiri.* Novosibirsk, U.S.S.R.: 1955.

Safronov, V. P. *Oktiabr' v Sibiri.* Krasnoiarsk, U.S.S.R.: 1962.

Shemelev, V. I. *Profsoiuzy Sibiri v bor'be za vlast' sovietov, 1917–1919gg.* Novosibirsk, U.S.S.R.: 1928.

Shornikov, M. M. *Bol'sheviki Novonikolaevska v period podgotovki i provedeniia Oktiabr'skoi revoliutsii.* Novosibirsk, U.S.S.R.: 1963.

———— *Bol'sheviki Sibiri v bor'be za pobedu Oktiabr'skoi revoliutsii.* Novosibirsk, U.S.S.R.: 1963.

———— *God semnadtsatyi. Bol'sheviki Sibiri v bor'be za pobedu Oktiabr'skoi sotsialisticheskoi revoliutsii.* Novosibirsk, U.S.S.R.: 1967.

Sibir' v period kapitalizma. Economicheskoe i obshchestven-no-politicheskoe razvitie Sibiri v 1861–1917g. Novosibirsk, U.S.S.R.: 1968.

Snow, Russell E. "The Russian Revolution in Transbaikalia, 1917–1918," *Soviet Studies* 23 (October 1971): 201–15.

Soskin, V. L. *Ocherki istorii kul'tury Sibiri v gody revoliutsii i grazhdanskoi voiny.* Novosibirsk, U.S.S.R.: 1965.

Suny, Ronald G. *The Baku Commune, 1917–1918: Class and Nationality in the Russian Revolution.* Princeton, New Jersey: Princeton University Press, 1972.

Treadgold, Donald W. *The Great Siberian Migrations.* Princeton, New Jersey: Princeton University Press, 1957.

Vilenskii, Vladimir D. *Bor'ba za Sovietskuiu Sibir' (Tsentrosibir') 1917–1918gg.* Moscow: 1926.

Wade, Rex A. "Irakli Tsereteli and Siberian Zimmerwaldism," *Journal of Modern History* 39 (December 1967): 425–31.

—— *The Russian Search for Peace, February–October 1917* Stanford, California: Stanford University Press, 1969.

Zol'nikov, D. M. *Rabochee dvizhenie v Sibiri v 1917g.* Novosibirsk, U.S.S.R.: 1969.

D. NEWSPAPERS

Izvestiia TsK.

Novaia Zhizn'.

Pravda.

Index